NEWSPAPER
JOURNALISM

st date

NEWSPAPER
JOURNALISM

PETER COLE AND TONY HARCUP

SAGE

Los Angeles | London | New Delhi
Singapore | Washington DC

First published 2010

SAGE Publications Ltd
1 Oliver's Yard
55 City Road
London EC1Y 1SP

SAGE Publications Inc.
2455 Teller Road
Thousand Oaks, California 91320

SAGE Publications India Pvt Ltd
B 1/I 1 Mohan Cooperative Industrial Area
Mathura Road
New Delhi 110 044

SAGE Publications Asia-Pacific Pte Ltd
33 Pekin Street #02-01
Far East Square
Singapore 048763

British Library Cataloguing in Publication data

A catalogue record for this book is available from
the British Library

ISBN 978-1-4129-3119-9
ISBN 978-1-4129-3120-5 (pbk)

Library of Congress Control Number: 2009922265

Typeset by C&M Digitals (P) Ltd, Chennai, India
Printed by CPI Antony Rowe, Chippenham, Wiltshire
Printed on paper from sustainable resources

FSC
Mixed Sources
Product group from well-managed
forests and other controlled sources
Cert no. SGS-COC-2953
www.fsc.org
© 1996 Forest Stewardship Council

CONTENTS

TABLES

ACKNOWLEDGEMENTS

Thanks to everyone who has helped make this book possible, including colleagues and students past and present; series editors David Finkelstein, Martin Conboy and Bob Franklin; and most of all to Mila Steele and her team at SAGE.

Part I

Newpapers Past and Present

1

THE CONTINUING IMPORTANCE
OF NEWSPAPER JOURNALISM

A newspaper's role is to find out fresh information on matters of public interest and to relay it as quickly and as accurately as possible to readers in an honest and balanced way. That's it. (Randall, 2007: 25)

So writes David Randall in his book *The Universal Journalist*, the much reprinted, all over the world, and excellent 'insider' book on journalism and what it takes to be a journalist. Randall loves journalism and newspapers, and unlike many manages to remain upbeat about both. He recognises the criticisms of both, and is intolerant of journalism that fails to meet his high standards, but he maintains that there is more good journalism than bad, and that there are more honest journalists than twisters of the truth. And he believes that journalism and newspapers can, and should, be an influential force for good, and often are. The authors of this book share that view, but also recognise that it isn't the whole story. A newspaper's role is fundamentally that put succinctly by Randall; and he enlarges on it:

It [a newspaper] may do lots of other things, like telling them [readers] what it thinks about the latest movies, how to plant potatoes, what kind of day Taureans might have or why the government should resign. But without fresh information it will be merely a commentary on things already known. Interesting, perhaps, stimulating even; but comment is not news. Information is. (2007: 25)

But beneath that lies a complex web of debates and issues surrounding and influencing that simple purpose. They involve the content of newspapers, how that content is selected and how it has changed over time; the economics of newspapers, who owns them and determines their policies, editorial and commercial; the threats to newspapers from competing media, even their survival; the extent to which society wishes to regulate or control newspapers, the freedom of a free press; the responsibility of newspapers with regard to matters such as privacy, taste and decency, the age-old contest between public interest and what interests the public. There are other issues currently being debated about the effects of the press we have (and deserve?) on public attitudes to politics and politicians, on the susceptibility of newspapers to the influence of an increasingly sophisticated public-relations industry, on whether newspapers are coping with declining sales by 'dumbing down', trivialising, or whether changes in the news agenda are simply a response to changes in society and its interests. An understanding of current preoccupations is informed by an awareness of how the press has developed over the centuries, a historical context. All this and more will be discussed in this book.

Newspapers not dead – shock

A newspaper has been described as a portable reading device with serendipity. You can take it anywhere and read it anywhere. You do not have to plug it in or recharge it. Newspapers remain fairly cheap; even the *Sunday Times*, Britain's first £2 newspaper, costs no more than a pint of beer in most places, rather less than in some, and less indeed than the DVD that will inevitably be provided free in the polybag that holds all the sections together. For that £2, if you were as interested in property as cars, sport as fashion and style, culture as business, you would get as much reading as you could accommodate in a week of Sundays. At the beginning of 2009 the most expensive dailies (excluding the specialist *Financial Times* at £1.80) were the *Independent* at £1 and the *Daily Telegraph*, *Guardian* and *Times* at 90p (Monday to Friday), with the mass-circulation redtops half the price or less. The serendipity comes in the surprise. You can turn the pages and come across something you find interesting. You weren't looking for it, because you didn't know it was there and you didn't know you would find it interesting.

The British have always been great consumers of news, comment and entertainment printed on paper, and we still are. We buy on average 11.2 million national newspapers each day and 11.8 million on Sunday (Audit Bureau of Circulations, October 2008). Readership of daily nationals is about 26.5 million and Sunday nationals 28.3 million (National Readership Survey, average issue readership April 2008 to September 2008). Set against an over-15 population of about 49 million, that is a lot of newspaper reading.

There is no correlation between the popularity of newspapers and the extent to which they are criticised and abused. It is the ultimate love–hate relationship. Expressions like 'Never believe what you read in the newspapers' have entered the language and become clichés, usually uttered by people who, rightly, believe most of the facts they read in newspapers. They tend to absorb more of what they read than what they watch or listen to, and what they read in the newspaper makes a significant contribution to conversation in the home and workplace, a welcome antidote to last night's *EastEnders*.

Despite (accurate) talk of the decline of newspaper sales in Britain, the fascination with them has never been greater. While debate goes on about the influence of newspapers over our national life, from politics to celebrity, the newspapers themselves are in the spotlight as never before. Politicians are to blame, for pandering to newspapers behind the scenes while in public attacking their malign influence on our national life. The public are to blame for buying the material they attack the newspapers for publishing, and for 'shopping' – and, in these days of mobile telephones doubling as cameras, photographing or filming – the misdemeanours of well-known figures they spot misbehaving. Newspapers themselves are to blame for their reluctance to admit their mistakes and excesses. Most dislike and disparage analysis and criticism of their practices, particularly when it comes from media academics. Rival media are to blame for deferring to newspapers and sustaining their reputation for remaining the most influential medium. So radio and television constantly review newspapers, rolling 24-hour news channels at length and repeatedly, with newspaper journalists doing it; current-affairs programmes discuss the content and views of newspapers, late-night phone-ins discuss issues they have read about in the press; print journalists appear on *Newsnight, Question Time, Any Questions,* anywhere a view is needed. It is of course partly because the electronic media are obliged to be impartial whereas print journalists take positions.

None of this is good for the egos of the print journalists who are so magnified across the electronic media. They run the risk of taking themselves very seriously and believing in their own wisdom. Worse, they are susceptible to that dangerous disease, celebrity journalism. There was a time when print journalists were neither seen nor named. Now the newspapers give some of them lavish billing and television gives them a programme. The car is not the star on *Top Gear;* Jeremy Clarkson is. When Piers Morgan turns his charms on tabloid celebrities in his television interview show, there is no question who the real celebrity is. Not the WAG or supermodel. Both Clarkson and Morgan were once simply newspapermen.

So it would seem that despite accusations from some quarters that newspapers today trivialise and are dumbed down – and there is arguably some substance in both claims – newspapers have at least as much presence as they ever did. The basic role of the newspaper, to find things out and tell people about them, in as accessible a way as possible, is still fulfilled. There is debate about what those things that are found out are, and whether they are worth finding out in the first place (the news agenda), but it remains the case that without newspapers much that those exercising power over the rest of us would prefer not to enter the public domain does so through the medium of the newspaper.

Newspapers occupy a crucial place in the 'public sphere', defined by Habermas (1984: 49) as 'a realm of our social life in which something approaching public opinion can be formed. Access is guaranteed to all citizens'. Harrison

(2006: 110) traces this public sphere for news from the conversations in the eighteenth- and nineteenth-century town halls and coffee shops to the present era of newspapers, broadcasters and the internet. This engages the public in politics and debate. But today's multi-media world is 'increasingly provided by a smaller number of large and powerful organisations, as well as by organised and well-resourced groups in civil society' (ibid.: 112). A decline in newspaper sales and an increasing concentration of ownership might undermine the access to a range of views.

Newspapers in the digital age

Journalism itself is more important than where its products are published, and one of the problems of the current media debate is the failure to distinguish between the two. So preoccupied have media owners and managements become with the process of publishing and the variety of opportunities modern technologies allow that debate over how and where to publish has drowned out the more important question of what to publish. The fashionable use of the generic word 'content' instead of news and information has a significance that goes beyond the semantic. Content is simply what occupies the space and to use it to describe the products of journalism is to devalue the spirit and practice of intellectual inquiry and analysis that is the hallmark of good journalism.

The debate over the future of newspapers and their place in a multimedia, multi-platform, converged media world is of course of great importance and fascination. It is crucial in a business sense because unless publishers make money they will not publish. But after a period of complacency – crisis, what crisis? – newspaper publishers realised that something had to be done. One or two titles – the *Guardian* for example, and for a short time the *Telegraph* – embraced, or at least acknowledged, the digital age before the turn of the twenty-first century. But many more decided to enjoy the profitability they were still experiencing, blink at the circulation figures and carry on doing what they knew how to do, produce newspapers. Managers and publishers had relatively recently come to terms with the post-Wapping benefits of the computer for newspaper production, and profits. They were slow to see that the computer would pose a much greater threat as a rival publishing technology. Most journalists felt equally unthreatened by those about them predicting doom, dismissing them as nerds and techies who never read anything anyway and preferred Apples to news. They could safely be left in 'cyberland' while real journalists got on with their newspaper reporting. As we shall see later, the newspaper mainstream, editorial and managerial, kept their heads in the sand and ignored the signs of change all around.

Table 1.1   *Percentage of adult population reading a newspaper*

	1983	1986	1990	1994	1998	2002	2006
All newspapers	77	73	68	61	57	54	50
Popular	57	50	47	46	42	37	33
Quality	10	11	11	11	11	12	12

Source: 24th British Social Attitudes Survey (2008)

Down and down: the decline of newspaper sales

Peter Preston edited the *Guardian* for 20 years from 1975 to 1995, and saw its circulation grow considerably over that period. Others did not have the same experience; decline had begun, and would accelerate. Reflecting on the general sales loss so preoccupying editors and owners today, Preston (2008: 642) describes the circulation falls over his professional life: thirty years ago the *Daily Mirror* selling 3,879,000, in June 2007 only 1,565,000. The *Daily Express* has fallen from 2,312,000 to 770,000, the *Daily Telegraph* from over 1.3 million to 892,000. 'Where have 1.5 million *News of the World* customers gone? And over three million *People* readers. Why are national daily sales down to 11.6 million when those with not-so-long memories can recall 14 million? Why is our universe contracting year after year, as though inexorably?'

Franklin (2008a: 3) is less gloomy. 'While the decline in newspapers' circulations is undoubtedly significant, the suggestion here is that newspapers are not about to vanish or disappear'. Rather they are 'changing and adapting their contents, style and design in response to the challenges they confront in the increasingly competitive market'. This is a world of other media platforms, the internet and mobile telephones. Franklin says this is not a 'complacent' argument, but a recognition that 'adapting to increased competition, often driven by new technology, is historically what has triggered change in the newspaper industry .... what newspapers have always done'.

The latest (24th) British Social Attitudes Survey (2008) provides data on newspaper readership, and reviews how that has changed over the years of the survey's publication. Regular readership (at least three days a week) is measured and divides newspapers into two categories, 'quality' (*Times, Telegraph, Guardian, Independent, Financial Times*) and 'popular' (*Mail, Express, Sun, Mirror, Star*). The figures in Table 1.1 show the percentage of the adult population reading any paper, a popular paper and a quality paper.

In their chapter of the Social Attitudes report *Where Have All the Readers Gone?*, John Curtice and Ann Mair (2008: 161–172) describe the decline as 'continuous and relentless', pointing out that regular adult readership of national newspapers in Britain has fallen from just over three quarters to just half. 'Collectively Britain's newspapers have lost a third of their readers and, instead of reaching the overwhelming majority of the population, are now regularly ignored by around half'. However, the authors note that readership of quality papers has remained steady at around one tenth of the population. 'The overall decline in newspaper readership has in effect been a decline in the readership of (once) popular daily papers'.

It may seem strange to be producing a book on newspaper journalism at a time when the industry is dealing with declines in circulation and readership by trying to get away from the limiting 'newspaper' descriptor of its activities, and placing more emphasis on its non-newspaper activities. Words like 'press' and 'newspapers' are being removed from company titles, usually replaced with the word 'media' (Guardian Media Group, Telegraph Media Group). So obsessed are they with newspaper sales and readership decline, amplified by the advertising decline of the economic recession of 2008–09, so prepared to take seriously the apocalyptic soothsayers predicting the end of newspapers, that they seem almost embarrassed to talk about the newspaper bedrocks of their businesses.

But there remain good reasons for concentrating on newspapers in a book such as this, and they are not simply historical. The newspaper industry, perhaps because it is perceived by some to be the most threatened media sector, is a key driver in the change that is coming about. Newspapers, more than any other sector, are driving convergence by adopting other forms of publishing – web, audio, video. The broadcast sector, with its own problems of falling audiences through the fragmentation brought about by digital multi-channel opportunities, is not moving into newspapers. And online publishers of news are not moving into journalism, except those already in journalism: newspapers and news broadcasters.

So far the elephant in the room has been newspaper decline, or even death in the foreseeable future. Temple (2008: 206) suggests the newspaper is at 'a critical crossroads, facing the most serious challenge to its future existence since the *Daily Courant* rolled off the presses in 1702'. Newspaper people have many strengths, but these often contribute to their weaknesses. They include looking on the dark side – bad news is usually bigger news; treating problems as crises; pessimism; and endless introspection. When journalists or media managers get together they seldom talk about anything but media matters. They also think in short time scales – after all newspapers come out every day or every week – so a set of poor circulation figures (despite the massaging to which the publishers have contributed) is a crisis not a problem. And a period of readjustment, albeit massive, is not the same as imminent death. Such panic attacks are not helped by an awareness that they were slow to wake up to the implications of online publishing, and when they did wake up it was in a state of hyperactivity.

It wasn't as though circulation decline was a new problem. Newspaper sales have been in decline in the UK for 30 years, but to extrapolate that to the rest of the world, as Franklin (2008b: 307) points out, 'articulates a curiously North

American and Euro-centric view of the press which seems blinkered to the explosion of new titles and readerships in other parts of the world'. Most people working in UK newspapers today have never known anything but decline. There have been individual successes that have bucked the trend for a period, but the high water mark of the 1940s and 1950s when the *Daily Express* sold 4.3 million and the *News of the World* peaked at nearly 7.5 million (Greenslade, 2003a: 5 and 120) will never come again. It is not sufficient to blame the rise of the internet. As Preston (2008: 643) puts it, 'The net may be delivering the *coup de grace*, but it's not truly to blame for what's gone wrong over decades. Human living patterns, changing, moving on, have done that'. During the golden age of newspaper sales television was just stuttering into life. And television as it was, analogue and fewer channels than the fingers on one hand, will never again have the audiences it had when everybody was watching the same few programmes – digital satellite and cable saw to that. So it is simply wrong to think that newspaper circulation decline is a result solely of the internet, broadband and online news. It started long, long before that.

Technology does not exist in isolation, of course. It emerges out of specific economic, social and political contexts. But technological change can make certain things possible, or more or less likely. Technology was no threat to newspapers in the 1980s when computer typesetting and direct input revolutionised the industry, transforming the economics in the direction of huge potential increases in profitability. That 'new technology' era allowed for enormous growth in the size of newspapers (pagination) with the resultant potential for growing advertising revenues. The current digital revolution allowing for the delivery of words, pictures and sound through screens and a vast (limitless) increase in the amount of information available through this medium is of course a challenge to newspapers, but not necessarily a terminal threat. It is that challenge newspapers are addressing now, in various ways, with varying investment and varying creativity and imagination. There is undoubtedly a lot of gloom to be found in newspaper offices these days, but that is not the whole story. It is also an exciting time for newspapers. Newspapers are not on death row.

Global newspaper trends

So loud is the noise made by the doom laden 'death of newspapers' faction (journalist and academic alike) in the UK that we tend not to look at the wider picture, to ask whether this decline is a global phenomenon. It is not as though the internet is a localised presence – the world wide web is just that, world wide, although broadband penetration, and thus mass availability, is still predominantly a feature of the advanced economies. But worldwide print publication of news remains buoyant, as data collected annually by the Paris-based World Association of Newspapers (WAN) demonstrate.

WAN's World Press Trends figures, published annually since 1986, are collated from 232 countries where newspapers are published. The data for 2007 show that worldwide newspaper sales rose by 2.6 per cent on the previous year and 9.4 per cent over five years. When free daily newspapers are included, global circulation rose by 3.7 per cent for the year and 14.3 per cent over five years. These figures are helped by huge growth in newspaper sales in India (up 35.5 per cent over five years) and China, the world's largest market with 107 million copies sold daily (up 20.7 per cent over five years). But sales were up in 80 per cent of countries surveyed. All over the world 532 million people buy a newspaper each day (486 million in 2003) and average daily readership is estimated to be 1.7 billion. But what about Europe, where internet use is large and growing and newspaper decline is considered widespread? In fact here too sales have risen in 11 EU countries, and if free newspapers are included circulations rose by 2 per cent across the EU in 2007. While most Eastern European paid-for titles increased sales, decline was more evident in Western Europe, with Sweden and the UK performing worst. Elsewhere significant falls were recorded in the United States, Australia and Oceania.

So there is some statistical support for the pessimists in Britain, but it cannot be simply explained as part of a global, or even European trend. It is not just a case of saying that newspaper readers are switching to the internet for their news wherever there is huge internet availability.

While there is evidence of a decline in sales in Britain, we should not forget just how many papers are still bought in this country. And even in our allegedly time-starved age we spend plenty of time reading our newspapers. The National Readership survey carried out its first 'Time Spent Reading' survey of this during the first half of 2007. As the NRS managing director Roger Pratt said, it showed 'just how robust the print medium is'. It demonstrated that 'consumers are committing substantial time to print media despite increasingly busy lifestyles and the proliferation of media channels'. The survey showed that a Monday–Friday national newspaper was read for an average of 40 minutes, a Saturday national newspaper for an average of 60 minutes (with 42 per cent reading for more than an hour), and national Sunday newspapers for an average of 70 minutes (with half of readers spending more than an hour on their paper) (NRS Time Spent Reading report, October 2007).

The *British Journalism Review* commissioned its own survey from the pollster YouGov on the nature of newspaper decline and findings were published in 2006 with a commentary from Steven Barnett, Professor of Communications at the University of Westminster (*BJR* Vol. 17, No. 1, p. 8):

> There are those inside and outside the newspaper industry who genuinely fear that the daily printed newspaper will soon become as anachronistic as the black Bakelite telephone, and that it simply cannot survive in the modern world. Can the newspaper continue to offer something different and unique in people's lives? Is it being overwhelmed by the immediacy of 24-hour channels and the internet? Is it too expensive, too opinionated,

too distrusted journalistically, or just too much to handle on a daily basis when there are so many other calls on people's time? Will it be on its deathbed five years from now?

The data revealed that 29 per cent read a newspaper less often than two years earlier, the figure rising to 32 per cent for national newspapers. But 13 per cent read a paper more often (10 per cent for nationals). Significantly, and perhaps unexpectedly, the 'more often' figure rose to 28 per cent in the 18–29 age group. The main reason given for reading less often was the availability of news elsewhere, particularly from the internet. However, 53 per cent of respondents said they still found things they liked in newspapers that they could not get elsewhere. While 18 per cent thought they would 'probably' give up reading newspapers over the next four or five years, 56 per cent took the opposite view. Barnett said that such figures could not be described as catastrophic, noting that the more negative figures about newspaper reading came from those who described themselves as 'occasional' readers (less than once a week):

> Our research suggests that newspapers may have a longer shelf life than many believed possible, and that the model of the cinema – adapting to the television age but not being overwhelmed by it – might be the more appropriate analogy. These data are indicative of a prevalent mood that seems better disposed towards the printed press than we might reasonably have expected. … There will certainly be continued circulation decline. But the evidence suggests that just as cinema going declined until the 1980s and then bottomed out and rose again, newspapers will find their plateau. In cultural and consumer terms, as long as the newspaper industry can continue to offer something of real journalistic substance, our data suggests that it will continue to find a willing and substantial readership. (ibid.: 14)

It is widely believed that take-up of online media, and the consequent reduction in the use of traditional media, is most prevalent among the young. Ofcom, the regulator of broadcast media in the UK, provided some data in this area in its 2006 market report. It found that all consumers, but particularly the younger ones, were using the internet more, spending less time reading magazines and newspapers, watching TV and listening to radio. Among 15 to 24-year-olds, 27 per cent said they read national newspapers less since they started using the internet, while 14 per cent of all consumers reported a similar shift in their habits. The five analogue terrestrial television networks made up 58 per cent of young people's viewing time compared with 74 per cent in 2001. However, Ofcom's chief operating officer, Ed Richards, remarked that old media would not be going out of business:

> It's not the death of any particular media. We are seeing an adjustment as a new medium, the internet, becomes more and more significant in people's lives. Other media will have to adjust and have to respond as they have been doing to that threat, and to respond in the way they use and position their current media. But we do not think any media will die as a result of this. All media will carry on and no doubt be successful.

Gavin O'Reilly, group chief operating officer of Independent News and Media, publishers of the *Independent* and *Independent on Sunday* in the UK, and many other titles from Ireland to South Africa, who is president of the World Association of Newspapers, takes a bullish view of the state of the newspaper industry worldwide, while recognising the circulation decline in Britain. He criticises media commentators and leading journalists for talking down the continuing success of newspapers and failing to celebrate how well they are adapting to the digital media world. Consumers will always want, he says, 'unique comment and analysis, well-crafted and well-edited content that has faced the rigours of a well-honed editorial process' (speech to Society of Editors conference, 4 November 2007).

Peter Preston (2008: 645) describes the pessimism in the British newspaper industry as 'the curse of introversion'. The industry is 'the very model of a great business bringing itself to dust in a welter of navel gazing. Day to day it remains wrapped in its own preoccupations'. Preston is sufficient of a realist to recognise what is going on in terms of circulation decline and the fall in advertising revenues as classified advertising – that's jobs, cars and houses – revenues fall, but says this represents inevitable and inexorable change which the industry has failed to adapt to. 'Introversion means we adjust slowly to change, if we adjust at all. Introversion means we don't notice the world changing around us. Introversion means a fatal lack of communication in the communications business, a blinkered refusal to make connections or form fresh alliances. Introversion brings a kind of imbecility along with it'.

But that adjustment to change is now coming about, and after several years of gloomy 'introversion' there are signs that the newspaper industry is beginning to adapt to the digital age. It is recognising that whatever the publishing platform information has to be gathered, and newspapers have traditionally been very good at that. It is recognising that journalism itself is more important than how it is published, and that newspapers know as much about journalism, probably more, than other media. How that process of change is developing will be discussed in detail in Chapter 6.

Why newspapers remain so powerful

Jeremy Tunstall (1996: 1), writing before the internet became the force it is today, argued that newspapers remained powerful in the video age. The arrival of television had greatly increased the significance of the mass media around the world, but in terms of broad political and societal power television had added to – and not subtracted from – the press in general and newspapers in particular.

Newspapers, he wrote, exercised a continuing prerogative both to bias the news and to slant the comment. 'It is the newspapers, not television, which go for the politician's jugular. Typically it is the newspaper which first spills the politician's blood; only then does television swoop in for the action replay'. Fewer people now read a daily newspaper each day but perhaps three or four times a week, but each newspaper was much fatter than that of a few decades ago. We were, said Tunstall, in an age of semi-regular newspaper reading. 'The somewhat reduced TV networks and the somewhat arthritic daily newspapers still tower and stoop over the fragmented new media'.

'Semi-regular' reading has increased, a fact disguised by the publication of newspaper circulation figures that average daily sales over the six publication days. Sales of Saturday newspapers, particularly at the 'upper' end of the market, are massively greater than Monday to Friday sales. Without the supplement packed Saturdays, more akin to Sunday newspapers than those published by the same title on other days of the week, sales of national dailies would look much worse than circulation figures suggest. The *Guardian*, for example, which averages an audited sale of around 350,000 across all six publishing days, sells about 200,000 more copies on a Saturday than on all the other days of the week.

The fatness is undeniable, with all national newspapers spawning more and more sections, again particularly at the upper end of the market. The number of words in one edition of the *Sunday Times* or *Observer*, or Saturday *Guardian* or *Telegraph*, would equate to that in many novels. This has resulted in the perception that news has been relegated in importance, whereas arguably there is at least as much news, or material presented as news in news sections, in all newspapers as there has ever been, in most cases more. A look at the pre-Wapping era of 'old' technology and the 16- to 24-page broadsheets that were then the norm reminds us that in many ways the scale and ambition, not to mention the value, of national newspapers has grown rather than diminished.

The propensity of newspapers to go for the politician's jugular remains, and some would argue this has gone too far. But it is the newspapers that continue to expose the news management of governments, the hypocrisy and manipulation of statistics. It is the newspapers that embarrass politicians and on occasion bring them down, whether over policies, financial impropriety or philandering. It is the newspapers that get bees in their bonnets, worry away, obsess. We may challenge the subjects of those obsessions, which range from the serious and important to the trivial, the inconsequential and sometimes the downright dangerous. But with as pluralistic a press as we have in this country a lot of different tastes are catered for. As long as newspapers provoke the strength of feeling that most do they are unlikely to become marginalised. When the *Guardian* and *Daily Mail* can both evoke such rage from different sections of the public (and each other), when both can be regarded by those who dislike them as so biased, so wrong, then there is clearly a choice and representation of different political outlooks. ITV or Sky News do not produce such reactions, and nor does Google News. The BBC does on occasion, partly because of its public funding via the licence fee, but mainly because the newspapers decide to whip up a campaign about some 'outrage' or other; another demonstration of the power of the press to set agendas.

Quite apart from the physical factors, the newspaper continues to offer a different approach to journalism from other media. It offers a range of content in one package, as opposed to requiring the consumer to go to different places for different things, as on the internet. It acquires character and attitude from the way it selects and what it selects. It is seldom bland. Newspapers, unlike other media, tend to reflect and reinforce the prejudices of their readers, painting a picture of the world the reader will recognise. Newspapers will understand the lives of their target audiences and publish material that is relevant to them, that fits in with their preoccupations, interests, working lives, family lives and leisure. While magazines are deliberately more specific, newspapers will seek to deal with all aspects of the readers' lives: their health, holidays, finance, homes, children, clothes, food, the things that excite them, enrage them, worry them and amuse them. All this in one portable package.

Newspaper journalism, even in the age of dramatic and technology-led change, still represents more than any other medium the essential of journalism: to find things out and tell others about them; to tell stories in a simple and accessible way; to explain; to root out hypocrisy and corruption among those who wield power, in so many ways, over the rest of us; to right wrongs and campaign; to provide the stuff of everyday conversation; to enrage and entertain; to shock and move; to celebrate and condemn. In the words of the American journalist H.L. Mencken, 'to comfort the afflicted and afflict the comfortable' or in the words of the former *Sun* editor Kelvin MacKenzie, to 'shock and amaze on every page'.

But young people entering journalism do not necessarily see it that way. They may see journalism as one way to make a difference. They may be interested in events and want to be close to them, explaining why they are important, interesting, dramatic or simply remarkable. Newspaper journalists work for commercial organisations but, although newspapers are businesses, they are not businesses like any other, because they are about life and not things; they are about us, and the ways we live and are organised and governed.

The good journalists ask the questions and question the answers. These days there are many places to publish information and the business of how and where to publish it is in transition. Newspaper publishers will publish (and are doing so) on a variety of platforms, but it will be a long time before the scope, the relative simplicity, of the newspaper becomes redundant.

Would Rupert Murdoch have spent £650 million on three new printing plants in Britain if he did not see a secure future for newspapers? Would the *Telegraph* titles be bought for nearly £600 million if the new owners, the Barclay brothers, simply wanted a website?

Murdoch, whose titles make up about about 35 per cent of UK national newspaper circulation, and who was a late convert to embracing news on the internet – he is now a zealous convert – does believe newspapers have a future, as part of a mix of publishing platforms where the most important feature is the brand (its credibility and the trust in it). During his series of 2008 Boyer Lectures on Australian radio he poured scorn on the pessimism of some journalists and the 'perverse pleasure' they took in 'ruminating on the pending demise' of newspapers. 'The newspaper,' he said, 'or a very close electronic cousin will always be around' (Murdoch, 2008).

The financial analysts would say in their formulaic way that newspapers will continue to form an important part of the media mix. We would suggest that newspapers will continue to represent the journalistic bedrock. Or as Gavin O'Reilly (2007) put it to the Society of Editors conference: 'We see newspapers as the ultimate browser, where in essence someone else has done the hard work for you, and delivered the serendipity of life to you in a concise, colourful and portable way, and all for the price of a cup of coffee'. He underestimated the price of a cup of coffee.

Structure of this book

In this introductory chapter we have set out why we believe newspapers continue to be so important and so fascinating, notwithstanding the rapid changes that are going on around them and indeed to them. Subsequent chapters will take particular aspects and explore the role of newspapers in more detail, pointing to particular examples and drawing out key themes. Chapter 2 will look in detail at the present state of the national newspaper market in the UK, the different market sectors and the audiences and relative performance of different national titles. It will provide current sales, readership and demographic data, and consider changes in the editorial agendas of different titles. The most significant change to newspapers in the past decade has been format change within the sector previously referred to as 'the broadsheets'. Three of those daily 'quality' titles (and two Sundays) have 'downsized' to what is now described as a 'compact' format, to the (at least initial) benefit of their circulations. The regional press has undergone a period of a great decline in sales, and the reasons for this and the response of publishers are considered in Chapter 3.

Chapter 4 provides a brief history of the press over the past three hundred years, considering the influence of key figures at particular moments in history and the emergence of titles still published today. The importance of developing technologies, in distribution as well as printing, of the radical press as well as what became the mainstream press, of government controls through the 'taxes on knowledge', and of the unabashed pursuit of political power through newspaper ownership, are all considered. Power and profit shifts between the different owners and titles dominating particular periods are described. Press history shows that there is nothing new in many areas of concern today: the power of individual proprietors, scurrilous journalism, tabloid agendas, special offers to induce purchase, price-cutting and ferocious competition.

Chapter 5 deals with the political economy of the press in the age of corporate newspapering. Colin Sparks (1999: 46) was unequivocal:

> Newspapers in Britain are first and foremost businesses. They do not exist to report the news, to act as watchdogs for the public, to be a check on the doings of government, to defend the ordinary citizen against abuses of power or to do any of the other fine and noble things that are sometimes claimed for the press. They exist to make money just as any other business does. To the extent that they discharge any of their public functions, they do so in order to succeed as businesses.

While most editors and journalists would take a loftier view, most proprietors and shareholders would agree with Sparks. This chapter looks at the ownership of the press, and its concentration. It looks at the reasons for large profits in a time of circulation decline and the effects of technological change. It considers changes in ownership and the attractiveness of media companies to potential purchasers. Has cost-cutting in recent years had a negative effect on journalism? What is the significance of the development of free newspapers? It was already clear by the end of 2008 that the global recession would have a profound effect on the UK newspaper industry.

Chapter 6 examines contemporary practices in newspaper journalism and how editorial emphases have changed. Has the broader agenda of the serious press to include popular culture and celebrity represented a 'dumbing down' or the democratisation of news? Is Brian McNair right when he suggests (2003b: 223) that the thesis of dumbing down is at least a 'contestable' or even 'elitist' response to welcome developments in journalism?

This chapter will consider McNair's argument in terms of consumer, lifestyle, popular culture and celebrity journalism. It will also deal with the debate initiated by John Lloyd in his book *What the Media Are Doing to Our Politics* (2004a). Lloyd believes the media, and particularly newspapers, contribute to the lack of respect for and trust in politicians. Their emphasis on negativity, he argues, can undermine the political process. He had an ally in the outgoing prime minister Tony Blair, who devoted one of his farewell lectures to the media, which he described as 'like a feral beast, just tearing people and reputations to bits' (2007). Blair went on:

> I do believe this relationship between public life and media is now damaged in a manner that requires repair. The damage saps the country's confidence and self-belief; it undermines its assessment of itself, its institutions; and above all, it reduces our capacity to take the right decisions, in the right spirit for our future.

Another current debate on newspaper practices emanates from a *Guardian* journalist, Nick Davies, who savaged his peers in a controversial book, *Flat Earth News* (2008). Much of the research for this was carried out by Cardiff University's School of Journalism, Media and Cultural Studies. Davies says that he feels 'forced to admit that I work in a corrupted profession' (2008: 3). Examining various stories he claims to have found 'falsehood, distortion and propaganda running through the outlets of an industry which is supposed to be dedicated to the very opposite, i.e. to telling the truth'. He and his Cardiff researchers put much of the blame on public relations and news agencies. Contemporary practices will also include the demands made of journalists in a multi-media age, questioning whether increasing their productivity dilutes the quality of their journalism.

Chapter 7 deals with ethics and regulation, which remains self-regulation in the case of newspapers. Mike Jempson (2007), director of the Mediawise Trust, observes that 'journalism is under scrutiny as never before'. There is more discussion of newspaper ethics today than at any time, with an emerging body of academic literature dealing with the subject. Newspapers subscribe to the Code of Practice of the Press Complaints Commission, a code developed by newspaper editors themselves. Many of the debates involving the academy, politicians, the public and newspaper editors themselves are around ethics and standards, and have to deal with a public that buys more newspapers when they feature scandals in public life while decrying press intrusion and telling pollsters of their lack of trust in the media.

Chapter 8 looks at investigative journalism, seen by many as having declined through a lack of investment. Painstaking investigations take time and may not yield a result, and cost-cutting managements are said to be unwilling to make the investment. Others will say that all reporting is investigative because it is about finding out, and the journalism of disclosure is still alive. Political donations and MPs' expenses are but two recent examples of the products of journalistic investigation. Since the supposed golden era of investigative reporting, *Sunday Times* Insight in the 1960s, the Freedom of Information Act has entered the statute book. This chapter will examine whether that is fulfilling the expectations of those who campaigned for it, or whether Britain's traditional culture of secrecy is alive and well.

The growth of the academic discipline of journalism studies and its many related subjects is examined in Chapter 9. It is fair to say that relations between journalists and academics who seek to research and analyse their practices and products have not always been warm. Journalists who spend their lives asking questions in an attempt to reveal the truth are often curiously averse to answering questions themselves and sometimes question the right or ability of those who do not 'do' journalism to research or analyse it. Equally, academics in the field have often approached journalism with preconceptions and a distaste for the popular end of the market. They have on occasion been disappointed that academic research methods are not employed by journalists working to a different time frame and for a different and much larger audience. But there are signs that some mutual understanding, not least of the differences between the two activities, is developing. Perhaps the growth of journalism education in universities and the movement of journalists into academic employment, the emergence of the so-called 'hackademics', has fostered that. The fact that this book draws frequently on the work of media academics but is written by two former hacks now working in the academy could be seen as bridge building. Equally the use in the book of sources from inside journalism, speeches and lectures by eminent journalists, and data emanating from the newspaper industry can be taken to indicate that a welcome two-way process is going on.

Chapter 10 returns to the themes introduced in Chapter 1 and looks back to the future, to the engagement of newspapers in the new, converged journalism. It describes the vast changes that have taken place very recently in the direction of multi-platform publishing. It looks at the demands on publishers and journalists alike as the new media age is addressed. And it recognises that there are more uncertainties than certainties about what lies ahead; we are probably nearer to the beginning of the 'digital revolution' than we are to its end, assuming there is one. Discussion of the future is perhaps inevitably based more on opinion than fact, which is one of the allegations against newspapers today. Two opinions from very well-known journalists underline the point. First John Humphrys, scourge of politicians, anchor of BBC Radio 4's *Today* programme, and quoted in the *Independent* (2006):

> The idea of society functioning without newspapers in one shape or form is simply preposterous. If they don't survive, heaven help all of us. The question is what form they take and I would be absolutely astonished if within the foreseeable future they didn't remain in their current form. We love newspapers. Obviously we are not buying them in the same numbers we did. They have been through this kind of crisis before and I have lost track of the times we have discussed the imminent demise of newspapers. But whenever a newspaper comes up for sale, you get killed in the rush; everyone wants to buy it. How come?

And Piers Morgan, former editor of the *Daily Mirror*, in the same *Independent* article (2006):

> Every newspaper has a great future online. End of story. Within five years every newspaper will be free and they'll all be online. And if not, they should be. There will still be a presence in print but that will be for older readers and you will find that anybody under the age of 35 will only read newspapers online.

Finally, this book has drawn on many books, journals, papers and articles that the authors would like to recommend. Newspaper journalism is a vast subject and the scope of this book has inevitably limited the extent to which each of its constituent parts, outlined above, could be explored. For that reason Chapter 11 is a critical bibliography, essentially recommended reading for those who wish to dig deeper into a fascinating subject.

We begin, in the next chapter, with a closer look at the present national newspaper landscape.

2

THE UK NATIONAL PRESS TODAY

We have in Britain the greatest variety of newspapers of any nation in the world, and that is particularly true of our national press. But what do we mean by 'national press'? In these days of devolved government, the *Scotsman* or *Herald* may see themselves as the national newspapers of Scotland, and the *Western Mail* has claimed to be the national paper of Wales. Therefore, to define the national press as those newspapers published in London and readily available across the UK could be seen as provocative; however, it remains a useful and commonly accepted description, and will be used throughout this book.

The fact that we have a thriving national press is due to several factors. London is the capital and the home of parliament, government departments, the senior courts, the royal family, financial institutions and the headquarters of many of our leading companies. It is, in short, the main centre of power. It is thus the source of most news of the institutional variety, from prime minister's questions to company annual general meetings, from major trials and appeals to state occasions and cultural events such as film premieres and theatre first nights. It is inevitable, then, that a press which seeks to engage a national audience will be based in the nation's capital. That is true of journalistic activity, but no longer necessarily of the production aspects of the newspaper industry.

London is also the transport hub of the country and historically that has been a major factor in the development of a national press. The growth of a rail network during the nineteenth century, radiating out of London terminal stations, provided the perfect basis for a speedy nationwide distribution of newspapers from London. In the context of a small and highly populated country the ability to provide newspapers full of national and international news, printed late at night, on breakfast tables the length and breadth of the country the next morning allowed the national press to develop rapidly. Distribution by rail continued until the 1980s. The great London railway stations were scenes of huge activity every night and into the early hours of the morning as bundles of freshly printed papers were carried from vans to trains with special provision for this cargo and sent to onward distribution points all over the land. Costs, rail cuts, the development of facsimile transmission of newspaper pages to satellite print works and the growth of the motorway network eventually moved distribution on to the roads, but rail had dominated for one hundred years.

All this, and perhaps a culture of nationalism rather than regionalism, led to the dominant influence of a national press in a way that never happened in other European countries or the United States, where, for reasons of the size of the country and the impossibility of overnight distribution, a tradition of big city and regional newspapers developed.

> Like other national presses the British press is highly idiosyncratic. The British press is an extreme case within Europe in the extent to which it is dominated by national newspapers published in one city. The leading publications are all London daily newspapers (and their even more idiosyncratic Sunday stable companions). Because they are so competitive, these newspapers have none of those inhibitions which semi-monopoly generates elsewhere. The London newspapers are less restrained than the leading newspapers of most other countries; they are all public companies, open to public and financial scrutiny. Their senior people are willing to be interviewed. As an extreme example of a press which is *national*, which is *competitive*, and which is a *newspaper* press, the British national press provides a case study of newspaper power which may be of some wider significance. (Tunstall, 1996: 2)

Britain's newspaper marketplace is highly stratified, although not as much as it was, and is influenced by class (or socio-economic group), education, occupation and self-image. We refer to the 'tabloids', meaning the redtops, the *Sun, Mirror* and *Star*, not the 'serious' tabloids like the *Independent* and *Times*, which refer to themselves as compacts. We talk of the 'mid-market', meaning the *Mail* and *Express*, and of the 'serious', 'quality' or 'broadsheet' market – the *Telegraph, Times, Guardian, Independent* and *Financial Times* – despite the fact that three of the broadsheets are now smaller format. Sales generally diminish as we work up these three tiers, although the *Mail*'s circulation breaks this rule.

The stratification is the same on Sundays, with the same publishers occupying the same areas of the market. So in the redtop tabloid sector we have the *Sunday Mirror* and *People* published by Trinity Mirror (publisher of the *Daily Mirror*), News International's *News of the World* as stable-mate to the *Sun*, and the *Daily Star Sunday* (Express group). In the mid-market we have the *Mail on Sunday* and *Sunday Express*, sharing publishers with the *Daily Mail* and *Daily Express* respectively. And at the quality end we have the two 'compacts', the *Observer* and the *Independent on Sunday*, published in the same formats by the same owners, of the *Guardian* and *Independent* respectively,

Table 2.1　Sales of national dailies in 000s – Sept. of year in question

Title	1977	1987	1997	2004	2008
Telegraph	1,327	1,186	1,130	901	851
Times	287	450	815	661	638
Financial Times	178	308	327	438	429
Guardian	267	473	428	376	349
Independent	n/a	360	288	265	220
Daily Mail	1,881	1,810	2,344	2,443	2,242
Daily Express	5,310	1,700	1,241	960	739
Sun	3,944	4,140	3,887	3,336	3,155
Daily Mirror	3,986	3,096	2,442	1,794	1,441
Daily Star	n/a	1,159	632	900	731

n/a = not applicable (i.e. yet to launch)

Source: Audit Bureau of Circulations

Table 2.2　Sales of national Sundays in 000s – Sept. of year in question

Title	1977	1987	1997	2004	2008
Sunday Times	1,342	1,277	1,449	1,370	1,221
Sunday Telegraph	847	758	938	702	622
Observer	700	766	498	462	453
Independent on Sunday	n/a	n/a	311	214	183
Mail on Sunday	n/a	1,834	2,322	2,338	2,239
Sunday Express	3,167	2,251	1,262	1,004	655
News of the World	4,990	5,191	4,620	3,889	3,242
Sunday Mirror	4,027	2,999	2,424	1,584	1,316
People	4,052	2,961	2,002	1,013	626
Daily Star Sunday	n/a	n/a	n/a	485	382

n/a = not applicable (i.e. yet to launch)

Source: Audit Bureau of Circulations

and two broadsheets, the *Sunday Times* and *Sunday Telegraph*, stable-mates of the daily *Times* and *Telegraph*. Rupert Murdoch's News International (redtop and quality) and Richard Desmond's Express group (redtop and mid-market) are the only publishers to have a presence in two of the three market sectors for both dailies and Sundays.

Tables 2.1 and 2.2 show sales of the national newspaper titles (daily and Sunday) over the past thirty years.

The redtop tabloids

Traditionally the redtop tabloids have been the most popular newspapers, targeted first at the working man, now more broadly at readers of both sexes from the lower socio-economic groups. Once referred to as the 'picture papers' because of the predominance of pictures over words – emphasised by the small format – they gave much space to sport, particularly football and horse-racing, the sports favoured by the working class for their links with betting. They featured show business (in the days before 'celebrity'), 'people' stories rather than politics, issues and foreign affairs.

Essentially redtop tabloids are about 'fun', a word encountered frequently by Sofia Johansson (2008) in her study of what attracted *Mirror* and *Sun* readers to their newspapers. She was told (2008: 404) 'it's a fun newspaper to read' and found 'this was a primary reason for buying the papers, with central experiences of amusement'. This study described the tabloids as having 'a typically sensationalist news style, a celebrity oriented and sexualised news agenda and the use of aggressive journalistic methods such as paparazzi coverage and chequebook journalism' (2008: 402).

This enjoyment factor in the popularity of redtop tabloids is stressed by Johansson's research sample. 'Sport and celebrity gossip dominated discussions of particularly well-liked reading material' (2008: 405). The papers provided 'a way to cope with experiences of events and circumstances of the surrounding world as threatening or depressing, where the newspapers would have a cheering-up function'. The emphasis on fun can be understood as 'a response to day-to-day routines, where the newspaper reading can work both as a way to release unwanted emotions and as dealing with general anxieties' (407).

It is all told in a language driven by its accessibility, its readability. It became known as 'tabloidese'. Martin Conboy (2006: 14) describes 'this systematic language use as rhetoric, not a high-flown, abstract style but a set of language devices used with the deliberate and consistent aim of confirming the existence of a national tabloid readership'. He quotes Teun Van Dijk (1991: 47) describing it as a 'range of language deployed by the tabloids to effectively inscribe a readership within its pages through the use of metaphor, irony, alliteration, rhyme or parallelism'.

Keith Waterhouse (1989: 26–27), until 2009 a *Daily Mail* columnist but for very many years a star of the then hugely successful *Daily Mirror*, described how in the mid-1930s that paper

> spat the plum from its mouth and began to speak in its own down-to-earth voice. … The *Daily Mirror* ceased to be fuddy-duddy and became brash and cheeky. Sometimes, it has to be said with hindsight, the paper's efforts to be bright and breezy had all the desperation of a fixed smile, and on occasion, anticipating the antics of today's tabloids, it could be so trivial as to appear featherbrained.

That style, refined and adapted by Murdoch's *Sun*, still defines the redtop, using short words and sentences, nouns as adjectives and expressions seldom spoken by anyone at all to provide the quick read the redtops believe their readers require.

As Jeremy Tunstall puts it:

> These daily papers focus on light news, the entertaining touch, and human interest; this in practice means focusing on crime, sex, sport, television, showbusiness, and sensational human interest stories. There is an overwhelming emphasis on personalities; such 'serious' news as is covered is often presented via one personality attacking another personality. Much material in these papers is 'look-at' material – there are many pictures, big headlines, and the advertising is mainly display, which again involves pictures and big headlines. The remainder of the tabloid is 'quick read' material with most stories running to less than 400 words. (1996: 11)

Although that broad Tunstall description of the redtop tabloids holds today, the papers have moved downmarket – 'dumbed down' (Johansson, 2008: 402) – and the environment in which they are published has changed. But they still provide a 'community' of readers, who enjoy discussing the trivia they read in the redtops. 'Tabloid reading was without exception described as a social activity' and was 'connotative of the warmth of human interaction, or belongingness and security' (409, 410).

The tabloids still sell in large quantities (the *Sun* sells ten times as many copies each day as the *Guardian*, for example) but they are losing sales faster than any other sector of the market. Over the past twenty years the *Sun* and *Mirror* between them have suffered sales losses of one third, or nearly 2.5 million. On Sundays the decline is significantly greater. The *News of the World*, *Sunday Mirror* and *People* have lost nearly half their combined sales over the same period, around 5.5 million. The rate of decline has increased over the past decade. So the popular press has become less popular, and the relative success of the *Mail* titles, to which we will come with the mid-market, has challenged the terminology.

The figures for individual titles over the past twenty years are stark: *Sun* sales down from 3.9 million to 3.1 million; *Mirror* down from 3.2 million to 1.6 million; *News of the World* down from 5.0 million to 3.3 million; *Sunday Mirror* down from 3.0 million to 1.5 million; and, most spectacularly, the *People* down from 2.9 million to 0.7 million (all figures audited ABC). So why the biggest decline in the most popular sector of the market? In order to answer this more specific question we will ignore the more general factors which apply to all newspapers, particularly the growth of alternative sources of news and information, and the variety of media on which they are available. Those who believe that the printed press has 'dumbed down' over the last twenty years would argue that this has been done for commercial reasons, that so-called quality has been traded for greater commercial success. In the case of popular newspapers this 'lowest common denominator' or 'pandering to the masses' argument only works if it brings the desired result. If we are talking about the mass sector of the newspaper market, then it has clearly failed. The tabloid sector has always targeted the mass market, always sought to be 'popular'. Tunstall argues that 'the full tabloidisation of both downmarket and mid-market British national newspapers was not completed until the 1980s' (1996: 9), but the diminishing popularity of the 'downmarket' part of that has been underway since then.

In the heyday of the *Daily Mirror*, the 1950s and 1960s, it was certainly a more upmarket product than it is today. In a period when class was a more clear-cut aspect of British society the *Mirror's* brilliance was in being able to inform comprehensibly and mostly without patronising while at the same time being entertaining. It rarely talked down to its working-class readership, while accepting that what we would now call their lifestyle, both work and leisure, was distinctive and definable. The *Mirror* dealt with politics and work-related issues. It was the friend of organised labour, up to a point, and of crowded football terraces where everybody stood. It drank in the public bar, not the saloon. It celebrated manual labour and holidays in British seaside resorts. And it recognised, as many then didn't, that intelligence and reflection were not matters of social position.

But then the social order began to change, youth culture became a recognisable condition that crossed traditional class boundaries, as did political affiliation, and the erosion of deference meant the erosion of distinct and separate agendas for the different sectors of the newspaper market. And in 1969 Rupert Murdoch bought the *News of the World* and the *Sun*. The latter was re-launched to compete head-on with, and subsequently defeat, the *Mirror*. The *Sun's* early, and hugely successful, editors, Larry Lamb and Kelvin MacKenzie, did not share the *Mirror's* aspirational view of the working man and his thirst for education but preferred instead to cater to his perceived (by the *Sun*) tastes for naked breasts, sexual innuendo (and activity), soap operas, military adventures and package holidays to Spain, and his distaste for scroungers, strikers, comers-in and 'toffs'. The initial sales figures suggested they had adopted the right formula. They caught the pre-Thatcher mood and grew in confidence through most of the Thatcher years. It was done with style and wit. The *Mirror*, helped by the catastrophic ownership of Robert Maxwell, was left standing.

But it was a re-interpretation of the old formula, and a more pessimistic view of its audience, that the *Sun* was exploiting, and it failed to take into account how the old order was changing. It failed to recognise that Thatcherism had destroyed working-class solidarity by making it aspirational, that owner-occupation and the decline of traditional working-class manual employment were expanding the middle class and the numbers who sought to join it or believed they had. Why else was the *Mail* gaining readers while the redtops were losing them? These newspapers for the masses took the soft route of following television, reporting the twists in soap opera plots as though they were fact not fiction, and turning soap actors, not to mention Page Three girls, into celebrities. They created a new aristocracy out of footballers and their wives. The *Daily Star* launched on the basis that if the *Sun* had prospered by going downmarket of the *Mirror* they could achieve the same by going downmarket of the *Sun*. They made their glamour pictures more soft porn and took the television symbiosis a stage further by devoting pages every day to 'coverage' of reality TV shows, particularly *Big Brother*. The *Mirror* lost its roots and the *Sun* never had any. They partied instead. They sent 3.00 a.m. girls to party with, and report on, the celebrities they had created, and their editors became celebrities in their own right. Kelvin MacKenzie, and then the new *Mirror* editor, *Sun*-trained Piers Morgan, encouraged by the fascination for the tabloids shown by editors of more serious newspapers, started to enjoy sharing the status, and the parties, that their creations lived for. Having removed themselves, and their newspapers, from the everyday lives of their readers, they depended on the voyeurism of these readers, their absorption in the vacuous lives of the rich and famous-for-very-little.

Those who were entranced by celebrities had other places to go, magazines whose *raison d'être* was reporting and sustaining the B-list. Magazines can handle fads – they can be closed when the fad passes, and new ones will then take their place. But newspapers, in whichever market sector they are located, need a soul, to stand for something. The danger for the redtops is that only focussing on ephemera runs the risk of making them ephemeral themselves. The circulation decline of the redtops would suggest that they are running that risk.

The Sunday tabloids, historically more racy than their daily counterparts, have suffered more. The *News of the World*, still the biggest-selling paper in the country, continues to investigate and has the journalistic talent to do it well, but too often the subjects are of too little consequence to merit the effort. Investigation in the celebrity era also often comes down to investigating celebrity infidelities paid-for kiss and tell accounts by the dumped or concerning the bedroom performance of the dumpers. There is a curiously old-fashioned tone to the shock (however hypocritical) expressed by the redtops at the morality of those they 'expose'. It may have worked in the days when they were amplifying the evidence delivered in salacious court cases, when public morality led to tut-tutting while enjoying the read. Today it is hard to believe that many are shocked, or much care, particularly when they know that cuckolded minor celebrities are touting their stories for money.

Away from the bedroom, investigations are too often contrived: the *agent provocateur* activities of the *News of the World*'s 'fake sheikh', the illegal bugging, the repetitive 'exposing' of security flaws by sending reporters with fake weapons through airports. In an age of real terrorist fears and real security the public-interest justification by the redtops for soft investigations no longer rouses the readers.

The *Mirror* made one attempt to put the clock back. Long after Maxwell, long after the *Sun*'s circulation lead looked irrecoverable, Piers Morgan, supported by Philip Graf, chief executive of the new owners, Trinity Mirror, decided he was sick of *Big Brother*, celebrity, kiss-and-tell, and wanted to return the *Mirror* to its former self. Leave aside his own massive contribution to the promotion of celebrity journalism, and his television programme in which he interviewed celebrities about what it was like to be the subject of celebrity journalism, Morgan was characteristically determined about his reinvention of himself and his newspaper.

At the 2001 Belfast conference of the Society of Editors, Morgan publicly renounced *'Big Brother* journalism'. The events of 9/11, he said, had redefined tabloid journalism. He recounted his Belfast speech in his volume of 'diaries':

> We all saw big sales increases through July and August thanks to *Big Brother*, the most inane television ever made. I remember sitting in my office one night as bidding for interviews with various occupants of the *BB* house reached ridiculous proportions, thinking: has it really come to this? Is my journalistic career going to depend on whether I can persuade some halfwit from Wales called Helen to take my company's £250,000 and reveal in sizzlingly tedious detail that she's even more stupid than we first feared? (2005: 302)

He said that he had detected a new hunger for serious news that had at first been driven by fear after 9/11 but was now born out of serious interest. Morgan recalled the words of a former *Mirror* editor, Sylvester Bolam: 'The *Mirror*'s a sensational paper, but sensationalism doesn't mean the distortion of the truth. It means the vivid and dramatic presentation of events so as to give them a forceful impact on the mind of the reader' (2005: 302). 'I genuinely believe we're on to something here,' said Morgan, and went on to change his paper radically. This meant serious content written by serious journalists. John Pilger, veteran *Mirror* man, was one who returned and the paper adopted a strongly anti-Iraq war stance, as well as a black title-piece rather than the former redtop. Celebrity gossip was out. Just 18 months later Morgan was sending a *mea culpa* email to his chief executive Sly Bailey (Graf had gone, a casualty of the *Mirror*'s decline) after monthly sales figures had, as he put it, 'fallen off a cliff'. He had misjudged the way many *Mirror* readers would respond to the start of the war, with his paper attacking it while the sons of his readers were under enemy fire in Iraq.

Maybe it was the latter point rather than the new seriousness of the paper, the issue rather than the philosophy. Whichever, it hardly sent out signals that changing direction was the route to recovery. The *Sun* increased the circulation gap, and has continued to do so. And it was Iraq that brought about the downfall of Morgan. He had printed pictures allegedly taken in Basra of British soldiers allegedly abusing Iraqi civilians. There were questions over the authenticity of the pictures, and then a huge row involving the government, the army and the *Mirror*. It was the beginning of the end for Morgan, and soon after he was sacked (Morgan, 2005: 1–12). The *Mirror* returned to competing with the *Sun* on its own ground; and the redtop tabloid market continued to decline.

The mid-market

The mid-market revival is the story of one newspaper, the *Daily Mail*, and its Sunday sibling the *Mail on Sunday*. The two have overturned the natural order of the newspaper market, where redtop tabloids sell more than mid-market papers, which in turn sell more than the serious or 'quality' papers. The *Daily Mail* today is the second largest-selling daily newspaper in Britain (to the *Sun*); the *Mail on Sunday* is the second largest-selling Sunday newspaper (to the *News of the World*). Both sell on average more than 2.3 million copies each publication day (audited ABC sales).

The *Mail* was founded in 1896 by Alfred Harmsworth, and unlike any other national newspaper (with the exception of the *Guardian*, which has a different structure being owned by a trust) has enjoyed the same ownership ever since. Associated Newspapers, the company running the Mail group, is headed today by the latest Lord Rothermere, and the family has never deviated from its support for its newspapers. They have had a chequered history, but the modern good times really started in the early 1970s when the company ended its involvement in the redtop tabloid market by closing the failing *Daily Sketch* and relaunching the broadsheet *Mail* as a mid-market tabloid. It started the *Mail on Sunday* in 1982. It owes the success of both newspapers to the journalistic flair and talent of David English, who became editor-in-chief, and after his death his successor Paul Dacre, the present editor-in-chief. These two editorial giants have led the *Mail* titles not only to a complete dominance of their market sector but also to an influence and regard across the national newspaper market. They are loathed by their liberal critics. *Guardian* columnists and leader writers regularly disparage the *Mail* and what it stands for, while the *Mail* regularly responds with disparaging comments about the *Guardian*. Since the overlap of readers is nearly non-existent, it is an 'insider' battle fought out in the public prints often to the bafflement of the readers of one or other newspaper.

The extreme end of liberal contempt for the *Mail* was articulated by Nick Davies in his wider assault on the current state of newspaper journalism, *Flat Earth News* (2008). He finds the *Mail* 'guilty of a certain kind of reporting. This involves something rather like the work of a gardener, who digs out and throws away weeds and stones and anything else which he does not want and then plants whatever he fancies. The story, in other words, is a model of the subtle art of distortion. Aggressive distortion' (2008: 357).

Nevertheless, the *Mail* is taken immensely seriously by politicians across the spectrum as representing a hugely significant and unignorable strand of British public opinion. The *Mail* titles exude confidence. The daily, with its longer history, sets the agenda, which is based on an intimate knowledge of its audience. The *Mail* is the embodiment of the idea that a successful newspaper both reflects and reinforces the prejudices of its readers. It believes it knows what these are, more than the politicians who seek their votes. The *Mail* is suspicious of what it sees as the metropolitan liberal consensus of the 'political and media classes'. It regards this as out of touch with 'ordinary voters', by which it means *Mail* readers. It despises political correctness and what Dacre refers to as the 'subsidariat'. Delivering the Cudlipp Lecture at the London College of Communication in January 2007, Dacre described this as the loss-making newspapers, those 'subsidised' by the profits of other publications in their group (he cited the *Sun* 'subsidising' the *Times* and *Auto Trader* 'subsidising' the *Guardian*) and the taxpayer 'subsidising' the BBC. He said of the loss-making newspapers:

> Their journalism and values, invariably liberal, metropolitan and politically correct, don't connect with sufficient readers to be commercially viable. Ah, say the bien pensants, but such papers are hugely concerned for the common good. But there is a rather unedifying contradiction here. For the subsidariat are actually rather disdainful of the common man, contemptuous even, of the papers that make profits by appealing to and connecting with millions of ordinary men and women.

That, in a nutshell, is the credo of the dominant influence on the *Mail*. It is articulated daily in a set of values that can be summarised thus: it espouses self-reliance and eschews dependency – it is for standing on your own feet, suspicious of welfare and relentless in 'exposing' cases of welfare abuse, or 'scrounging'. It is more concerned about crime than the causes of crime, and prefers what it calls 'traditional' values to 'liberal' values. That means a belief in marriage and family life, and concern about working mothers. It campaigns against bureaucratic interference, or 'meddling', and celebrates achievement above equality of opportunity. It takes a negative line on the European Union, the BBC and the 'nanny state'. At the same time it campaigns, more vigorously and bravely than others, for justice for Stephen Lawrence and a range of 'victims' – pensioners, teachers wrongly accused of misconduct against pupils, employers wrongly accused of discrimination.

Unlike the redtop tabloids the *Mail* cannot be accused of ignoring serious news. It is a tabloid that puts the emphasis on text and is never afraid to run long stories over more than a page. It invests heavily in editorial content and promotion and has more long-serving distinguished journalists than any other paper. It is ruthlessly edited, commissioning far more material than it publishes, and it projects its columnists whom it hires to project its prejudices in a more extreme form than represented in its leaders. The *Mail* likes to give space to a rant. It has a strong record of exposure stories that frequently make waves and influence or even set the political agenda. At the same time it has led the way on lifestyle features, particularly in the area of health. It has the highest proportion of women readers of any national newspaper. While the mass-selling redtops have failed to recognise changes in British society, the *Mail* has embraced them, identifying the growing middle class as its target audience and understanding that many of them do not subscribe to liberal values. It is often portrayed as the voice of 'middle England', of the 'silent majority'. Its success suggests that this constituency exists.

In his Cudlipp Lecture Dacre took on those of the 'liberal establishment' who sought to curb the excesses of the press, who argued that the 'irresponsibility of Britain's media was making good governance all but impossible' and that 'more civic journalism' was needed. He said:

> This argument, while being a brilliant defence of such newspapers as *Pravda*, profoundly misunderstands the nature of Britain's popular press. Such papers need to be sensational, irreverent, gossipy, interested in celebrities and human relationships and, above all, brilliantly entertaining sugar coated pills if they are to attract huge circulations *and* devote considerable space to intelligent, thought provoking journalism, analysis and comment on important issues. And any paper that manages both to entertain and engage millions of readers with brilliantly written serious journalism on the great issues of the day is playing an important role in democracy and the judges and the subsidariat ignore the sugar coated pill argument at their peril.
>
> Of course the British press, pretty much all of it, has flaws: under pressure of deadlines it is, regrettably, too often careless, too often insensitive and clumsy in its headlong rush for a story, it over-states and over-simplifies, it prefers the dramatic to the mundane, the sentimental to the compassionate. Above all it lives for the day and is often risibly short term in its view of things.
>
> But I also believe passionately that the popular press has great virtues. At their best, popular papers – that are far more sensitive than politicians and opinion polls to national moods – articulate the anxieties, apprehensions and aspirations of their readers. Genuinely democratic – I mean, you try persuading people to fork out 45p for a paper on a rainy day – they give voice to millions of ordinary people who don't have a voice.
>
> And because they have this symbiotic, almost tactile responsiveness to their readers, such papers are often able to identify and highlight great truths – truths that are often uncomfortable to a ruling class that is increasingly dismissive of ordinary people's views. (Dacre, 2007)

The *Daily Express* was notoriously dismissive of its readers' views when it was owned by the TV mogul and New Labour peer Clive Hollick. The

Express, the creature of one of the most famous of all proprietors, Lord Beaverbrook (see Chapter 4), had dominated the market from the 1930s to the 1960s, when it entered its period of decline, which continues and is unlikely ever to be reversed. In the golden days it too knew its audience and its times, deeply patriotic, royalist, conservative and imperial. It was selling over 4 million copies a day in 1955, and around three-quarters of a million today. It never really recovered from the end of empire, consistently losing sales throughout the sixties and most years since. After it moved out of Beaverbrook ownership it went through a succession of proprietors, and changed its editor with the same regularity of a premier league football manager.

But it was Hollick, acquiring the paper in 1996, who defied every theory of running a successful newspaper by deciding to sack the readers. In its heyday the *Express* was the confident upholder of all things Conservative (with a capital 'C'), and until Hollick bought the paper it had remained staunchly right wing. Hollick decided it should overnight become New Labour, and brought in as editor Rosie Boycott to supervise the change. Suddenly the colonels from Cheltenham found themselves reading about the case for legalising marijuana over their toast and marmalade. They did not like it. Hollick had forgotten the first rule of newspapers, that it is so much easier to lose readers than to gain them. And when you tell all your readers that this is now a different newspaper of a wholly different political and social outloook, then it is likely they will depart. They did. The *Mail* gratefully took them in. Hollick sold to Richard Desmond, who had built his reputation and fortune publishing in the cellophane wrapped, top-shelf end of the magazine market. Then in 2004 the *Express* readers had another opportunity for confusion. The editor, Peter Hill, signed a front-page editorial explaining his 'historic decision' to return to normal service and 'back the Tories'. Sales continued to fall.

The new Tory *Express* developed a new kind of newspaper formula: iden-tify a small number of stories that research shows interest the readers and always lead the front page with them, whether or not anything has hap-pened. Initially it was house prices, mortgage rates and inheritance tax. Then they seized on Princess Diana and turned the conspiracy theory into an art form. Day after day they led the paper on new twists in the already very old story, using seldom identified 'sources' to back up increasingly unlikely 'news' stories about the circumstances of Diana's death. Day after day these stories sank without trace, but it never deterred the paper from coming up with more. In 2007, while never suspending its commitment to the Diana conspiracy, it adopted a similarly obsessive approach to the abduction of Madeleine McCann. Of course this was a story that had absorbed the British public for many weeks after the child's disappearance in Portugal, and there had been saturation coverage from all the media. But the *Express* con-tinued to lead the paper day after day, under the label in red type 'Madeleine', with tenuous stories seldom appearing anywhere else. In March 2008 the *Express* (together with the sister *Daily Star* and the two papers' Sunday stable-mates) were forced to publish prominent apologies and pay substantial damages to Madeleine's parents, Gerry and Kate. Today the paper, which has had editorial costs stripped out to leave a much smaller staff than its competitors, is much diminished in reputation, as well as sales.

The *Mail* – 'brilliant and corrupt, the professional foul of contemporary Fleet Street' (Davies, 2008: 369) – is always controversial, always talked about by journalists and politicians. But the mid-market is now *Mail* (loved and loathed) territory, weekdays and Sunday, and these papers attract upwardly mobile readers from the redtop sector as well as competing with right-of-centre titles in the quality sector.

The serious or 'quality' sector

No longer can we call them the broadsheets, because three of them aren't. The so-called 'compact revolution' is dealt with in detail later in this chapter, because it has been a significant development and has contributed to the relative success of the upmarket sector during the recent years of newspaper circulation decline. It is the sector that has undergone the most change, not only in format but also in editorial content, bulk and in driving multi-media publishing. It is the sector that features most often in the 'dumbing down' debate (see Chapter 6) because occupying the higher, more serious, more issue-driven ground, it has more potential for descent and its natural readers tend to occupy the higher socio-economic and intellectual area of society, and include the politicians and decision takers, those who run society. The serious newspapers, traditionally strong on text and debate, less interested in human interest, tittle-tattle and popular culture, have a presence and influence way beyond their relatively modest circulations.

The five serious dailies – *The Times, Telegraph, Guardian, Independent* and *Financial Times* – account for (at the end of 2008) an average 2.48 million sales (audited ABC), fewer than the *Sun* alone and just 0.4 million more than the *Daily Mail*. The four serious Sundays – *Sunday Times, Sunday Telegraph, Observer* and *Independent on Sunday* – have combined sales of 2.48 million, fewer than the *News of the World* alone and only 0.27 million more than the *Mail on Sunday*. Competition and profitability, however, are not simply about sales; they are about sales to certain kinds of people. Revenues from popular, mass-circulation newspapers come predominantly from the cover price, whereas the serious newspapers, which sell at a higher price, are much more dependent on advertising revenue, for which they can charge higher rates because of the higher socio-economic status, and affluence, of their readers.

As Tunstall (1996: 14) puts it:

> In terms of commercial income, upmarket papers are primarily in the advertising business, while downmarket papers are primarily in the sales business. Upmarket papers must sell to upmarket people, for whom they can charge high advertising rates per thousand readers. These contrasted forms of revenue, it can be said, exaggerate the real differences between their two sets of readers. But there is also a further form of polarisation or exaggeration; while downmarket papers simply focus on selling more copies (thus maximising sales revenue), the upmarket papers tend to focus upon the more affluent (and more attractive to advertisers) readers even within their middle-class audience.

It thus becomes highly significant that the popular newspapers are losing sales (on which they are more dependent) faster than the serious titles. And it goes some way to explaining why the serious titles have been earlier and more enthusiastic adopters of web publishing, in that they are more concerned, have more to lose, from a shift of advertising from print to online, and have a readership who are more active online.

The *Financial Times*, the pink one, needs to be distinguished from the other serious titles. It is basically a specialist business newspaper, seeing its natural rival as the *Wall Street Journal* (acquired in 2008 by Rupert Murdoch), and it has an international audience, publishing in the United States and the Far East as well as in London. It has a large institutional sale, with a heavy presence in boardrooms and financial institutions. Its audited sale, always included in the monthly ABC data, and thus compared with the other serious papers, is, however, very different in character. Its sale of 452,000 (Oct. 2008) includes 297,000 (66 per cent) outside the UK and Ireland. *The Times*, in contrast, sells 29,000 of its 630,000 circulation (5 per cent) overseas. The other qualities show roughly similar proportions to *The Times*.

However, in recent years the *FT* has enjoyed a great circulation growth and has added to its general content while in no way diluting its business and finance base. It is highly regarded for its political and international coverage, and for its commentary. It has developed its website into one of the strongest. Although it does not have a Sunday sibling it produces a Saturday edition which is distinctively different, and has more general appeal, from its Monday to Friday product, and this is on sale on Saturdays and Sundays, making it Britain's one declaredly 'weekend' newspaper.

The four general serious dailies and their four sibling Sundays have readerships that are 80 per cent ABC1 (the professional and managerial classes) and 50 per cent AB (the senior members of those classes). They are educated, affluent (to varying degrees), cultivated (ditto) and influential. They span the mainstream political spectrum, with the *Independent* and *Guardian* left of centre (the *Independent* more agitprop, the *Guardian* more social democrat) and *The Times* and *Telegraph* to the right. This is reflected in the

Sunday publications, although the *Observer*, the *Guardian's* stablemate, will take a rather different line from the daily on certain issues, most notably the Iraq war. The *Sunday Times* tends to be more vigorously right-wing than the daily, and has a very different character. All but the *Telegraph* titles, *Sunday Times* and *Financial Times* have changed to the compact format (see later in this chapter). Despite that maintenance of the status quo the *Telegraph* has in almost every other way been through a massive change – new owners, new editors for daily and Sunday, new offices and a new and rapidly developing commitment to the digital age. Traditionally the most conservative of newspapers, with its most conservative audience, it is now offering readers pods, blogs and online TV, all with a constant cross referencing in the newspapers to its digital output.

Each of the serious newspapers has a distinctive personality, often caricatured, often used as a descriptor for a certain kind of person, defined by the newspaper he or she reads. *The Times* is probably the most famous British newspaper, known as the paper of the establishment, even, years ago, advertising itself as the 'top people's paper'. It was read by the political and professional classes, and carried the law reports. It had its famous letters' page, the establishment noticeboard, where the ruling elite could air their views and assume, often rightly, that note would be taken of them. Historically *The Times* was the 'newspaper of record'. It would provide the most comprehensive account of parliamentary debate, law reports and the activities of the royal family. It probably remains the most famous British newspaper across the world – *The Times* of London – despite being unrecognisable from its former self. Today, in common with the rest of the serious, quality press, it has a much more general, even populist, agenda. The change began when Rupert Murdoch bought it.

The *Telegraph*, the largest selling of the serious dailies, is traditionally the Conservative house journal, appealing to swathes of the traditional middle class across the country. If *The Times* was defined by its letters' page, the *Telegraph* was defined by its births, marriages and deaths columns. It seemed that no self-respecting member of the middle class would be born, betrothed, have children or die without these events being posted in the *Telegraph*. It sustained the congratulations and condolences shared, by post, among the readers. And to a certain extent it still does. *Telegraph* readers were not necessarily very successful or very rich, although a significant number were; however, they were above all respectable, professional, God-fearing people supporting what they considered to be traditional values. They tended to go to church, pay for education, drive Rovers and respect the upper and officer classes, or the 'natural order'. They did not like 'state interference'. They did like state occasions, field sports and Sunday lunchtime drinks parties. They sympathised with those unable to maintain their stately homes and country houses. Such people as still exist still read the *Telegraph*.

But this newspaper, like *The Times*, now has to appeal to a broader audience, or at least to the sons and daughters of the traditional one, to Fulham as well as Gloucestershire.

It may have moved on from defence correspondents with a rank in their bylines, but it still gives a high priority to defence matters, recognising that commissioned officers still feature highly among the readership. It still debates problems associated with nannies and paying the school fees, and it still has its 'country life' agenda. But it is now more streetwise, even if that street is likely to be Sloane Square or Lombard Street. It assumes its readers would rather buy their chickens, pheasants or smoked salmon from expensive mail-order specialists rather than Marks and Spencer, and it recognises than the Rover has given way to a Range Rover. It knows that readers are more likely to live in the city than the country, but assumes they own, or aspire to, a weekend place in the country. It also believes its readers buy shares and worry about inheritance tax. And it maintains some of its former excellence in its sports coverage.

The *Guardian*, perhaps more than any other newspaper, is the one that is stereotyped by its critics and referred to satirically or derogatorily by its right-of-centre rivals. It in turn is equally obsessed by other newspapers, particularly the *Daily Mail*. The *Guardian* used to be characterised as wearing open-toed sandals, and aiming at fell-walking social workers or teachers of a woolly liberal persuasion. That dated back to its Manchester non-Conformist roots, and the influence of its remarkably long-serving, bearded and bicycling editor C.P. Scott, who set up the trust that owns the paper, and the *Observer*, today. But the *Manchester Guardian* moved to London in the 1960s, dropped the Manchester, and gradually became the metropolitan liberal national newspaper it is today. Under its two wholly London editors, Peter Preston and Alan Rusbridger, it has taken on a new character and through its online product, Guardian Unlimited, has established an international reputation. It has a relatively small circulation – only the *Independent*'s is smaller – but a deeply committed and engaged readership of articulate, educated, mainly middle-class people. It takes itself very seriously, and so do its readers.

It still attracts a bedrock of public-sector readers, mainly teachers and social workers, for whom it provides supplements and from whom it has developed a profitable classified advertising business. It has also dominated the media jobs advertising marketplace, and runs a media news and comment section, and associated website, that are read avidly by media professionals. It speaks up for the Third World, for immigrants and ethnic minorities, the planet and climate change, for comprehensive education and for Europe. It is demanding of the Labour Party, to which it gives qualified support and which it frequently irritates. It sees itself at the cutting edge of metropolitan fad and fashion and ahead of the game in terms of culture, both popular and high. It some times seems embarrassed by the affluence of its audience while at the same time catering for those who eat in expensive restaurants and take exotic holidays. It is often surprised that more people do not agree with it, or worse, accuse it of hypocrisy. It agonises over those less fortunate than itself while appealing to a fashionable, liberal, London elite.

It does, however, provide a conscience for left-of-centre politics, and has a sound record for exposing inconsistency and sometimes corruption in those in power. It has influential columnists, a youthful second section, and it remains the preferred choice of the more earnest university student who still buys a (subsidised) newspaper.

The *Independent* achieved the near impossible by starting and continuing to exist. It was the brainchild of Andreas Whittam Smith and two *Telegraph* colleagues who had a dream of a new national newspaper not financed by one dominant proprietor or group. They raised money in relatively small tranches from venture capitalists and were able to claim true 'independence' when they launched into a booming and yuppie 1986. Although relatively conventional in appearance – it was a broadsheet then – it was innovative in content (it was the first paper to provide comprehensive listings and the first broadsheet to run large pictures) and became immediately fashionable. Its slogan 'It is. Are you?' – independent, that is – resonated at a time when the passions roused by Murdoch's move to Wapping were great. The marketing people used the word 'badge' – it enhanced the image of those seen carrying it. It sold more than 400,000 copies for a while, but then suffered from the economic downturn of the early nineties.

The ownership structure could not sustain it, and 'independence' gave way to corporate ownership, first by the *Mirror* and then by Tony O'Reilly's Independent News and Media. It has tried to maintain the values of its founders editorially if not in terms of ownership, but circulation continuously declined until the paper pioneered the reduction in size to the compact format (see later in this chapter). It is now declining again, with a circulation approaching half of that seen in its heyday. A Sunday stablemate was launched in 1990, the *Independent on Sunday*, again innovative with its well-designed Review. That paper too has suffered from declining sales, more than the daily, and both titles are now bottom of the sales league in their respective markets.

Both are relatively under-resourced in terms of editorial staffing and budgeting, and neither makes a commercial case for existing. But O'Reilly finds them helpful to his profitable international portfolio, likes to own national newspapers in Britain, feels affection for them, and supports them. Under the editorship-in-chief of Simon Kelner, who understands the need to compensate for a lack of resources with distinctiveness and niche appeal, the *Independent* then set off in a new direction when it adopted 'poster' front pages, dealing with a single issue and making no claim for impartiality. Kelner coined the term 'viewspaper' and saw that there was an (albeit limited) market for a paper that overtly campaigned, took a line, in its news coverage. It was consistent, and ahead of British public and newspaper opinion, in its opposition to the war in Iraq, and in Robert Fisk possessed a reporter with attitude whose every word underpinned that stance. After embarking on the 'viewspaper' strategy the *Independent* sought out other issues to take on with the poster treatment. It often seemed there were not enough, with the paper having to contrive an 'issue' for the front page poster treatment rather than simply choosing the most important or interesting story of the day.

In 2008 Kelner moved from the editor to managing director role and brought in as his successor Roger Alton, who had previously edited the *Observer* with some circulation success. He took a more conventional approach to the front page and introduced a new sports supplement. He could not stem the circulation slide, but was hardly helped by a price rise to £1 (Monday to Friday) that made it the most expensive general interest daily. The *Independent* still has critical respect, but more affection than readers.

Who reads what? The demographics of newspaper audiences

The preceding sections on the three sectors of the national newspaper market have concentrated on the qualitative descriptions of the titles making up each sector, the audiences that they cater to and their success in this objective. A quantitative analysis of audience characteristics also helps to describe a newspaper, and marketing departments regularly collect data, both to tell the publisher about the audience their title has, and to identify those worth pursuing. This can lead to editorial developments, to the targeting of certain groups through particular content. It is of great interest to advertisers who are much more precise targeters than editors. The advertiser will base decisions on where to buy space on the demographics of the readers of the newspaper, and the likelihood of their being interested in buying the product or service being advertised. BMW does not advertise in the *Sun*.

The National Readership Survey continuously polls a representative sample of 35,000 people a year at the rate of 3,000 a month to provide first figures for the readership of papers (as opposed to sales, where ABC audits the sales figures provided by publishers) and then demographic data about those readers. It is an independent, non-profit organisation, and its methodology is agreed on by both advertisers and publishers, who take the results very seriously. The following tables can tell us a lot about the typical readers of each title. The first four contain NRS data for the period April to September 2007.

Although women are the majority in the adult population, most newspapers have a larger male readership than female. The one exception is the *Daily Mail*, as we have seen above the most commercially successful newspaper of the last twenty years. The *Mail* deliberately targets women in several ways. Its designated Femail and health sections appeal to women, as do the human interest, lifestyle and 'relationship' stories of which the *Mail* is

Table 2.3   *Newspaper readership by sex*

Newspaper	Readership male %	Readership female %
All adults (15+)	48.6	51.4
Daily Telegraph	55.1	44.9
Financial Times	69.6	30.4
Guardian	57	43
Independent	60.9	39.1
Times	58.4	41.6
Daily Express	53.6	46.4
Daily Mail	48	52
Daily Mirror	53.1	46.9
Daily Star	69.1	30.9
Sun	57	43

Source: NRS 2007

Table 2.4   *Newspaper readership by age*

Newspaper	15–24	25–34	35–44	45–54	55–64	65+
Daily Telegraph	7.4	7.8	11.2	14.6	20.9	38.1
Financial Times	12.1	22.1	22.8	20.7	11.5	10.8
Guardian	11.1	16.2	25	19.6	15.3	12.7
Independent	15.2	18.9	19.2	22.8	12.7	11.2
Times	13.3	13.5	18.3	16.6	19.4	18.9
Daily Express	8.1	6.5	11.3	18	20.4	35.7
Daily Mail	9.2	6.9	14	17.1	21.7	31
Daily Mirror	14.5	12.5	13.8	16.8	15.8	26.6
Daily Star	21.1	21.2	23.6	14.9	12	7.2
Sun	19.9	17.8	19.2	14.8	13.6	14.6

Source: NRS 2007

so fond. It is the newspaper most influenced by magazines in its approach to subject matter, presentation and narrative writing style. It uses magazine writers and makes extensive use of features. The *Daily Star* and *Financial Times* have the highest proportion of male readers, for entirely different reasons: soft porn in the *Star*, money in the *FT*. Of the redtops, the *Mirror* has the highest proportion of women readers.

Newspaper editors are always chasing young readers. The argument is that the sooner you get them the longer you will have them, and that papers with an older readership lose them at a faster rate because they die. That theory depends on the loyalty of readers to stay with one title – 'We've always taken

Table 2.5   Newspaper readership by social grade

Newspaper	A	B	C1	C2	D	E
Daily Telegraph	16.1	43.3	27.7	7.2	3.1	2.5
Financial Times	20.4	56.1	19.7	2.7	0.5	0.5
Guardian	13	49.9	28	3.2	3.3	2.5
Independent	11.2	45.4	33.4	6.2	2.8	0.9
Times	14.7	48.1	26.3	6.2	2.8	1.8
Daily Express	2.3	24	36.5	22.3	9.2	5.7
Daily Mail	5.2	26.6	34.2	19.4	10.4	4.2
Daily Mirror	1.2	10.5	28.5	29.5	21.5	8.6
Daily Star	0.3	6.8	21.5	32.1	29.4	9.9
Sun	0.8	9.8	25.5	30.9	22.9	10.1

Source: NRS 2007

the *Express* in our house' – and the assumption that young readers are attracted to newspapers at all. These assumptions are questionable, as is the belief by many advertisers that young people have more purchasing power and are more suggestible in terms of buying new products. Several factors counter that conventional view. Newspaper purchasing and reading habits have changed: even loyal readers of one title will buy it only on certain days ('occasional regular readers'); home delivery has declined massively; and more young readers than old are using the internet as their primary source of news. Increasing life expectancy means that there are more loyal older readers for longer, and the 'silver economy' is recognised as increasingly significant. So as long as older readers are replaced a perfectly viable newspaper market can exist at a time of changing demographics with an older age profile.

The successful *Daily Mail* has 70 per cent of its readers over the age of 45. The highest-selling title in the serious sector of the market, the *Daily Telegraph*, has 74 per cent. The *Guardian*, in contrast, has 53 per cent of its readers under 45, as does the *Independent*. The *Sun* has an even spread of readers across all age groups, but only 43 per cent over 45. The *Daily Star* has the starkest profile: not only the highest proportion of male readers but also the highest proportion of young readers, 38 per cent under 35 and 58 per cent under 45.

There is a clear class or socio-economic basis to the UK's newspaper readership, and the figures supporting this are of great relevance to advertisers who seek precision in targeting those most likely to buy their goods and services. The serious or 'quality' newspapers draw more than 60 per cent of their readers from the AB social grades, apart from the *Independent* with a figure of 57 per cent and the *Telegraph* with 59 per cent. The AB categories (26 per cent of the adult population) include senior- and middle-management

Table 2.6 *Newspaper readership by ethnic origin*

Newspaper	White	Black	Indian subcontinent	Chinese/ other Asian	Other	All non-white
Daily Telegraph	90.5	0.9	1.7	0.8	0.6	4.0
Financial Times	74.8	2.7	10.5	2.6	0.4	16.2
Guardian	81.3	4.9	1.9	3.3	1.4	11.5
Independent	83.7	3.9	2.9	2.3	2.6	11.7
Times	87.4	1.7	2.7	0.7	0.5	5.6
Daily Express	90.4	1.1	2.9	0.7	0.5	5.2
Daily Mail	89.5	1.2	2.3	1.3	0.6	5.4
Daily Mirror	84.5	5.7	3.9	1.2	1.1	11.9
Daily Star	92.4	2.5	2.5	0.7	0.8	6.5
Sun	88.3	3.4	2	1.1	1.1	7.6

Source: NRS 2007

professionals, from business, education, medicine, the civil service, law and the public sector. C1 (29 per cent) is the social grade describing all others doing non-manual jobs and manual jobs with specific qualifications. C2 (21 per cent) describes skilled manual workers, D (16 per cent) semi-skilled and unskilled manual workers, and E (8 per cent) those with the lowest levels of income (descriptors used by Ipsos MORI). The *Sun, Mirror* and *Daily Star* all draw more than 60 per cent of their readers from the C2, D, and E social grades, with the *Star* having the highest figure of 71 per cent. Again, the *Daily Mail* breaks through the usual market-sector barriers, with 65 per cent of its readers in the non-manual ABC1 categories, and 32 per cent in the top AB professional grouping. As it regularly points out, its substantial circulation in comparison with the serious sector of the market means it has more AB readers than all the quality titles.

The minority-ethnic population is about 13 per cent of the adult population as a whole, a figure that is not reflected in the minority-ethnic readership of most daily newspapers. The *Daily Telegraph* minority-ethnic readership makes up only 4 per cent of its total readership, the lowest figure of any title. *The Times, Daily Express* and *Daily Mail* have a figure of around 5 per cent, with the *Sun* significantly higher at 7.6 per cent. The two centre-left serious newspapers, the *Guardian* and *Independent,* have the highest proportion of minority-ethnic readers, 11.5 per cent and 11.7 per cent respectively, apart from the *Financial Times* which has easily the highest figure, 16.2 per cent, thanks to its high readership of readers of Indian subcontinent origin.

Voting intention data in table 2.6 (overleaf) comes from MORI and were collected in the year before the third Labour general election victory. Clearly they are dependent on the state of the parties at that time, but give a clear

Table 2.7 *Newspaper readership by voting intention (%)*

Newspaper	Labour	Conservative	Liberal Democrats
All adults	35	33	22
Daily Mirror	60	16	17
Daily Star	53	18	15
Guardian	46	6	37
Sun	41	32	13
Independent	35	13	39
Express	27	46	17
Times	27	39	28
Financial Times	25	43	24
Daily Mail	21	55	16
Daily Telegraph	16	63	16
No paper	35	28	26

Source: MORI 2004

picture of the party political inclinations of the readership of individual titles, and editorially the political views of those titles. The *Daily Mirror* has the highest proportion of Labour voting readers (60 per cent) and the *Daily Telegraph* the highest proportion of Conservative voters (63 per cent). The *Independent* attracts the highest proportion of Liberal voters. Apart from the *Mirror*, the *Guardian*, *Star* and *Sun* have a preponderance of Labour voters, while the *Telegraph*, *Express*, *Times*, *Financial Times* and *Daily Mail* are dominated by Conservative voters.

Compacts

The 'compact revolution' within Britain's broadsheet press was brought about by the failure of the *Independent* to recover from falling circulation and a series of changes to its ownership and editor (six in seven years). It had failed to sustain its dream of independence from traditional ownership. The economic climate had changed for the worse within five years of its successful launch, and the cost of launching the *Independent on Sunday* in 1990 stretched the *Independent* too far. There then followed a series of ownership arrangements, none of which were true to the original concept, until Tony O'Reilly, the former Heinz executive, took full control in 1998.

While in many ways a traditional newspaper baron, he had a relationship with the paper he was to save that went beyond that. He was prepared to suffer huge losses from the moment he took over, and while that inevitably led to reducing the editorial staffs of both the daily and Sunday titles, he persevered. His appointment as editor-in-chief of Simon Kelner, a talented sports-production journalist who had been on the *Independent* at the start before moving to executive positions on the *Sunday Correspondent, Observer* and, moving out of sport, as editor of the *Daily Mail* supplement Night and Day, changed the uncertain atmosphere on the papers and brought stability, even if it failed to halt the circulation decline. O'Reilly also brought in as chief executive Ivan Fallon, who had run his lucrative South African operation. Earlier Fallon had been the business editor and deputy editor at the *Sunday Times*.

Sales of the daily were down to 220,000 at the end of 1998, as these three men considered the state of the *Independent* at the start of a new era of ownership. It was no small achievement for a new national newspaper to still be there more than a decade later, but this was dependent on O'Reilly underwriting it. After a series of strategies to rebuild the titles had failed, Kelner and Fallon came up with the 'big idea'. They would re-launch the *Independent* as a quality tabloid, or 'compact' as Kelner relentlessly described it, to differentiate it from the mass-circulation redtops. O'Reilly endorsed this decision.

It was not in fact a new idea. As Roy Greenslade notes (2003a: 258) the mid-market *Daily Mail*, then a broadsheet and losing sales, went tabloid in May 1971 to coincide with the closure of its sister (tabloid) title the *Daily Sketch*. Lord Harmsworth, the chairman of Associated Newspapers, publishers of the *Mail*, referred to the re-launched newspaper as a 'compact', but back then the word never caught on. The *Mail* was selling 1.8 million before its 1971 re-launch. Today it sells 2.3 million.

The arguments surrounding the *Independent*'s decision were not new, even to the quality sector of the market. Under Peter Preston's editorship of the *Guardian* (1975–1995) tabloid sections had been introduced, but even though Preston (a lover of Spanish and Italian small-format quality newspapers) seriously considered going all the way and making the main news section tabloid the risk was considered too great, the belief that broadsheet equalled quality being too deep rooted to be put aside.

Kelner and Fallon thought it all through again. They knew that market research carried out by broadsheet titles had repeatedly drawn a pro-tabloid response, particularly among commuters on crowded trains, younger readers and women readers, categories of great interest to advertisers. There was the long tradition of smaller-format quality papers in mainland Europe. There would be considerable initial publicity in changing format. And it was likely that sampling, even a gain in sales that stuck, would follow the re-launch. Against that there was the peculiarly British association of the word tabloid (simply a measure of size, half a broadsheet) with the downmarket, redtop sector of the market. Would there be accusations of 'dumbing down' if a serious broadsheet downsized? There were problems, too, about advertising revenue. Would advertisers pay the same for a full page in a tabloid as a full page in a broadsheet? It was clearly less risky for the *Independent* than for papers with more conservative, and larger, audiences like *The Times* and *Telegraph*. *Independent* readers were younger, less resistant to change. And its low and declining circulation meant it had more to gain and less to lose by the change in size.

The *Independent* chose to hedge its bets, first printing the compact version alongside the broadsheet (a costly exercise, but one minimised by the small sale of the paper). The compact was launched inside the M25 on Tuesday, 30 September 2003, Monday to Friday only. It performed very well; the audited circulation for October 2003 was up 17,000 on the previous month. Better figures were to come as the compact was rolled out across the country. By November it was up another 5,000, by the following April a further 20,000. A Saturday compact was introduced on 31 January 2004, and the final step, to stop printing any broadsheets, came on Friday, 17 May 2004. A sale of 261,000 was recorded for that month, an increase of 40,000 year on year. Many of them came from the *Guardian*.

'For the first five years of my editorship', Kelner told *Media Guardian* (26 July 2004), 'on those afternoons when the monthly sales figures arrived, I used to look at them at a distance. Now I embrace them. They're phenomenal. We're 50,000 copies ahead year on year. We've gone up almost 40 per cent in some places'.

Although the public pronouncements from the rivals were dismissive, they were not entirely convincing; it was clear that they were worried. They too had done their market research and produced dummies of tabloid versions of their own newspapers. The *Independent* had stolen a lead, and whatever the rivals did now, however they explained it, they would be following. This worried the *Guardian* more than *The Times*. Rupert Murdoch told his *Times* editor, Robert Thomson, to prepare for a tabloid launch. Just seven weeks later it arrived, on Monday, 24 November 2003, with the compact selling alongside the broadsheet, just like the *Independent*. Thomson was forced to drop his attacks on the *Independent*. 'It is an undoubted success for which they deserve credit', he told *Press Gazette* (16 July 2004). 'We are grateful to them for having done the market research on how the audience would receive a compact quality newspaper'. *The Times*'s own compact research was reported (in *The Times*, 9 July 2004) by Brian MacArthur. It showed that 'nearly half of compact readers are aged between 25 and 44, 60 per cent are in full-time work, that 78 per cent are ABC1s and that about 40 per cent work in the business sector'.

Some thought *Times* readers would be more resistant to change than the *Independent*'s, that to the lawyers, businessmen and politicians who read the paper a compact would not reflect their self-image. Murdoch had dealt with such concerns before – by ignoring them. He had cut the price, and been greatly criticised for that; but he had also increased the circulation in doing so, taking *The Times* to a secure second place in the quality sector. Again he was rewarded for his speedy reaction over changing the format. *The Times* also increased sales by 5 per cent over the first year, not as dramatic as the *Independent*, but it was starting from a much higher base, with per centage increases in sales smaller.

The two other broadsheet titles had different problems with changing the format. The *Daily Telegraph*, with its 'middle-England' audience, older than its rivals, more conservative, more dispersed from London, was probably at greatest risk of reader resistance to a smaller format. Its then editor, Martin Newland, had also explored the tabloid option. But at this time the *Telegraph* editor and management had more important things to worry about. In the wake of the Conrad Black scandal the paper was up for sale (see Chapter 5).

The *Guardian* was in a different trap. It also had circulation problems and was a more direct competitor of the *Independent*. Its lead in sales had shrunk from 177,000 when both newspapers were broadsheet to 112,000 a year after the *Independent's* compact launch. The gap continued to contract, to 86,000. The *Guardian* was also more sensitive to accusations of imitating the *Independent*. It had its own reputation for innovation, in typography, supplements and marketing. It too had developed tabloid dummies, and many expected it to follow the *Independent* and *Times*. But Alan Rusbridger, the editor, had profound reservations about the tabloid, and probably even more about following the lead of its lower-circulation rival. He was concerned about the effect on content and the nature of the paper tabloidisation would bring. He watched the *Independent* and *Times* carefully, measuring stories, comparing the content and presentation of the two versions of each paper. Rusbridger (2005) described the effects of shrinking the size of the two serious papers that had already gone compact: 'Punchy front pages; opinionated copy: views before news; picture-led layouts; striking, lively, focussed presentation; headlines with attitude; take-no-prisoners writing'. The two papers, he said, were claiming they were 'exactly the same ... just more convenient for the reader'. He was not, he claimed, saying the two papers were worse than the broadsheets that had preceded them. 'All I can say is that two of our most important newspapers have changed, quite strikingly, in ways beyond mere shape. And that is not without significance. How journalists tell stories has an effect on the civic process. Ask anyone in public life'.

Rusbridger could hardly launch a 'tabloid compact' after that. And anyway he was already determined to do something different. Thus was born the 'Berliner' concept, adopting for the *Guardian* not the well-known, in Britain, tabloid format, but the bigger, in-between format of the famous European papers like *Le Monde*. Rusbridger commissioned designs, and set a team to work on internally producing a daily Berliner-sized version of the *Guardian*. 'We started thinking about the Berliner size because it works so well. Tabloid forces change in terms of layout, one main story a page, one

Table 2.8   Compact effect

Title – compact launch date	Last true broadsheet sale – month	One year later – increase over broadsheet (%)	Three years later – increase over broadsheet (%)	Today – increase over broadsheet (%)
Independent 30 Sept. 2003	219,000 Sept. 2003	265,000 21% Sept. 2004	265,000 21% Sept. 2006	221,000 +0.9% Sept. 2008
Times 24 Nov. 2003	656,000 Oct. 2003	691,000 5% Nov. 2004	654,000 0% Nov. 2006	638,000 –3% Sept. 2008
Guardian 12 Sept. 2005	358,000 July 2005	389,000 9% Sept. 2006	349,000 Sept. 2008	349,000 –3% Sept. 2008
Independent on Sunday 16 Oct. 2005	203,000 Sept. 2005	234,000 15% Sept. 2006	n/a	183,000 –10% Sept. 2008
Observer 8 Jan. 2006	437,000 Nov. 2005	444,000 2% Jan. 2007	n/a	453,000 +4% Sept. 2008

Month of 'true' last broadsheet sale is last full month broadsheet and excludes 'untypical' months like December and August

Source: ABC

picture. It changes editorial and pushes you to an *Independent*-style front page. With the Berliner you don't fall into that trap. You have calmer typography, and it is less intrusive. You can linger on a spread. It has a calming effect' (interview with Cole, 2005).

But there were major, and expensive, problems in taking this path. There were no presses in Britain configured to print a Berliner. The *Guardian* had to make a huge investment, more than £50 million, in new presses to print the new format. And the time taken building them was time spent as a broadsheet competing with a compact *Independent* and *Times*. The Berliner *Guardian* launched on Monday 12 September 2005, two years after the compact *Independent*, gaining 9 per cent in the first year. The *Independent on Sunday* went compact a month later, increasing sales by 15 per cent in its first year (ABC); the Berliner *Observer* launched in January 2006, putting on an initial 9 per cent. Apart from the *IoS* the increase was nothing like as dramatic as that of the first compacts. By now the *Times* and *Independent*, familiar as compacts, had passed through the early surge although they were still enjoying a circulation that had much increased over their previous broadsheets. Table 2.8 shows the effect to the end of 2008 of the compact re-launch on the titles that chose this path, showing compact gain or loss in circulation compared with final broadsheet month.

The *Independent*, the paper that started the compact revolution, and thus publishing in the new form for the longest, was just ahead of its last broadsheet figure, and so was the *Observer*. The *Guardian*, *Times* and *Independent on Sunday* had all slipped back to below their last broadsheet figures. All gained initially from the transition and enjoyed two or three years of higher sales. Then the declining circulation continuing across the newspaper market kicked in and the compacts started to suffer also. But it has to be remembered that at the time they went compact all the broadsheet titles were losing sales, so it can be assumed that their figures today would be worse if they had not changed their format. In the end the public became used to compact 'broadsheets' and the decision to purchase or not was based on other factors. But Simon Kelner's initiative changed the face of the serious national press in Britain. As he said himself (interview with Roy Greenslade: *Media Guardian*, 26 July 2004)

> We've certainly made people think seriously about how their newspapers are packaged and delivered, and we've challenged the prejudices and preconceptions about whether it's possible to do an upmarket quality tabloid. Whether we've revolutionised the entire newspaper market we'll only know when the revolution is over. It's just the beginning.

It has been followed all over the world. The World Association of Newspapers estimated in its 2006 World Press Trends report that around 80 titles had adopted the compact format; but it also warned, prophetically, that circulation increases tended to disappear over time (World Association of Newspapers, 2006).

We now look at the non-London press – at the regions and nations, as the BBC refers to that which is not the metropolis.

3

BEYOND FLEET STREET: NEWSPAPERS IN THE REGIONS AND NATIONS

Berrow's Worcester Journal claims to be the oldest surviving British newspaper (or non-official newspaper, as the British Library describes it), and its history encapsulates in microcosm the development of printed, purchased regional newspapers in this country. It was founded, as the *Worcester Post Man*, a newssheet publishing irregularly, in 1690, beginning regular weekly publication as the *Worcester Journal* in 1709. It has been published continuously ever since. The paper was created as William and Mary came to the throne, supporting the new king and queen in a town that had been traditionally Stuart in its loyalties. The first printing press in Worcester had been set up in 1548, and several books had been printed on it (www.berrowsjournal.co.uk/history).

William Caxton had introduced the first English printing press in Westminster in 1476, some thirty years after Johan Gutenberg had invented moveable type. The first newspapers were beginning to be seen in Britain in the early years of the sixteenth century. But they were slow to develop since the population was largely illiterate, and relied on town criers to shout them the news (see Chapter 4).

Although the *Worcester Journal* was published and sold locally, over an area covering Wolverhampton, Tewkesbury, Gloucester and Birmingham as well as Worcester, it carried no local news at all. Those who bought the paper, who were, at a time of limited literacy, the richer and more educated, apparently wanted only news away from the city, news of war, politics and parliament. Today the role of the weekly local newspaper is to carry only local news, community news. This has increased over the years, so that the more local, the more grassroots the news, the more successful the paper.

While papers have become more local in content, their owners have become bigger and bigger. When *Berrow's* started as the *Worcester Post Man*, its first proprietor was Stephen Bryan, who was also the printer and editor. Bryan died in 1748, just a few months after selling his paper to Harvey Berrow. For a few years he published the newspaper as the *Worcester Journal*. But there was competition in those days, and a competitor tried to sell a rival paper under the same name. Harvey Berrow inserted his own name into the title, to prove it was the real thing, and it has remained there ever since, despite the family having long since ceased any connection with the *Journal*.

Berrow was the third son of a curate and chaplain and was a Peterborough apothecary. This was not unusual at this time when the early newspaper proprietors would sell medicines alongside their newspapers. Harvey Berrow would promote his elixir for dropsy, his powder for gout and his royal chemical washball in his paper, just as Rupert Murdoch's newspapers today often promote Sky TV. Berrow sold the paper to a local consortium but his name was retained in the title. There were mergers and acquisitions. A public company, Berrow's Newspapers Ltd, was formed after the Second World War, and its majority shareholder was the *News of the World*.

In 1982 it was taken over by Reed International, a paper manufacturer and one of the leading newspaper publishers of the time (it published the *Daily Mirror*). Relaunches and redesigns followed. *Berrow's* became a county newspaper in 1983 and then a free newspaper for the city of Worcester in 1987. A new, more upmarket county newspaper was launched in 1988. Reed International put the paper up for sale and there was a management buy-out in 1996, soon followed by a take-over by Newsquest, now the third largest publisher of regional papers in this country. Newsquest owns 210 titles and distributes around 9 million copies a week. *Berrow's* accounts for just 48,000 of those and they are distributed free. Newsquest is itself owned by the huge American publisher Gannett. So tiny *Berrow's*, which once sold just a few copies locally for tuppence ha'penny, contained five pages and was owned by a single proprietor, is today distributed free, has a website and is owned by a mighty transatlantic media conglomerate. In its tiny way it exemplifies the way in which the regional newspaper world has developed and changed.

A source of truly local news

Temple (2008: 94) notes that the local newspaper was almost unknown at the start of the eighteenth century but by the middle of that century was well established with some 130 titles being published. Like *Berrow's*, the early arrival, they carried little local news but concentrated on national and international affairs, just like the developing national newspapers. 'The local paper was local only in the sense that it was published locally' (Franklin, 1997: 76). Later, and to the present day, that was reversed with the local (and to a lesser extent regional) press concentrating on their own 'patches'. This was their unique selling point. They provided the only source of truly local news, and that remained the case when the electronic competitors, radio and television, arrived. Local radio and television were always regional rather than local and never attempted the 'community' news that has been the bedrock of modern provincial print journalism.

The end of the 'taxes on knowledge' (see Chapter 4) in 1861 spurred the growth of the local press as much as the national. The provincial press really came of age in the nineteenth century (Franklin, 1997: 77). By 1854 there were 290 provincial newspapers with five in Manchester and 12 in Liverpool alone. The *Manchester Guardian*, founded as a weekly in 1821, had the highest provincial circulation of 8,000 copies. Temple (2008: 96) records the flourishing of the provincial press in the mid-Victorian era when there were 18 London-based newspapers and 96 provincial dailies. But the birth of a mass national daily press, following the establishment of the *Daily Mail* in 1896 (see Chapter 4), was to 'reap havoc on the provincial morning press'. Consolidation of ownership began in the early part of the twentieth century with 'growth in newspaper chains' (Temple, 2008: 96) and has continued ever since. Competition in big conurbations gave way to local monopolies. Between the world wars there was a 'spectacular consolidation of the regional chains' (Curran and Seaton, 1997: 43), with the percentage of regional evening titles controlled by the five big chains rising from 8 per cent to 40 per cent between 1921 and 1939, and of morning titles from 12 per cent to 44 per cent. The number of towns with a choice of evening newspaper fell from 24 to 10 and of morning papers from 15 to seven.

The other significant change was in newspapers' identification with a political party. Curran and Seaton note that in contrast with the 'early militant press' the 'new local daily press (of the 1850s) encouraged its readers to identify with the political parties controlled by the dominant classes' (1997: 39). Ten of the new local dailies that emerged between 1855 and 1860 were affiliated to the Liberal Party, and 18 started between 1860 and 1870 to the Tory or Liberal Party. Today, with proprietorial or baronial ownership replaced by corporate control, and local competition replaced by local monopoly and thus the need to 'include' all the target audience rather than divide them along politically partisan lines, the political allegiance of most regional and local newspapers has been replaced by a weak and ill-defined 'community interest'.

Sectors of the provincial press

The regional and local (generically the provincial) press can, like the national marketplace described in the previous chapter, be divided into different sectors. Unlike the national press, this is not based upon the socio-economic profile of the audience, or the 'weightiness' of content, but on the time and frequency of publication, and the geographical size of the area covered. It is further divided into whether the newspaper is sold or given away. So we have the small 'daily' sector, the larger 'evening' sector, the larger still 'weekly' sector, and the very small Sunday sector.

The dailies are morning newspapers, analogous to the national dailies, with similar production schedules, serving regions (or nations, as we shall see) rather than cities or towns, giving more editorial attention to stories concerning or about their own regions, but also covering major national and international stories albeit mostly via agency copy. They pay more attention to business than other provincial sectors, and thus tend to draw their readers from higher socio-economic groups. Some of their editors and publishers see them (optimistically) as an alternative rather than a supplement to a national daily. Typical provincial dailies are the *Yorkshire Post*, published out of Leeds and distributed across the county of Yorkshire, and the *Birmingham Post*, distributed across the West Midlands.

The evenings (sometimes referred to as 'afternoon' newspapers), historically the largest-selling and most profitable provincial newspapers, are published throughout the day in the larger towns and cities. They are sold (distributed in the case of the frees) on the street. Historically, again, they provide up-to-the-minute news of the day, covering events happening too late for the dailies. Typical big-city titles are the *Manchester Evening News* (now both a paid-for and a free – see Chapter 5), the Newcastle *Evening Chronicle*, the *Birmingham Mail*, the *Nottingham Evening Post* and the *Bristol Evening Post*. The evenings concentrate on local news across their circulation areas, only covering national stories when they are of major significance or interest, particularly when they are breaking during the day, and will only feature in the daily papers the next day.

The weekly sector contains the largest number of paid-for and free titles, more than 500 of the former, more than 600 of the latter. Almost every town in the country, including those too small to sustain an evening title, has its weekly paper. These are more local in their coverage, covering stories and issues of relevance to those who live in the community. They will stray outside the circulation area only for a story concerning somebody who lives in it. Sunday provincial newspapers have never found it easy to gain a market, which is why there are so few. This is particularly true in England, where only the *Sunday Sun*, circulating in the north-east, and the *Sunday Mercury*, circulating in the West Midlands, have sales of any significance. Table 3.1 shows the number of titles in each sector. Local newspaper closures accelerated in 2008, as recession deepened and advertising revenues declined. In the 13 months from January 2008 to January 2009 there was a net loss of 42 titles (Greenslade, 2009a) – 53 closures and 11 launches. Newspapers closed from Morecambe to Staines, from Huddersfield to Wandsworth. Most were owned by the major regional publishers, with Trinity Mirror closing most of all.

Nations or regions?

There are understandable sensitivities about the description of some of the papers published in Scotland (particularly) and Wales as 'regional'; the Republic of Ireland and Northern Ireland are different again, and we will

Table 3.1   *A breakdown of the UK's provincial press*

Newspaper	Number
Daily and Sunday titles	
Paid morning	19
Free morning	13
Paid evening	73
Free evening	8
Combined evening	2
Paid Sunday	13
Free Sunday	5
Paid weekly titles	506
Free weekly titles	623
Combined weekly titles	18
Total	1,278

Source: Newspaper Society figures for July 2008

come to them. The debate is political, involving nationhood and devolution, and the concept of what constitutes a 'national' newspaper in the United Kingdom. Scotland has long had a thriving press and produces newspapers that are available over its length and breadth – and, as in politics, has 'exported' great numbers of respected journalists to London and the UK's national press. But increasingly, with the advent of devolution and the growth of support for Scottish independence, there are many in Scotland who refer to a distinct 'national press' in Scotland and feel insulted by the inclusion of what they regard as their national papers under the umbrella of the UK's regional press. The debate is further confused by ownership, with most of the Scottish 'national' press being owned by major conglomerates operating across the UK.

Aldridge (2007: 118) says that Scotland has its own national newspapers that concentrate on parochial concerns. After studying the ways in which the Scottish and UK press covered an election to the devolved Scottish parliament, Michael Higgins concludes that the press has a crucial role to play in 'political public spheres at the national and sub-national level'. His study demonstrated that the Scottish press covered the political process extensively whereas the UK nationals were more concerned with the end result, thereby emphasising 'the importance of the correlation between the political coverage of newspapers and the "deliberative spaces" established around democratic and media institutions as they stand and as they emerge' (Higgins, 2006: 40).

Temple (2008: 102) points to the extensive coverage of the Scottish Parliament provided by the Scottish 'national' papers and the fact that until recently none of the major Scottish titles were Scottish owned. That changed when Johnston Press bought the Edinburgh-based *Scotsman* and *Scotland on*

Sunday in 2006 from the Barclay brothers, now owners of the London-based *Telegraph* titles. True, Johnston Press has its head office in Edinburgh and its history in the Scottish regional press. But since 2002, when it bought Regional Independent Media, it has grown to become the second largest publisher of regional titles in the UK, and is no longer thought of as a 'Scottish' publisher. And during the ownership of the *Scotsman* by the Barclay brothers the paper, and its sister title *Scotland on Sunday*, were under the operational control of Andrew Neil. He might be a Scotsman but he had made his name in London editing the *Sunday Times*, managing Sky TV and building a BBC television career covering Westminster politics. He appointed English editors and pursued a strongly anti-independence editorial line.

Putting politics, semantics and national pride to one side, it should be noted that ABC, the Audit Bureau of Circulations, includes the major Scottish newspapers in its monthly audit of UK national newspaper circulations. This highlights the empirical fact that a key component of newspaper purchase in Scotland is the London-based national press. It could be argued that in terms of newspaper description 'national' implies availability all over the country, and the London-based nationals meet that criterion, while the Scotland-based papers do not. However, they are available all over Scotland, and thus meet the criterion if Scotland is regarded as a nation. And so the circle returns to a definition of nationhood, and politics.

The London-based nationals increasingly chase circulation in Scotland, with offices and reporting teams in Scotland and much editionalising of news to provide a Scottish emphasis. Temple (2008: 102) points out how the *Sun*, *Mail* and *Express* have added the prefix 'Scottish' to the titles of their Scottish editions. This has led to a vigorous competition for sales between titles based in London and Scotland, with the data suggesting there is little resistance to UK nationals in a market where Scottish nationals are available, as Table 3.2 shows.

ABC provides a geographical breakdown of its audited sales figures which shows that the *Sun* is the best-selling daily among Scotland's 5 million population, as it is in the UK, just outselling the *Record*, Trinity Mirror's Scottish tabloid which sells alongside the same company's *Daily Mirror*. The *Daily Mail* repeats its UK performance in Scotland, outselling all but the *Sun* and *Record*. At the top end of the market, where political coverage is most significant and the particular politics of Scotland might be expected to be highly significant, the *Scotsman* outsells *The Times* during the week (although the combined sales of the London quality papers – *Times*, *Telegraph*, *Guardian* and *Independent* – in Scotland are 78,500, over 50 per cent greater than the *Scotsman*) but on Sundays the *Sunday Times* sells more copies than the *Sunday Herald* and *Scotland on Sunday* combined. The biggest sale in Scotland, 430,000, is recorded by the *Sunday Mail*, the *Record's* Sunday stablemate and an entirely Scotland-based title, although owned by Trinity Mirror.

Table 3.2   The Scottish newspaper market

Title	Publisher	Published in	Sale in Scotland	UK sale
Scotsman	Johnston Press	Edinburgh	49,660	50,327
Herald	Newsquest	Glasgow	62,458	62,887
Record	Trinity Mirror	Glasgow	347,165	380,231
Mirror	Trinity Mirror	London	30,783	1,439,692
Daily Mail	Associated	London	120,509	2,230,457
Sun	News International	London	375,558	3,106,630
Times	News International	London	28,786	621,178
Sunday Herald	Newsquest	Glasgow	44,263	44,560
Scotland on Sunday	Johnston Press	Edinburgh	61,693	65,064
Sunday Mail	Trinity Mirror	Glasgow	429,509	469,463
Sunday Post	D.C.Thomson	Glasgow	259,337	388,293
Sunday Times	News International	London	68,720	1,190,098
Mail on Sunday	Associated	London	109,149	2,210,331
News of the World	News International	London	276,182	3,190,797

Source: ABC June–November 2008

Wales is a slightly different story. As Temple (2008: 103) notes, 'unlike Scotland, Wales lacks a national newspaper and the overwhelming majority of morning papers bought in Wales are produced in England'. The Cardiff-based *Western Mail*, regarded by both ABC (which does not publish separate circulation figures for Wales) and the Newspaper Society as a regional newspaper, does describe itself at 'the national newspaper of Wales'. However, the bulk of its sales are in the south of the country. The dominant title in the north is Trinity Mirror's *Daily Post*. It used to be a North Wales edition of the Liverpool *Daily Post*, which it greatly outsold, until the publisher decided to give it a separate, Welsh, identity and relocate offices and staff to North Wales.

In Northern Ireland as well the London-based national press is accepted, although also criticised for its lack of coverage of domestic politics and news, even during the thirty years of the 'Troubles'. London-based coverage was at best spasmodic and it was always the case that bombs on the British mainland gained significantly more coverage than more frequent killings in Northern Ireland. Temple (2008: 103) notes the quantity and influence of the province's local newspapers, the majority of which 'still serve a sectarian audience'. The *Belfast Telegraph*, once a Trinity Mirror title, now owned by Independent News and Media, publishers of the *Independent*, is the dominant Northern Ireland title and comes nearest to achieving a cross-community readership. McLaughlin (in Franklin, 2006: 61) identifies an unusual feature of local newspaper publication in Northern Ireland – competition. He explains that there are 73 weekly papers in the province, a very high number for the size of the population.

This is because for every unionist newspaper in a large town, there is a corresponding nationalist title; it is unusual to find. To find a local weekly that serves a mixed readership. In effect, therefore, these newspapers have not needed to compete with each other – they have survived on restricted readerships and advertising markets.

As in Scotland, the London-based national press has made strong efforts to gain circulation in the Irish Republic, with Irish editions being produced that are often quite distinct in tone and content from the UK versions of the same titles. The *Sun* sells 101,000 copies in Ireland, the *Daily Star* 99,000 and the *Daily Mirror* 66,000 (ABC, June to November 2008). The *Sunday Times* and *Mail on Sunday* both sell more than 100,000 copies. By way of comparison the Irish owned and published *Irish Times* sells 118,000 copies a day.

Profitable decline before anyone had thought of the web

One thing the UK's provincial press shares with its national counterparts is a decline in circulation, certainly of paid-for titles. Another is the gloomy tone and crisis talk that have dominated so much discussion of the press in the last few years, well before the recession of 2008–09. There is a tendency to think that newspapers' difficulties were all brought about by technology in the form of online publishing. But the regional press has experienced falling circulations for much longer than that. The reason that it was seldom seen as a crisis in the past was the continuing profitability of regional publishing. Some major publishers decided to sell their businesses, but there were always others waiting to pay large prices for them. Consolidation, in progress for many decades, continued with new players, like Newsquest and Johnston Press, emerging to form ever bigger corporations bent on further acquisition and bigger profits. The regional newspaper industry may have been changing, but the revenues were holding firm.

Franklin (2006: xvii), while providing Newspaper Society data that emphasised the continuing popularity of the local press – 85 per cent of adults (more than 40 million people) reading a regional or local paper; 67 million copies, paid-for and free, distributed weekly in 2005 – identifies significant changes that have radically altered its essential character:

- A continuing decline in the number of local newspaper titles and their circulations
- Consolidation of ownership of local newspaper ownership, centralising production in large regional centres, separating journalists from their readers and local community

- Reduction in number of journalists employed, increasing editorial reliance on news agencies and public-relations sources
- Increasing competition from expansive local radio and regional television
- Digital technologies providing increasing challenges to the local press

Aspects of all those changes can be recognised; the emphases can be challenged. Prior to the advent of the web (clearly the most relevant technological change, but not until the end of the twentieth century) societal changes and changing patterns of ownership emerge as the dominant factors. The decline of the evening papers, consistently the most profitable through their relatively large circulations and their lucrative classified advertising markets in local jobs, property and cars, best exemplifies the changes that have come about.

In its heyday the evening paper was predominantly bought by workers emerging from factories, reading the paper on the bus journey home, then taking it into the home where it was read by other members of the household. These were workers who tended to live in the place where they worked, took an interest in the town, followed the local football team and had no other access to news. The factories closed through de-industrialisation. The car replaced the bus as the favoured form of transport to and from work. According to McNair (2003b: 218): 'Some sections of the press – in particular the regional evening papers – are finding that the emergence of the post-industrial city and the dispersal of populations to the suburbs – a process which has occurred throughout Britain, but is most evident in the huge industrial conurbations such as Glasgow – are eroding traditional markets'. Home was increasingly on a suburban development out of town. There was now television there which deterred newspaper reading at home. Less Saturday working and more domestic distractions, like shopping, meant smaller audiences for a Saturday purchase. The decreasing interest in attending Saturday-afternoon football meant less identification with the local team, and buying the football special. Football itself changed dramatically through live matches on satellite television played by teams which were not local but better to watch and irrelevant to the local evening paper football special (and anyway the matches were frequently not played on Saturdays).

The evening papers believed the answer to this sales decline lay in content. In many cases the old staples of crime and court cases were discarded, to be replaced by 'lifestyle' stories deemed to be 'relevant' to the modern reader. If it worked for the *Daily Mail*, ran the thinking, it would work for the local paper. But they didn't have the resources, the access to celebrities or the journalistic talent of the *Mail* to make it work. It was not so much soft news as inconsequential news. You didn't need it, so you tended not to buy it.

Provincial papers as 'cash generation units'

Other factors came into play through the new-style corporate ownership. These corporations were driven by their share price and shareholders had no identification with hundreds of local communities spread across the country, their papers owned instead by one proprietor. Corporate owners knew that shareholders cared only about share price, and that share price was driven by the relationship between profits and turnover. That in turn was driven by costs, or rather cost-cutting. There were various consequences of this, most obviously the size of the staff and the amount they were paid. Staffing levels were cut repeatedly, district offices were closed, and pay for local journalists fell behind the norms in other occupations. It affected recruitment and retention because while journalism remains a popular career it is now predominantly a graduate career and graduates bearing huge student debts struggle on local newspaper wages.

The new proprietors looked at their new acquisitions and saw they had valuable high-street premises on prime sites. They sold up and moved out to greenfield sites and business parks, cut off from the communities they served. The public they needed to buy their papers no longer looked at the photographs in the front window or called in to talk to a reporter. The reporters mingled less with their readers and their subject matter. They left the office less, because there were fewer of them and because they might as well make a phone call. Local reporters (and editors) were less likely to know the area they were reporting on. Reporters came from university and college and did not necessarily want to return to their home towns. Editors in a large corporation were moved around the country as part of their career development and often had no connection with the locality in which they worked. It made it harder for a paper to identify with its readers. More importantly it made it harder for readers to identify with their paper. They stopped being readers.

And, as with the nationals, the owners of provincial newspapers were able to take advantage of the post-Wapping changes in technology and industrial relations. This represented the greatest cost-cut of all and, with the other savings detailed above, allowed the new corporate owners to aspire to, and progressively achieve, profits on turnover of more than 30 per cent, sometimes more than 35 per cent. But the response to the opportunities offered by these record profits was to assault the key selling point of the evening newspaper, its topicality. Where with old (hot metal) technology newspapers were priding themselves on the speed with which they published on-the-day stories, with the new technology and its capacity to deal even faster with publication they gave up. Today's evening newspapers are not that at all. Most of the content is written and edited the day before, small numbers of pages are altered on the day, and for most papers anything delivered after

10.00 a.m. is too late for today; even 10.00 p.m. the night before is too late for some. This has given rise to a majority of news stories carrying the word 'has' in the first paragraph, a crude device for disguising when an event has actually happened. In an age of instant news, rolling news, online news, 24-hour news on radio and television, none of which can provide the local service of which the local paper is still capable, the evening papers have abandoned their territory.

Preston (2008: 643) points out that the London *Evening News* and the *Star* were killed off long before the net was invented. And the decline in evening newspapers around the country is the fault of owners who have turned them into 'single-edition late morning papers, updated on the net in a further burst of suicide fever fuelled by imbecile accountancy'. Rather than 'fighting back with investment, zeal and ingenuity, they cut back on news and shelved editions'. In short, says Preston, they 'gave up the ghost.'

Another example of newspaper proprietors 'giving up the ghost' has been the relentless reduction in the numbers of different local editions produced. Editionalising was once the norm across the sector, providing local news within a paper covering a wider area. Peter Sands, former editor of the *Northern Echo*, recalls: 'We tried [in the early 1990s] to reach our diverse audience with six different editions that included slip pages of local news, which changed for every geographical area, and regional pages that stayed throughout. In Darlington [the head office site] there could be as many as 10 broadsheet change pages each morning' (quoted in Preston, 2009). But the number of editions of morning and, particularly, evening papers has been progressively cut in order to cut costs – with the predictable consequence that this has also cut readers.

It is significant that the lowest rate of decline has been in the local weekly sector, which was the last to show any decline at all, although it is now beginning to follow the pattern of decline of morning and evening regional titles. There is however still a desire, particularly among older readers, for truly local news and advertising, for parish-pump editorial. This is evidenced by the fact that tenth in the list of 87 regional newspaper publishers is Tindle Newspapers. Sir Ray Tindle, who once owned more mainstream local papers in Surrey, such as the *Surrey Advertiser* based in Guildford, before he sold out to the *Guardian*'s regional arm, has deliberately set out to build a portfolio of very small local weeklies. His 27 paid-for weeklies sell an average of 9,000 copies each. The distribution of his 36 free weeklies averages 30,500 (Newspaper Society, July 2008). His business is profitable and growing. His formula is simple: keep it local, and then more local. He caters for the traditional editorial imperatives: people like to see their name in the paper, so fill it with local names from sport and a variety of local activities. There is no competition for this sort of news. Wainwright (2008) describes Tindle newspapers as 'sacredly local. Editors print lists of funeral mourners and flower show winners that once gave the weekly *Somerset Guardian*

Standard 125% penetration in Frome. That's a quarter of the town buying more than one copy a week'.

The majority of the weekly newspapers owned by today's dominant publishers exploited the high penetration of their titles, regarding them as secure and not in danger of suffering from cuts in editorial budgets. The lucrative local classified advertising would continue to flow in, they believed, and the editorial copy surrounding it was less important. Tiny, inexperienced editorial staffs meant fewer reporters to cover the courts and the council, the villages, local societies, golden weddings and funerals. Tindle recognised the importance of these staples; they didn't. They did not understand that the attraction of the local weekly which brought about its popularity was the importance of community in an age when mobility of labour and the dispersal of the extended family undermined it. Local schools, local crime, planning controversies, new traffic systems and parking restrictions, wheelie bins and locations of supermarkets: these were the things local people were interested in, talked about and wanted to read about. These interests remained, relatively uncovered by the local weeklies. But the advertising slipped away, and with it the easy profits.

Two small examples are indicative of the attitudes undermining the traditionally resilient local press. Reporters on a Home Counties weekly newspaper were incredulous when they received an email from their editorial director in October 2008, announcing an end to the daily delivery of national newspapers to editorial departments and the reimbursed purchase of weekend newspapers by reporters. The reporting staff should in future rely on Google and other newspaper websites. The irony of the instruction was not lost on journalists trying to sustain a printed weekly newspaper. Second, in a BBC radio interview in November 2008 on the fall in profits and collapse in share price of Johnston Press, the company's then chief executive Tim Bowdler described his group's newspapers as 'profitable cash generation units'.

As the recession of 2008–2009 gathered momentum, with a consequent fall in advertising revenues through the collapse of the property market and the credit crunch, the crisis in the provincial press became increasingly serious, reflected both by journalists losing their jobs and by a steep decline in the share prices of the major publishers. The share price of Johnston Press, for example, fell by 94 per cent in a year (*Sunday Times*, 4 January 2009). The newspaper quoted Bowdler as describing the situation as 'a hell of tough time'. But he went on to say: 'There is gloom that newspapers will cease to exist. That is utterly wrong. There is still great interest in the local community. Newspapers need to become local portals with new revenue streams'. He left the company the next day. By then announcements of staff cuts by all the major publishing groups were coming out almost daily.

Many journalists and observers are now questioning how many of the 1,278 titles featured in Table 3.1 will survive into the second decade of the twenty-first century. Strategies for survival include a switch to free distribution of the printed product and the further development of online publishing, and these will be discussed further in Chapters 5 and 10 respectively. But first, having now outlined the current state of the newspaper industry both nationally and regionally, how did we get to this point? The next chapter helps to answer that question with a brief history of newspapers.

4

HEADLINES FROM NEWSPAPER HISTORY

There is nothing new about news. Throughout recorded history people have craved to discover news out of what Kovach and Rosenstiel (2003) call the 'awareness instinct. They have a need to know what is going on over the next hill beyond their direct experience. Knowledge of the unknown gives them security, allows them to plan and negotiate their lives. Exchanging this information becomes the basis for creating community, making human connections' (2001: 21). Temple (2008: 3) puts it more intimately: 'We have always loved to gossip and exchange our little titbits of information with our family and neighbours. It appears reasonable to assume that the oral transmission of news dates back to the first human civilisations'. Kovach and Rosentiel (2001: 21) suggest the Greeks had a 'kind of pre-journalism', the oral journalism of the Athens marketplace where everything of importance was in the open – providing, of course, that you were not a woman or a slave. As democracy developed, as in Greece, so there was more news and information available to the public. And as societies became more authoritarian in the Middle Ages 'communication waned and written news essentially disappeared'.

Early days

The earliest recorded examples of the dissemination of news as we understand it today occurred in Roman times with the *acta Romana* or *acta diurna*. Conboy (2004: 6) attributes these to the writings of Tacitus. 'They seem to refer to a variety of practices which publicised events in ancient Rome, from the daily news of police courts, accidents, deaths and the range of public events which constituted Roman urban experience, to the reporting of municipal councils, courts of law, even the Senate'. These daily reports – produced in manuscript as there was no form of printing – were posted outside public buildings, where citizens would gather to read, or be read aloud to, about what was going on. Rumours flourished, but 2000 years ago the Romans understood the importance of information.

Progress in the dissemination of news was suspended for hundreds of years after the Romans, and the 'modern' history of newspapers cannot really be said to have started until the fifteenth century. There were other steps along the way, as Franklin (1997) notes, which could be regarded as precursors of the printed newspaper. One, the 'first modern sheet of news' (1997: 73), appeared in Venice in 1536 and told Venetians about the progress of the war in Turkey. The monthly manuscript was often read out around the city. The printed pamphlet and 'news book' was an increasingly common form of news transmission from the sixteenth century, as were ballads and broadsheets. The first known surviving news pamphlet was printed and distributed by royal authority in 1513, and dealt with the Battle of Flodden (Conboy, 2004: 9).

The essential preconditions for the existence of newspapers are literacy and printing, and these were to be a long time coming. The subsequent development of newspapers as we know them today continued to be influenced by changing social, political and economic contexts, by technology, entrepreneurialism and royal or governmental attitudes. Although movable type was probably invented by the Chinese long before (Temple, 2008: 7), Johann Gutenberg is credited with the invention of printing as a mechanical way of making books in Germany around 1450. If he had not done it then, somebody else would have because, as historian John Man notes, it was 'an invention waiting to happen'. Within just 50 years, between 15 and 20 million copies of books had been printed in Europe, in a communications revolution that places the recent development of the internet in context:

> Printing changed things so utterly that it is hard to imagine a world without it … Suddenly, in a historical eye-blink, scribes were redundant. One year, it took a month or two to produce a single copy of a book; the next, you could have 500 copies in a week … Hardly an aspect of life remained untouched … Gutenberg's invention made the soil from which sprang modern history, science, popular literature, the emergence of the nation-state, so much of everything by which we define modernity. (Man, 2003: 1–2 and 216)

Including newspapers, of course. And it did not take long for the printed word to demonstrate its ability to offend those in power. Just ten years after William Caxton set up the first English printing press in Westminster in 1476, Henry VII was warning against 'forged tidings and tales'. By 1542 the Privy Council was taking action against individuals for printing 'seditious', 'unfitting' or 'unsemely worddes' (Engel, 1996: 15, 18). In the following century, during the English Civil War, with authority breaking down, the first regular newspapers started to appear: *Mercurius Britannica* for parliament, *Mercurius Aulicus* for the King, giving alternative interpretations of events. Under Cromwell control of the press was quite loose for a while, but later under Charles II laws restricting newspapers were re-imposed, and became stronger under James II (1996: 18). Only the official *London Gazette* was left alone. But when James was deposed and left the country, six new newspapers soon emerged.

The mid-seventeenth century saw the development of the coffee houses as centres of the dissemination of news. Conboy (2004: 80) describes these as 'the space of exchange which corresponds to Habermas's public sphere' and led to 'the enhancement of news consciousness and the creation of a discourse of public opinion which would shape how journalism emerged'. Charles II tried to close them down in 1675 but was forced to give up, and they then had their most active and influential phase for the next fifty years. They spread from London to most major cities, and mixed political discussion, usually anti-establishment, with the gathering of news for print in papers and pamphlets and the distribution of those papers and pamphlets. Temple (2008: 11) writes of the courage of the early journalists of this time contributing to 'a public opinion formed without coercion and by a process of mutual understanding [which] continues to inform (however controversially at times) British press and broadcasting in the twenty-first century'.

The seventeenth century also saw the development of 'differentiated readership' (Conboy and Steel, 2008), targeting printed material at defined audiences. In the early part of the century this differentiation was along broadly Royalist and Parliamentary lines, but after the Restoration of the monarchy in 1660 there was more control on the publication of news, particularly of political news. After the lapsing of the Licensing Acts this differentiation became more apparent with readerships 'expressed in terms of their lifestyle, tastes and broadly emergent bourgeois identity' (Conboy and Steel, 2008: 651).

The 1689 Bill of Rights provided for freedom of speech and freedom of debate in Parliament. In 1695 the liberal philosopher John Locke successfully argued for the abolition of the Licensing Act that controlled the press 'and for the next 17 years there was brief but luxuriant flowering that produced Britain's first daily paper, the *Daily Courant*, in 1702, as well as Daniel Defoe's *Review*, the *Tatler* and the *Spectator*' (Engel, 1996: 18). The first regular publications, which developed audiences through their regularity, were the thrice-weeklies, which maintained their popularity after the arrival of the *Courant*. The first of these was the *Flying Post*, started in 1695, and soon profitable. The *Courant* was started by Samuel Buckley and had 'an eye on the public appetite for news of war' (Conboy, 2004: 86, 87). The *Courant* ceased publication in 1735.

Stamp duty on newspapers was first introduced in 1712, taxing the press at a penny a paper and having a great impact on their profitability. It also brought more control of the press by the executive. It ushered in an era of corruption as publishers sought to offset the tax by taking bribes. Engel (1996: 19) recounts how Sir Robert Walpole 'not merely paid journalists to support him, he bribed Defoe to write pieces that ostensibly opposed him'. The tax was steadily increased, but it did not prevent the launch of a stream of new newspapers. By the mid-eighteenth century London had five daily papers and six thrice-weeklies, with a combined circulation of 100,000 copies (around a million readers) a week (Allan, 2004: 11). By 1800 the figure for London papers was more than 50, and the regional press numbered 100 titles (Temple, 2008: 14). The place of the newspaper in Britain was firmly established, its future assured. It was the 'great era of consolidation for daily newspapers, accomplished through a growing emphasis on consistency of appeal to a particular audience' (Conboy and Steel, 2008: 652).

Times leads the way

The most significant of the new newspaper launches – 'paradigmatic of the gravitation of journalism towards mainstream political life' (Conboy, 2004: 114) – in that it connects to the present day, came in 1785 with the arrival of the *Daily Universal Register*, which became *The Times* in 1788. The ninth London morning paper, it was started by John Walter as part of his publishing and book company. Hush money or subsidy was still a feature of newspaper publishing, and Walter for years received a 'subsidy' of £300 a year from the Treasury in recognition of its support of government policy and opposition to the party of the Prince of Wales. 'Three hundred a year "as a reward for the politics of the Paper", in the words of John Walter, was a fair sum for a newly founded journal' (*History of the Times*, vol. 1: 213, cited by Conboy, 2004).

In 1792 came the Libel Act. Journalists became legally responsible for their reports, but were no longer vulnerable to prosecution by ministers. They had the right to a jury trial and juries tended to be sympathetic to the press. These early days of daily newspapers showed much evidence of the eccentricity, even craziness, of those involved, a feature of newspaper life that has survived to the present day. Alexander Andrews (cited by Engel, 1996: 19) in his 1859 *History of British Journalism*, described the press as 'run by besotted geniuses … the business of their profession keeping them out of their beds half the night, they kept out the remaining half of their own choice; and the little hours were consumed in tavern hilarity … (but) the reign of the rackety ones was drawing to a close'.

Walter's son, John Walter II, took over *The Times* in 1803, and appointed Thomas Barnes, a former drama critic, as editor in 1817. They were a powerful combination, and together made *The Times* the first British newspaper in a form we would recognise today. It reported serious political news, both from home and abroad. It invested in its journalism. And it was a sophisticated commercial operation. As Conboy (2004: 114) put it:

> The Times was not spurred on by abstract concerns for the reputation of good journalism …
> but by sound commercial considerations of the value of an increasing reputation for

independence which flattered the political convictions of its primary readership, the commercial middle classes, and the desire of advertisers to be associated with a newspaper with the ear of such an affluent and influential clientele.

The emergence of the influence of advertising is stressed by many newspaper historians, who usually put it in a positive light. It was said to have offset the cost of the stamp duty, the 'tax on knowledge', to have freed newspapers from the corruption of political interference and bribery, in short to have funded the freedom of the press. And it is the commercial model that has survived to the present day. Not all scholars, however, are convinced of the benign influence of advertising. James Curran and Jean Seaton (1997: 9) set out to 'reappraise the standard of view of press history... to re-examine critically the accepted view of the historical emergence of a "free" press ... to stand it on its head'. Concentrating on mainstream commercial newspapers and ignoring the parallel development of a radical press, argue Curran and Seaton, is a selective perspective, and only by following it can 'the conventional view of advertising as a midwife of press independence' be sustained. They put this 'conventional view' thus:

> A section of the commercial press became politically more independent largely as a consequence of the growth of advertising. This additional revenue reduced dependence on political subsidies; encouraged papers to reject covert secret service grants; improved the wages and security of employment of journalists so that they became less susceptible to government bribes; and above all financed greater expenditure on news gathering so that newspapers became less reliant on official sources and more reluctant to trade their independence in return for obtaining 'prior intelligence from the government'.

We are concentrating here on the commercial press, and *The Times* in its early years 'thundered' its independence and built up its news-gathering operation, its authority and reputation. It established its reputation for foreign reporting, most famously during the Crimean War when William Howard Russell became the first 'celebrity' foreign correspondent, and covered many other wars in a then unique and colourful eyewitness manner. For the first half of the nineteenth century, and particularly after the arrival as editor in 1841 of John Delane, perhaps the first 'great' newspaper editor, *The Times* was the leading title.

> It had such an ascendancy with its networks of couriers, translators, correspondents, its reputation for influence and impact, its circulation and its quality that it could claim to have established by the mid-century a position of absolute dominance in terms of its effect on bourgeois public opinion and in defining a position for the political role of a newspaper in bourgeois society. (Conboy, 2004: 118)

Technology too had played its part, as it has done throughout newspaper history. Walter I had started the *Register* primarily as a means of demonstrating a new printing system called logography; his son made the much more significant technological development of introducing the Konig Bauer steam press to print the paper from 1814. With many echoes of Wapping more than 150 years later, Walter had the new press delivered secretly to avoid sabotage by print workers, and only told them later (Engel, 1996: 21).

The Times at its height became 'the textual identification of confident, aspiring professional classes and an upper bourgeoisie' (Conboy and Steel, 2008: 652). It maintained its circulation lead over all other legal titles until 1855, selling more than twice as many copies as all its main rivals put together. These were the *Morning Herald*, the *Morning Chronicle* and the *Morning Post*. The figure was still only a little over 30,000, but this was before the era of massive sales, and readership of each copy was much higher than it is today. And *The Times* was targeted at an elite sector of society. At This time the dominant titles for the masses were the radical, illegal (they did not pay stamp duty) papers referred to by Curran and Seaton (above), papers such as the *Political Register, Black Dwarf* and *Poor Man's Guardian*.

At the same time as *The Times* was dominating the legal daily market Sunday newspapers were emerging, and in the case of many setting the long-lasting trend for papers which were different from the dailies, often much dirtier. One not in that category was the *Observer*, founded in 1791 and the oldest surviving Sunday paper. But the big seller was, as today, the *News of the World*. It was started in 1843 by John Browne Bell, and provided lurid crime stories, usually of particularly horrific murders. And it began to publish the sort of 'dirty vicar' stories for which it would be renowned across the years. As Engel (1996: 26) puts it: 'In essence nothing has changed in more than two centuries: carnal business and secret sins remain the business of the popular Sunday press, and though the veil of morality has become almost wholly moth-eaten over the years it has never entirely been tossed away'. By 1854 the *News of the World* was selling 100,000 copies a week, a vast amount for the time.

One of the major turning points in press history was the abolition of the taxes on advertising in 1853 and stamp duty in 1855. The arguments in parliament for this abolition included Gladstone's, that it would help to educate the common man. But opponents argued that it would have a corrupting influence, promoting greater sales of popular papers representing far from Victorian moral values. Most newspapers took a penny off the price, bringing it down typically to four pennies. One new entrant to the market, the *Daily Telegraph and Courier*, sold for two pence. It was to end the forty years of *Times* market domination, and itself led for most of the rest of the nineteenth century. It was founded by Colonel Arthur Burroughes Sleigh on 29 June 1855. Three months later Sleigh was broke and sold the paper to his printer, Moses Levy, who was already the owner of the *Sunday Times*. The price was cut to a penny, and the *Telegraph* sought to distinguish itself from *The Times*, and sell more copies. It succeeded in doing both.

It quickly established an identity that distinguished it from the deliberate elitism of *The Times*. 'The *Times*, the paper for the City merchant, and the *Daily Telegraph*, the paper for the clerk and shopkeeper' (Brown, 1985: 246, quoted by Conboy, 2004: 120). The *Telegraph* soon overtook *The Times*'s circulation, to become the dominant title until the turn of the century. Although Engel (1996: 35) describes it as 'a rather Pooterish paper for rather Pooterish people' and those who bought it as 'the very ancestors of the suburban ladies and Lt Cols (rtd) who still buy it today, the great British complaining classes' it was then more 'popular' in its choice of stories than it is today. But its successor as Britain's most popular daily newspaper was just around the corner.

Mail takes over

As the nineteenth century drew to a close the *Daily Mail* was launched. It came to 'embody the aspiring lower-middle class's views of themselves in similar ways to the dominant newspapers of the twentieth century' (Conboy and Steel, 2008: 653). The progenitors of truly popular journalism and mass circulation newspapers (Franklin, 1997: 80) are generally accepted to be Alfred Harmsworth, later Lord Northcliffe, and his younger brother, Harold, later Lord Rothermere. They were born in Dublin, two of 14 children, but the family moved to London when the boys were young. Alfred was initially the driving journalistic force, founding his school magazine and, at the age of 20, *Bicycling News*, then *Answers to Correspondents*, where he was joined by Harold, (Engel, 1996: 53). *Answers* was targeted at the 'thirst for knowledge' market, significant in those days, and soon sold about 30,000 copies an issue. Engel recounts the legend of how Alfred and Harold were walking along the Thames Embankment when they met a tramp who told them happiness was £1 a week for life. In 1889 *Answers* ran a competition with that as the prize: 700,000 entered and its circulation soared.

Still in their twenties, Alfred and Harold produced new magazines at the rate of two a year. In 1894 they acquired the failing *London Evening News* and turned it round. On 4 May 1896 they launched the *Daily Mail*, which has been in the family ever since. There were 11 morning London papers at the time, most of them not very good, having changed little since the abolition of stamp duty 40 years earlier. Raw materials and technology had changed. Paper was better and cheaper. Linotype machines were setting type at speed; rotary presses were printing papers at speed; the rapid growth of the railways provided fast nationwide distribution. Everything was in place for the expansion of the national newspaper market. And the *Daily Mail*, describing itself as 'the busy man's daily journal', more than any other was equipped and ready to dominate it.

There was nothing very revolutionary about the new *Daily Mail*. 'The newspaper that was to set the tone for the next hundred years looked exactly like the newspapers of the previous hundred years. ... the front page was covered with advertisements (this would continue until the Second World War) – it might have been the *Times* or the *Telegraph*. This was precisely the idea' (Engel, 1996: 59). The journalist community, however critical of the *Mail's* editorial prejudices, would say today how 'professional' it is. It is admired even where it is hated. It was the same when it was launched. Alfred Harmsworth, with so many successful publications behind him, had an extraordinary knack of getting it right, of understanding the audience. He understood aspiration. One of his many dictums on journalism was that the man in the street on £100 a year was 'tomorrow's £1,000 man – or so he thinks' (Engel, 1996: 59). He understood the importance of campaigning. He knew that the newspaper people read was part of their self-image; it would be called a badge today.

Four other national newspapers had launched over the few years before the *Mail's* birth, but they could not compete with the newcomer. It was aimed not at *The Times's* elite readership, not at the *Telegraph's* suburban middle-class readership, but at everyone. And by the dawn of the twentieth century it had overtaken the *Telegraph* and achieved a dominance that would last many years.

Conboy (2004: 173) identifies how Harmsworth saw the 'link between advertising, capital investment and circulation' and how the *Mail* represented the real start of the commercialisation of journalism:

> It laid the emphasis on the lighter side of life while remaining respectable in tone. It had a breadth of appeal in its articles, fashion pieces, personalities, and increased background on politicians in the news. Its style was more conversationally based. Above all, however, it had more news than its rivals.

Alfred continued his love of acquisition. He bought the *Daily Mirror*, the *Observer* (which he soon sold), and, secretly, *The Times*. He became increasingly obsessed with his own power, seeking political influence during the First World War. In his final years he became clinically insane. He died in 1922, regarded to this day as one of the greatest and most influential newspapermen ever. Harold took over. But by then there was a challenger to the *Mail's* domination. The Great War had drawn a line, and the post-war era needed a different kind of dominant newspaper.

The age of the *Express*

This was the *Daily Express*, which brought with it a proprietor every bit as large as life as Lord Northcliffe. Lord Beaverbrook was the next of the great newspaper barons. The *Daily Express* was launched on 24 April 1900 as a rival to the *Daily Mail*. The founder was C. Arthur Pearson, another magazine publisher and a quiet and modest man. Its launch advertisements proclaimed that it would 'aim to PLEASE, AMUSE and INTEREST, by gathering News and Witticisms all the Wide World Over' (Engel, 1996: 93). It was the first national daily newspaper, in many decades, to put news rather than advertisements on its front page. But under Pearson it never achieved half the *Mail*'s circulation.

Max Aitken, the future Lord Beaverbrook, was a Canadian. Like Alfred Harmsworth before him, he was interested in newspapers from an early age, and had started his own school newspaper. He became a lawyer and then a businessman, and in 1910 he moved to Britain, bought and sold the Rolls-Royce company, met Andrew Bonar Law the year before he became leader of the Conservative Party, and as a result found himself in the role of Conservative MP for Ashton-under-Lyne less than six months after coming to Britain. The same year he met Ralph Blumenfeld, editor of the *Express*. Impressed, he started investing in the paper, and in 1916 took control. He became Lord Beaverbrook the same year (Engel, 1996: 97).

His philosophy for the *Express* was that it should be a newspaper that would interest him. It appealed to an increasingly mobile population, to the conservative working class. It was intensely patriotic and the paper of the Empire. Beaverbrook made a speech in Sheffield in 1922 in which he said it was 'the duty of newspapers to advocate a policy of optimism in the broadest sense and to declare almost daily their belief in the future of England'. Beaverbrook was a controlling proprietor, a shameless user of his paper for his own political purposes, and he exerted considerable influence over everything that went into the *Express*. Its success came more gradually than that of the *Mail*. Although the latter was starting its decline, partly as a result of the increasingly eccentric behaviour of Lord Rothermere – support for Mussolini, and for Oswald Mosley and the Blackshirts – it maintained its market leadership for many years after the Beaverbrook *Express* started its assault. It took until 1927 for it to overtake the *Mirror* and get the *Mail* in its sights. It took the appointment of Arthur Christiansen as editor in 1933 to finally prevail over its rival. Christiansen, regarded as one of the greatest among all editors, held the job for twenty-four years, but it took just three to overhaul the *Mail*. By 1936 it was selling 2.25 million copies a day, the highest circulation in the world, and this would rise much higher. It consistently predicted there would be no war, and was still doing so in July 1939. It was the world's best seller. Engel (1996: 141) sums up the *Express*'s performance thus:

> And so the war came, as the Abdication had come, and television, and flight, and electrified trains, and everything else the *Express* and *Express*men had said would never happen. Christiansen had evolved the most brilliant technique for telling ordinary people about complex matters in simple terms. But the *Express* had fed them nonsense. It was

a defining moment for British journalism. No paper has ever reached out across the class divide of Britain more than the *Daily Express*; but it could not be trusted.

Mirror re-defines popular journalism

The *Daily Mirror*, the next dominant title, was born on 2 November 1903, as a 'woman's newspaper'. Like the *Daily Mail*, the paper he had founded seven years earlier, it was the brainchild of Alfred Harmsworth, soon to be Lord Northcliffe. It sold for two pennies, twice the price of the *Mail*, and was expected to be, like everything Alfred Harmsworth ever touched, a success. It was not. Harmsworth's original announcement of the *Mirror* said it would arrange its material so that 'the transition from the shaping of a flounce to the forthcoming changes in Imperial defence, from arrangement of flowers on the dinner table to the disposition of forces in the Far East, shall be made without mental paroxysm or dislocation of interest' (Engel, 1996: 147). Its editor, leading a team of mostly women, was Mary Howarth. But it sold relatively few copies, and a re-launch came soon.

Much more significant than the failure of the original concept was the success of the next, and this was again driven by use of technology. One of Harmsworth's magazine editors, Arkas Sapt, a Hungarian editing *Home Sweet Home*, had invented a new system for publishing a number of pictures on a single spread, and two months after its disappointing, women-oriented launch the *Daily Mirror* became the *Daily Illustrated Mirror*, the first successful picture paper (Engel, 1996: 149). It was for men and women. It focussed on photo-journalism, reportage, beauty contests and human interest. Ten years later its circulation was heading for a million. But Lord Northcliffe lost interest in the *Mirror* and sold his shares to his brother Lord Rothermere. The *Mirror* was popular in the Great War, through its ability to provide graphic pictures from the front, and spawned a Sunday picture paper from the same stable, the *Sunday Pictorial*, which would become the *Sunday Mirror* in 1963, still publishing today.

The *Mirror* was in decline in the 1920s. Lord Northcliffe had died, and Lord Rothermere was not investing in the free gift war that was obsessing other publishers. He was becoming more interested in political issues. In 1931 he lost control of the *Mirror* and other great names came to the fore. Guy Bartholomew, who through his work on the picture desk had been a major influence on the success of the picture paper, became editorial director in 1934, in control of the paper, and Hugh Cudlipp became features editor. Between them over the next few years these two men would transform the *Mirror*, turning it into the first true tabloid as we understand them today – mass-selling papers for the working man. There were pictures everywhere, plenty of them featuring girls in various states of undress (glamour but not topless); there were advice columns, celebrity columnists, readers' letters and sensational stories.

Despite interviewing Hitler in 1936, and finding the experience unthreatening, and reporting 'peace' after Munich in 1938, the *Mirror* was the truly popular paper of the Second World War, and it continued its dominance and circulation growth for the next twenty years and more. It was always a staunch supporter of Labour and the trade unions, and when Labour returned to power in 1964 under Harold Wilson it could count on the *Mirror*'s dedicated support. That was the year the *Mirror* – which had overtaken the *Express* to become the best seller in 1949 – achieved a sale of five million copies. Hugh Cudlipp, who became Lord Cudlipp in 1974, remained the presiding genius, never actually editing the paper but running it as editorial director and editor-in-chief. The *Mirror* of the 1960s remains iconic, revered to this day by those of its then staff still alive, a reverence added to by nostalgia, and what came next. It was upmarket by present tabloid standards, presenting serious political analysis brilliantly written and presented accessibly to its mass audience. It was investigative. It had cerebral star writers such as John Pilger and Paul Foot. It had Mirrorscope explaining complex issues simply. And it had overwhelming confidence. In 1969 it even launched a magazine, which was not to last. It was, Cudlipp believed, the first quality popular paper. But Cudlipp himself retired in 1973, and by then a new rival was catching up fast.

The *Mirror* was, ultimately, the victim of the new post-war age of 'corporate newspapering'. Cecil King, and his International Publishing Corporation, was perhaps the most effective chairman and worked very closely with Cudlipp. He was succeeded by Cudlipp himself after a boardroom coup in 1968. The company merged with a paper group, Reed International, in 1970 and was sold to Robert Maxwell in 1984. After his notorious death by drowning in 1991 – leaving financial chaos and a depleted pension scheme – and a difficult post-Maxwell period trying to sort out the mess, the Mirror Group was acquired by Trinity, the leading publisher of regional newspapers in the UK, in 1999. By then the *Mirror*'s decline was such that it was selling half the number of copies of its new rival, the *Sun*.

Sun arise

Rupert Murdoch arrived in British journalism in 1969. To the influential, controversial, charismatic and dominant figures who have littered this brief history of British newspapers was added another, the latest, with an additional adjective – global. His impact has been at least as great as the Harmsworths, Beaverbrook and Cudlipp, although, alone among them, he is not a baron. Murdoch is the apotheosis of what Jeremy Tunstall describes as the 'media mogul'. Tunstall has identified four stages to the development of newspaper ownership. First comes the 'old style Press Lord' – Northcliffe, Beaverbrook – successfully accumulating newspapers and less successfully trying to promote specific political policies through them. Then come the Crown Princes – Rothermeres – trying to imitate a more dynamic father, usually also trying to maintain the family tradition but accepting maintenance rather than growth, comfortable rather than dramatic levels of profit. The Media Mogul – Murdoch – is driven by acquisition, profits and growth, with political influence as an amusing extra. And finally there is the Chief Executive, not a major owner, thinking about profits, dividends and share options, and keeping the share price up and the proprietor happy (Tunstall, 1996: 80). As Conboy observes, Murdoch chose the ground on which he would do battle with his commercial rivals:

> The key moments of the tabloiding of British newspapers are defined initially and literally by the reformatting into tabloids of the *Sun* in 1969 and the *Daily Mail* in 1971. The *Sun* is widely acknowledged as having triggered a war of attrition over the dominant popular newspaper paradigm for the late 20th century. The *Daily Mirror* already a tabloid in format but identified with a previous era was drawn into a competition for the blue collar readership on terms dictated by the political and commercial ambition of Rupert Murdoch. The rise of the tabloid as the dominant contemporary format within journalism was forged in the 1970s and the competition between the *Sun* and the *Daily Mirror* for the position of leading articulator of the popular. This shifted popular journalism definitively away from public affairs (Rooney, 2000: 102) and the *Mirror's* blend of campaigning populism on political causes became consigned to the past. The 1980s saw the *Sun* establish its ascendancy in the market, sexualising popular culture as a central strategy in its success (Holland, 1998) and other popular papers such as the *Mirror* and the *Star* followed suit. (Conboy, 2004: 182)

Rupert Murdoch was born in Australia in 1931, the son of Keith Murdoch, owner of the most powerful newspaper group in Australia, Herald and Weekly Times. Rupert went to Oxford University, became a subeditor on the *Daily Express*, and then returned to Australia to inherit the *Adelaide News* and found the *Australian*.

As mentioned earlier in this chapter, the *News of the World* had been founded in 1843 and instantly become the major Sunday newspaper with a formula which has lasted down the years (it remains the largest-selling national newspaper today). Its circulation peaked in 1950 at around 8.5 million and it continued to sell 8 million until 1954 (Engel, 1996: 230). In 1891 it was bought by Lascelles Carr, owner of the *Western Mail*, and it remained in the Carr family for the next eighty years. Lascelles Carr appointed his nephew Emsley Carr as editor, a job he held for fifty years of great success. By the 1960s the majority of the shares were owned by Sir William Carr and his cousin Professor Derek Jackson, who in 1968 decided to sell up. The first person seeking to buy them was Robert Maxwell, then Labour MP for Buckingham. There was resistance to this from Carr himself, then ailing, and the unions, and alternative buyers were sought. Within a few weeks Rupert Murdoch was in London securing a deal with Carr whereby on buying the shares Murdoch became managing director of the *News of the World* and Carr became chairman. Three months later Murdoch successfully sought Carr's resignation (Engel, 1996: 241).

The *Sun* emerged in 1964 as successor to the *Daily Herald*, Mirror owner IPC's attempt to defend the readership of a paper now out of its time. Hugh Cudlipp was behind the launch and the paper was targeted at 'a middle class couple, aged 28, living in Reading' (Engel, 1996: 250). It was not a commercial success and IPC let it be known that it was for sale. Murdoch, again seeing off Maxwell, bought it cheaply in 1969, a daily newspaper to set alongside the Sunday title he had acquired the previous year. He had no intention of continuing either the small broadsheet format or the 'Reading' editorial content. He had, from the start, his sights set on the *Mirror*, and he believed he knew the formula, one that would sit happily alongside the *News of the World*. He was about to turn the tabloid market on its head. It would be 'an honest and straightforward newspaper with strong convictions. It would offer sex, sport and contests' (Engel, 1996: 253).

It offered all that and more. It put the expression 'Page Three' into the language, played a major role in the development of celebrity journalism, with its 'Bizarre' column of after-hours antics in the nightclubs and its kiss-and-tell stories of the infidelities of pop stars and footballers alike, and it was pithily and unambiguously direct in sharing its views with its readers. Over the years these have included support for 'our boys' in the services, derision of so-called political correctness, a celebration of the British (hard-) working man and opposition to Europe of a sometimes xenophobic nature, leading to accusations of racism (Searle, 1989). Throughout, one of its dominant characteristics has been its sense of humour, which has tempered some of its less pleasant characteristics; but it has also been accused of 'cruelty' towards its victims, especially those who cannot afford expensive libel lawyers (Pilger, 1998: 448).

The *Sun* has had two outstanding editors: Larry Lamb, later to be knighted, and Kelvin MacKenzie, later to became a celebrity in his own right. MacKenzie was the personality of the newspaper who wrote the great headlines and had bright ideas such as, 'Ten things you never knew about … '. He was described as being everything from a bully to a genius – often both at the same time – and he was undoubtedly a journalist who 'could pick a one-paragraph story off the spike and turn it into front-page news' (Melvern, 1986: 52). This gut instinct usually put sales figures up, but on occasion it could lead to embarrassing own goals, as will be discussed when we look at ethics in Chapter 7. It was the *Sun* that first seized upon, then articulated, and then promoted Thatcherism. It captured the anti-union, conservative working class and, like Margaret Thatcher herself, realised they were a new political force; more importantly for the paper, they could also be a new circulation force. And conveniently it presented an ideological divide between the *Sun* and the *Mirror*. It probably never was 'the *Sun* wot won it', as it famously claimed after the 1992 general election, but it didn't hurt to claim it.

The *Mirror* hardly put up a fight. The *Sun* was selling two million in 1971, two years after its launch, three million in 1973, and then overtook the *Mirror* with just under four million in 1977. Hugh Cudlipp retired in 1973, aware that the *Sun* was unstoppable and reluctant to follow it down an editorial path he found objectionable. When Murdoch acquired the loss-making *Times* and highly profitable *Sunday Times* in 1981 his domination of the British market was achieved. He turned his attention to satellite television, where he was equally successful, but before that he had to bring off the most seismic shift in newspaper publishing of the post-war era: Wapping.

Wapping revolution

The technology made it possible but it would not have happened without a proprietor determined to introduce it and a political climate that encouraged him to do so. As with website publishing later, Rupert Murdoch was not the first adopter, but unlike with website publishing he was quick to see the potential and to use his industrial and commercial power to exploit it. Quite simply, it was the use of electronic means, computer technology, to produce newspapers, and it was a revolution as great as any in the history of newspaper publishing. It meant a quicker, cleaner, more controllable method of moving words and pictures from their originators to the printed page. It dramatically increased the role of editorial (journalists) in the production process, with a consequent marginalisation of the printers. At a stroke it reduced the power of the print unions. And it had the potential for dramatically reducing production costs and (in the interests of Murdoch and other proprietors) increasing profitability. All this was self-evident. How you got from there to here was not.

The power of the print unions was great in the post-war period. A variety of them, with names like SOGAT, NATSOPA, SLADE, were traditional craft unions and their members were organised at plant level into 'chapels' led by 'fathers of the chapel'. They had direct and regular access to the senior management of newspapers and their work practices were rigid, demarcated and regularly negotiated, as was their remuneration. The print workers were highly skilled, highly paid, dynastic, proud of their elite position in the hierarchy of craft unions and their strength with regard to their employers.

Different parts of the production and printing processes were the preserve of specific unions, and so-called 'demarcation disputes' were not unusual. But when it came to disputes with management there was usually a united front. Their power, in essence, derived from the frequency of publication of newspapers. Every night, there were very tight schedules designed to produce thousands of copies of daily newspapers and deliver them to railway stations in time to meet specific trains, in time to deliver copies around the country to wholesalers who would pass them on to retailers, so that they were on sale to readers early in the morning. A few minutes' disruption to the process of setting type in hot metal, putting that type into chases with metal blocks carrying pictures, turning those 'metal pages' into papier mache flongs and then into metal plates to attach to printing presses, and then running the presses to print the newspapers, could mean missing the trains and losing the revenue from sales and advertising. It could not be recovered. A daily newspaper has a short life. Tomorrow there will be another newspaper.

The post-war period, particularly up until the early seventies, was a time of large circulations and huge profits. Managements tended to be weak, or pragmatic, in conceding quickly (there was no time for protracted negotiation if the paper was to come out) to union demands. The cost of concession was always much less than the cost of lost production. Pagination could not be increased, extra editions added, unscheduled page changes made, without the prior consent of the print unions. Besides, by colluding with the print unions to keep staffing levels and wages so high, the newspaper owners helped make it virtually impossible for any newcomer to encroach on their territory. Start-up costs for new newspapers were prohibitively high, and that suited many of the established proprietors for a long time.

Now the technology existed to remove the traditional printing methods. Words could be written into computers by journalists. Pictures could be handled by computers. Pages could be designed and output on computers. Every stage of the process up to printing (in which computers were also increasingly involved) could be undertaken without the traditional skills of the traditional printers. Managements began negotiations with the unions about the introduction of the new technology, but these were never going to be less than bloody – thousands of jobs were about to be erased. The political climate of the Thatcher government was hostile to the trade unions and confrontation was becoming common. New industrial relations legislation requiring strike balloting and outlawing secondary picketing had been introduced. But the newspaper owners were nervous. While the gains from change were obvious, the cost of getting there could be horrendous. Rupert Murdoch took a different route.

He was not in fact the pioneer of the newspaper revolution. That description belongs properly to Eddy Shah who fought and defeated the print unions in Warrington, Cheshire. He had built up a chain of free newspapers around Manchester, the *Messenger* series. He was opposed to the restrictive practices, as he saw them, of the print unions and in 1983 stared to hire non-union staff at his Warrington printing house. The National Graphical Association, one of the most powerful of the print unions, in Fleet Street as well as the rest of the country, was opposed to the new Thatcher trade union laws and chose Warrington to put up a fight. Pickets were mounted and soon there were battles in the streets as the police fought with the printers. It was precursor of what was to come in Wapping. Shah won a series of High Court actions against the NGA and eventually also won the 'Battle of Warrington' as pickets were withdrawn.

Shah's victory in the north, and the relationships he built with Fleet Street publishers, convinced him he should start a non-union, computer typeset national newspaper. He found financial backing and *Today* – non-union, new technology – launched on 4 March 1986. After a series of crises and changes of ownership and editors it finally closed in November 1995; its impact on the rest of the national press, however, had been great. As Brian MacArthur (1988: 214), its first editor, recalled: 'Eddy Shah may have failed when he tried to launch a national newspaper ... but he was a man who seized hold of an idea whose time had come'.

Tunstall (1996: 18) describes the Wapping revolution as having 'all the necessary news value ingredients; there was a sudden event, bitter conflict and a central personality, a hero/villain in the shape of Rupert Murdoch'. He quotes the then senior executive on the *Financial Times*, Frank Barlow:

> Sunday January 26 [1986] was the day on which Fleet Street, as we have known it for all our working lives, ceased to exist. That was the day on which Rupert Murdoch proved that it was possible to produce two mass circulation Sunday newspapers without a single member of his existing print workforce, without using the railways, and with roughly one fifth of the numbers that he had been employing before.

Rather than put his company's energy into negotiation – although negotiations about reductions in staffing went on – Murdoch went for the 'Big Bang', covertly. He acquired a site by Tower Bridge in Wapping; he installed printing presses; he equipped newsrooms with computers; he even established a company to distribute his newspapers by road, fearing the inevitable support of the rail unions for the print unions when the crunch came. Murdoch put up various smokescreens to disguise what was really going on. You could not hide a huge plant like Wapping, although you could protect or obfuscate what was going on inside it. The rumour was put round that Murdoch was preparing to launch a London evening paper called the *Post* to compete with the *Evening Standard*. This was believed by many.

Most journalists on Murdoch newspapers were completely ignorant of what was going on in late 1985. They continued their daily work in their old buildings, bringing out the *Sun* and *Times*, the *News of the World* and *Sunday*

Times. A small planning group of senior editorial (and other) executives worked in extraordinarily well-maintained secrecy to prepare for Wapping. Andrew Neil, *Sunday Times* editor, and Kelvin MacKenzie, editor of the *Sun*, were prominent among them. Towards the end of January 1986 journalists on the four papers were told what was happening. They were moving to Wapping; the Fleet Street offices were closing; there would be payments for making the move, but those who refused to do so would be dismissing themselves. Most moved to the new plant, and from 26 January all four titles were published out of Wapping.

A dispute over the sudden move ensued, with the journalists who had refused to go – known as the 'refuseniks' – and the redundant print workers picketing the Wapping plant. There was enormous bitterness and verbal abuse of the majority who crossed the picket line to work in the Wapping plant. There was a constant police presence, often with horses, and some violence. The picketing lasted for more than a year.

But the revolution could never be unpicked. It was the beginning of the end for Fleet Street as other publishers, with more negotiation and less confrontation (that had been the case in Wapping), followed the same new technology route to greater profits. Roy Greenslade, then a senior executive on the *Sun*, who himself made the move to Wapping, records (2003a: 477):

> A rival executive estimated that Murdoch's costs were instantly reduced by £80m a year after Wapping. His papers immediately became immensely profitable: News International's profits in the year up to June 1986, just six months after the move, were up on the previous year by 74.2% to £83.3m. The *Sun* alone made 40% more than in the previous 12 months. The following year, up to June 1987, NI's profits rose to £111.5m.

Or, as Tunstall (1996: 18) put it, 'the conflict was about Power and Money. The result was a major shift away from the trade unionised labour force and in favour of owners, managers and editors'. That shift created the conditions under which newspapers have been produced in the UK over the past two decades. Getting rid of the print unions would finally leave journalists in editorial charge of newspapers – that had been the promise that encouraged some reluctant journalists to move to Wapping. It still left the corporate managers in charge of the size of editorial staffs, as waves of redundancies in 2008–2009 were to demonstrate.

A question of (Scott) Trust

While this necessarily brief history of newspapers in Britain has concentrated on the dominant and influential newspapers of successive eras, it cannot end without mentioning the two national papers at the top end of the market that have the lowest circulations but disproportionate fame, reputation and clout. Neither falls into the traditional or modern commercial model; one is very old, the other very new. These are the *Guardian* and the *Independent*. The *Guardian* is the liberal regional paper that became a national; the *Independent* the realisation of a dream that you could produce a national paper without a baron or a mogul behind you.

The *Guardian* is different. Different in its ownership. Different in its origins. It holds a distinct place in the quality-newspaper market, has an engaged audience that claims an almost proprietorial influence over its newspaper, which is itself notable for its lack of a proprietor. It is scorned by its opponents, loved by its supporters. Millions who have never read it believe they know what it represents – and they are often wrong. It hangs its conscience on its sleeve. Its critics accuse it of an unworldly disconnection from the concerns of 'ordinary people', but then *Guardian* readers do not see themselves as ordinary people. Its critics regard it as holier than thou, but then its readers believe they stand for a better world. They accept that there are no easy answers, but at least they care. They care very much, and that includes caring about the *Guardian*.

It was launched on 5 May 1821 as the *Manchester Guardian* by John Edward Taylor. At first it was a weekly, publishing twice a week from 1836, and becoming a daily in 1855 when stamp duty was removed and the price was cut to two pennies. Taylor started the paper to 'promote the liberal interest in the aftermath of the Peterloo Massacre'. As the *Guardian*'s own short online history records: 'Taylor was a reformer. His newspaper declared that it would "zealously enforce the principles of civil and religious Liberty … warmly advocate the cause of Reform … endeavour to assist in the diffusion of just principles of Political Economy and … support, without reference to the party from which they emanate, all serviceable measures"'.

In 1872 Charles Prestwich (C.P.) Scott was made editor of the *Manchester Guardian* at the age of 26, a position he held for the next 57 years (*Guardian* editors still serve longer than most, but not that long). Scott, another giant of newspaper history, bought the paper in 1907 following the death of Taylor's son, pledging to maintain the principles set out by John Taylor. Scott amplified these with one of the most famous quotes in journalism in an essay he wrote at the time of the *Manchester Guardian*'s centenary. 'Comment is free, but facts are sacred. The voice of opponents no less than that of friends has a right to be heard'. When Scott retired in 1929 he passed control of the paper on to his two sons, John Russell Scott as manager and Edward Taylor Scott as editor. The two agreed that if one of them was to die the survivor would buy the other's share of the ownership.

Such planning turned out to be prescient because C.P. Scott died in 1932 and Edward was killed in a boating accident on Lake Windermere four months later. Inheriting the sense of duty of his father, John Scott realised that the aims of the founder would not be honoured were he to die and death duties be imposed. John Edward Taylor, when he sold the paper to

C.P. Scott, wanted it to be 'conducted in the future on the same lines and in the same spirit as heretofore'. John Scott sought a way of ensuring that this would be the case when he died, and the Scott Trust was devised.

John Scott created the Trust in 1936, renouncing all financial interest in the business for himself and his family and putting all his shares into the Trust. It is this trust which owns the *Guardian* today, and all the associated businesses that have grown up around it. The Scott Trust owns the *Observer* and the *Manchester Evening News*, founded in 1868 and bought for the *Guardian* by John Scott in 1924, as well as regional newspapers in the north west and south east of England. These include the *Rochdale Advertiser* series, the *Stockport Advertiser* series, the *Surrey Advertiser* and the *Reading Evening Post*. It owns radio stations and a highly profitable car-sales magazine, *Auto Trader*. All are there to underpin the central purpose of the Trust: 'To secure the financial and editorial independence of the *Guardian* in perpetuity: as a quality national newspaper without party affiliation; remaining faithful to its liberal tradition; as a profit seeking enterprise managed in an efficient and cost-effective manner'.

So there are no share holders, no distribution of profits. The Scott Trust appoints the editors, and while the Guardian Media Group, as it is today, has a conventional management structure and *modus operandi* it is answerable to the Scott Trust, which owns the business. This has resulted in imperatives that are different from those of its competitors.

The *Guardian*'s hybrid position as a Manchester-based regional newspaper with a national agenda and increasingly national sales was resolved progressively in the 1950s. The editor then was Alastair Hetherington, and together with the senior director and descendant of C.P. Scott, Laurence Scott, he decided to recognise that the *Manchester Guardian* was now in many ways a national newspaper by dropping the Manchester prefix from the title. On 23 August 1959 readers were told that this change 'acknowledges an accomplished fact. Nearly two thirds of the paper's circulation now lies outside the Manchester area' (Greenslade, 2003a: 124). However the *Guardian* continued to be edited from Manchester until 1964, with London fulfilling the role of a district office, albeit a rapidly growing one. From 1964 all the growth concentrated on London, with a consequent reduction in the Manchester contribution over the years. There were financial problems and discussions in the mid-sixties with *The Times* over the possibility of merger. But Hetherington was firmly opposed to such a course, and independence was maintained.

The role of the Scott Trust has continued to be central, and a distinguishing aspect of the *Guardian*. Its overriding purpose, to secure the *Guardian* 'in perpetuity', has meant long periods of subsidy from other parts of the group, historically the *Manchester Evening News*, more recently *Auto Trader*. *Observer* losses have been sustained since the *Guardian* acquired it in 1993. But the absence of the need to distribute profits to shareholders has allowed the *Guardian* to invest in the future when others have been more cautious. Most notably, it allowed the *Guardian* to take a ten-year lead in the development of its website by identifying the need early and not having to justify to shareholders the huge investment needed to build and develop the new publishing platform. In October 2008 the Scott Trust announced a 'reorganisation of its structure to strengthen the protection it offers the *Guardian*'. It would be replaced by The Scott Trust Ltd, with the trustees becoming directors of the new company. It cannot pay dividends and no individual is allowed to profit personally from directorship (Scott Trust, 2008).

It is, are you?

No one, and that includes the founders, would deny that Margaret Thatcher and Rupert Murdoch made the *Independent* possible. Thatcher had created the economic climate, had reduced union power and encouraged venture capital, or private equity as we call it today. The buzzword of the eighties was 'yuppie', the 20- and 30-somethings populating the City of London, making money for themselves and accessing start-up money for those who wanted to begin their own businesses. Murdoch, however controversially, had broken the power of the print unions through his Wapping revolution and taken full advantage of the profits potential of the new computer technology for producing newspapers.

Andreas Whittam Smith was no yuppie himself – he was a dour, rather academic, clergyman's son – but as a business journalist on the *Daily Telegraph* he was well able to read the economic climate. He realised that if ever there was a time to start a new newspaper – until then unthinkable unless you had vast financial backing and could persuade the print unions to cooperate – this was it. With two *Telegraph* colleagues, Stephen Glover and Matthew Symonds, he determined to set up a new, upmarket daily newspaper, independent in character, *Independent* in name. Its simple slogan when it went to the public was: 'The *Independent*: It is, are you?' As Greenslade (2003a: 482) says:

> Wapping was to prove one of the *Independent's* greatest assets, helping to attract both staff and readers. Many journalists from the *Times* and *Sunday Times*, worried by the ethics of union-busting, and conveniently overlooking the fact that they were about to work on a non-union paper made possible by Murdoch's move, wanted to cleanse themselves of Wapping.

The three founders set out to be free of traditional proprietorship. They went into the venture-capital market and raised about £18 million in relatively small sums, sufficient, they believed, to launch a new daily. There was no dominant investor. There were share options for the staff, and the founders were as central to the management team as to the editorial concept and development. Printing and distribution would be subcontracted. It was, determinedly, not a corporate newspaper. One of the founders, Stephen Glover, recalled:

> Proprietorless, independent and now with money, the newspaper represented for many a journalistic ideal which in the age of Murdoch and Maxwell had seemed unattainable. In fact, of course, the *Independent* was merely a creature of a different sort of capitalism with different sorts of owners, but in those early days it was possible for journalists to believe that this was a kind of workers' co-operative, in some deep sense their own paper. Whereas in the companies from which they had escaped journalists were regarded by management as a regrettably necessary part of producing a newspaper, here the management was dominated by journalists who encouraged everyone to attend meetings and express a view. (Glover, 1994: 81)

The *Independent* launched on 7 October 1986. It looked traditional, deliberately, with its broadsheet format and low-key design. It used pictures that were bigger and better than the other broadsheets. It pioneered the concept of 'listings' in newspapers. But all the traditional, and in a quality newspaper expected, features like obituaries and law reports were also included. It was an immediate success, becoming fashionable with the yuppies and the intelligent young in general. Although by background and attitude the three founders were hardly of the left, the new newspaper, despite its free-market stance, was perceived as a largely liberal anti-Thatcherite paper (Greenslade, 2003a: 485). It reflected the growing unpopularity of Thatcherism; it became a 'badge', *the* fashionable newspaper to be seen carrying. Sales soared. The *Guardian* suffered. By the end of 1987 the *Independent*'s circulation was approaching 400,000.

But the good times were not to last. The economic boom of the eighties was coming to an end. As the excitement of start-up and initial success wore off, there were internal disagreements, between staff and founders, among the founders themselves. Whittam Smith, the editor and driving proprietorial force, became more and more dominant. And the realities of running a newspaper in a deteriorating economic environment soon became clear. Further funding was secured early on, but the time eventually came when the *Independent* was forced to seek money where it had so adamantly refused to go – from other, more traditional, publishers.

Eventually, after suffering badly from Murdoch's competitive price cutting of *The Times*, after a failed attempt to buy the *Observer*, the *Independent* entered talks with major investors from the newspaper industry which would bring its independence to an end. After a great deal of very public to-ing and fro-ing, Newspaper Publishing, the *Independent*'s publishing company, moved into the hands of two publishers: the Mirror Group with its chief executive David Montgomery brokering the deal, and Tony O'Reilly, a wealthy publisher of newspapers in Ireland, who had made his initial fortune with Heinz of baked beans fame. Troubled times followed, as the editorial staff came to terms with the end of the dream and muttered about the amount of money the founders had taken out of the company, and muttered more about 'the way the paper was going'. The relationship with Mirror Group was never happy, and O'Reilly, by now a global player with newspaper interests in South Africa and Australia, sought to buy them out. He succeeded in 1998 in securing complete control of the *Independent* and its Sunday sister which had been launched in 1990.

O'Reilly marked the arrival at the *Independent* of a newspaper mogul with a touch of the baron. He has been content to run the newspaper at a loss, the 'badge' of the post-launch period attractive to him in a very different way. Today, now, as described in the last chapter, compact (the upmarket descriptor for the tabloid size), the *Independent* has a small but very loyal group of readers. It sells around 220,000, the lowest figure of any national daily; it is an opinionated 'viewspaper', as its editor until 2008 Simon Kelner (who then became managing director) likes to describe it; it supports issues supported by the more radical young. It has become a respected niche product with a precarious existence. Quite how precarious was demonstrated when management revealed plans for the *Independent* to leave its own offices and rent space in the *Daily Mail*'s headquarters in 2009, allowing it to cut costs and maybe backroom staff (Ponsford, 2008).

And now we are at the beginning of a new chapter in newspaper history. Newspapers no longer publish only on paper. The twenty-first century has taken newspapers online, and newspaper companies have become media groups trying to reconcile their historic role and success with the challenges of the digital age. In the next chapter we will examine how the present-day successors to the pioneer owners are dealing with this changed environment.

Part II

Contemporary Practices and Current Debates

5

THE CHANGING POLITICAL ECONOMY
OF THE PRESS

The 'Wapping revolution' of 1986 marked not only the end of the power of the print unions but also the solidification of the corporate age of newspaper publishing. Some of the long established newspaper dynasties survived, most notably the Rothermere/Harmsworth control of the group publishing the *Daily Mail*. But other changes in ownership, of the Telegraph and Express groups, heralded a new era in which owners were not necessarily well-known individuals but public corporations with shareholders and stock market prices to concern them – to a considerable extent, businesses like any other. Wapping had changed the cost structure of newspaper publication and, in theory at least and often in practice, had made the potential for generating huge profits a very real one. That was surely the reason why in the few years after Wapping a number of new titles came on to the market. Start-up costs were lower; the new industrial relations climate brought in by the Thatcher government gave the employers dominance in their relationship with organised labour; the new technologies for newspaper production simplified the process, made it cheaper, more flexible and more profitable; and the economic climate made investment capital from a variety of sources, including venture capital, readily available.

A golden age for newspapers?

Franklin (1997: 83) describes the years between 1986 and 1990 as representing 'something of a Golden Age for British newspapers, with 10 new national newspaper launches'. The golden age soon lost its sheen, as the economy turned downwards. Of the ten new titles listed by Franklin – *Today*, the *Independent*, the *Sport*, *Sunday Sport*, the *London Daily News*, *News on Sunday*, the *Post*, the *Sunday Correspondent*, the *Independent on Sunday* and the *European* – only the two *Independent* titles (now under corporate ownership, both selling least in their market sectors) and the *Sport* titles (hardly newspapers and hardly selling) have survived. The one national newspaper launch since then has been the *Daily Star Sunday*, in 2002. Like its daily counterpart it is targeted at the very bottom of the redtop market. *Sunday Business* launched in 1996, as a descendant of the *European*, which had by then joined the Barclay brothers stable, and then closed. *The Business*, which it later became, had a teetering existence but a committed friend in Andrew Neil, who, as managing director of the political and weekly *Spectator*, was later able to turn it into *Spectator Business*. It is anyway better regarded a magazine than as a newspaper.

Wapping promised a new age of plurality in the national press, a public sphere enriched by a plethora of new titles through cheaper and easier access to the newspaper market (Temple, 2008: 80). But while new titles appeared most of them were short-lived. 'So where was the abundance of new titles the introduction of new technology had promised?' The answer, argues Termple, is that 'there could and should have been more successful titles: despite the high production costs prior to new technology these were a relatively small percentage of the overall costs … What the Wapping revolution did achieve was to allow newspapers to start making money. Some existing newspapers, for example the *Telegraph* titles, were arguably saved from extinction by a move out of expensive leased Fleet Street buildings and the adoption of new technology' (2008: 82–83). The real beneficiaries of Wapping were the established publishers who were well used to riding the ups and downs of the economic cycle and were now enjoying huge reductions in costs and consequent increases in profits. The new entrants were soon experiencing their first economic downturn, the recession of the early nineties. While the *Independent* titles were the most notable survivors of those who had exploited the Wapping opportunity, their business model of a number of small investors was soon to be challenged and replaced by the more traditional model.

From family affairs to corporate ownership

When newspaper closures brought an end to the brief 'golden age', the old order returned in the sense that the old titles dominated at the turn of the millennium. However, ownership of those titles was a different matter. Jeremy Tunstall (1996: 79), as described in Chapter 4, has argued that the nature of proprietorship has changed over the last fifty years, and changed more since the 'Wapping revolution'. The era of the traditional press lords came to an end, although some remained as 'crown princes', and there was a 'new pattern of media moguls and, after 1986 and Wapping, a new wave of macho managers'. The media mogul's 'driving urge is acquisition', according to Tunstall (ibid.: 80). Profits, growth and financial performance come first. The final Tunstall category is the 'chief executive, who is not a major owner, typically has predominantly commercial motivation … [and] also has to keep up the share price as a defence against hostile take-over'. We might better describe this as 'corporate ownership' in which the owning corporation and its dominant figure may not necessarily have a media tradition.

If we examine the political economy of the national press in Britain today we can apply Tunstall's model. We have in the present Lord Rothermere, the 'crown prince', the latest in the Harmsworth line of press barons, but one who presides over a corporate structure rather than a baronial fiefdom. Associated Newspapers, the publisher of the *Daily Mail* and *Mail on Sunday*, also own the Northcliffe regional newspaper chain and the free *Metro* series, *London Lite* and *Loot*. The Rothermere approach to the national flagships has been to entrust content and significant management responsibility to an editor-in-chief, in which role there have been two hugely influential men, the late Sir David English and the present incumbent Paul Dacre. Their dominant leadership has been responsible for the continuous success of the group over three decades. Associated Newspapers represents corporate management under a crown prince, but above it all it represents a continuity of ownership for more than one hundred years.

The *Express* newspapers, after their dominance of the mid-market they shared with the *Mail* titles in the mid-twentieth century, moved from Press Lord (Beaverbrook) ownership to a succession of changes of proprietor between 1977 and the present day. After a period of a not very successful 'crown princedom', the group moved through a period of corporate owner-ship when the Aitken family, direct descendants of Beaverbrook, sold up in 1977 to a shipping and construction company, Trafalgar House (they owned the famous shipping line Cunard). They were taken over in 1985 by the large and profitable regional newspaper group United Newspapers with its powerful chief executive David Stevens. United sold to a new media mogul Clive Hollick, who had built his empire in television, in 1995. Five years later Express Newspapers were taken over by Richard Desmond's Northern and Shell company, supported by a German bank (Greenslade, 2003a: 667). He was a self-made publishing man, deriving his fortune from the soft-porn end of the market – his magazines were to be found on the top shelves of newsagents. If Desmond is a media mogul – which, from the point of view of his business interests and history of launch and acquisition, he is – he comes from the seedier end of publishing and his entry into mainstream newspaper ownership should be seen as a corporate takeover. He has ruth-lessly stripped out costs and journalists, and the decline of the *Express* titles has continued under his profitable stewardship.

The modern history of the *Mirror* titles is also one of corporate takeovers by other publishers. Ownership by the International Publishing Corporation (IPC), dominated by Cecil King and Hugh Cudlipp, moved to Reed International, long a supplier of newsprint (paper) to the *Mirror* titles, in 1970. 'It was the first time a non media company had come to dominate a newspaper publishing group in Britain' (Wintour, 1972, cited in Greenslade, 2003a: 211). This then was the start of the new age of ownership.

Robert Maxwell, however, was in some ways a throwback. He saw himself as a latter day press baron, with all the qualities of megalomania, authoritarianism and the desire to acquire political influence through newspaper ownership that had been present in his baronial forbears. Another self-made publisher (of books) and a politician (he had been a Labour MP), he made repeated unsuccessful attempts to buy into national newspapers until he acquired the big prize in 1984 of Mirror Group newspapers. His bizarre, often crazed, stewardship is much chronicled, no aspect more than his death by drowning. Was it an accident? Was it suicide? Was it murder? Debate raged, particularly when the complexities of the financial mess he left behind emerged. He had stripped his employees' pension fund and left his company to sort out the chaos that survived him. He 'disappeared' off his private yacht cruising by the Canary Islands in the autumn of 1991, and was found floating in the sea some hours later.

The Mirror Group's situation was grave in the extreme and after much negotiation with the banks a rescue package involving David Montgomery as chief executive was put together. Montgomery, a former journalist (he had edited the *News of the World* and *Today*) turned media entrepreneur, had no aversion to unpopularity and ruthlessly cut costs and staff. He is a classic example of the new corporate newspaperman, and continues his activities in mainland Europe today. He ran the Mirror Group until 1999 when bidders were sought and later that year the group was bought by the largest regional newspaper group in the country, but with no experience of running national newspapers, Trinity, which was renamed Trinity Mirror. It became another example of corporate ownership, and has proved a difficult acquisition for Trinity. Circulations have declined, particularly of the Sunday titles, the *People* and *Sunday Mirror*, and this has coincided with a decline in the regional market.

Rupert Murdoch, *the* press baron and media mogul of the corporate age and the chief executive answerable to the board but identified in the public consciousness as the autocratic 'owner' of all he controls, is the first and only truly global media player with a name bigger than his companies. He is thus hard to categorise, but his power and influence are universally recognised. He is not a seeker after political influence in the sense of the press baron as described by Tunstall; he is first and last a businessman. Any political agendas he may have – and the extent to which he 'controls' his editors and 'orders' the political line is ferociously debated – are related primarily to his business strategies, not his political ambition. The influence of his papers is undeniable, not least for their dominance of the markets, and there is plenty of evidence that he is courted by political leaders seeking the support of his various papers. But Murdoch is more interested in financial policy and corporate regulation, and how these affect his business interests, than he is in the minutiae of domestic social policy. Britain was Murdoch's stepping stone from Australia to the world, and he controls a large proportion (see below) of national newspaper sales in Britain, as well as Sky Television. He operates a conventional corporate structure, with a global network of chief executives, and moves his key players from country to country. For example, his acquisition of the *Wall Street Journal* in 2007 led to the transfer from London to New York of his UK chief executive, Les Hinton, and the editor of *The Times*, Robert Thomson. Murdoch bought the *News of the World* and the *Sun* in 1969, *The Times* and *Sunday Times* in 1981. He had, or soon would have, the biggest selling Sunday and daily newspapers in the country, the biggest selling Sunday title in the quality sector, and the most famous title in the world. He set about consolidating his position in Britain, a process which led to Wapping in 1986.

The *Telegraph* moved from 'crown prince' to 'media mogul' when Lord Hartwell's family lost control in 1985 to the Canadian Conrad Black's Hollinger company. Black had much of the old style press baron about him – he was a larger than life, controlling presence, an intellectual with a desire to be accepted in British political circles, but he was modern in the sense that he ran a company with a board and shareholders to whom he was answerable. The fact that he tended to forget this corporate side of his position led eventually to his downfall, prosecution and imprisonment for misusing company funds. In 2004 the *Telegraph* titles were sold to the Barclay Brothers (David and Frederick), who eschew publicity and exercise quiet control from the sidelines, or rather Sark in the Channel Islands. They are another example of the modern corporate owner.

The *Observer*, more than two hundred years old, was the family business of the Astors and had the last owner/editor in David Astor. He realised he could no longer afford to maintain it and sold it in 1976 to the giant American oil company, Atlantic Richfield. They sold up in 1981 to another business with no media involvement, Lonrho, which had considerable mining interests in East Africa and was run by another larger than life entrepreneur in the person of 'Tiny' Rowland. Lonrho's ownership was fraught, with many questions asked about the relationship between the *Observer*'s journalism in East Africa and Rowland's commercial interests. The relationship came to an end in 1993, with Lonrho facing mounting debts and needing to shed the loss-making newspaper. The *Observer* was bought by the *Guardian* and thus ended seventeen years of corporate ownership. The *Guardian* is owned by The Scott Trust Ltd, with the trustees holding all the shares which pay no dividends. Its constitution ensures that no individual can profit personally and that its prime aim is to secure the *Guardian* in perpetuity.

Table 5.1   Daily sales by publisher

Group	Titles	Daily sales (000s) and % of market
News International (Murdoch)	Times, Sun	3,668 34.7%
Associated Newspapers (Rothermere)	Daily Mail	2,194 20.8%
Express (Desmond)	Daily Express, Daily Star	1,466 13.9%
Trinity Mirror	Daily Mirror	1,400 13.2%
Telegraph Media (Barclay Brothers)	Daily Telegraph	836 7.9%
Pearson	Financial Times	449 4.2%
Guardian Media	Guardian	358 3.4%
Independent News and Media (O'Reilly)	Independent	201 1.9%
Total sales		10,572

Source: Computed from ABC headline circulation figures (November 2008)

So the transformation of the political economy of the British national press is complete, with all the family owners except the latest Lord Rothermere gone, and the new breed of corporate owners, susceptible ultimately to bids and takeover, with the romance or ideology of journalism subordinate to making profits (not that they all do), in control. Dominant individuals, big personalities, names better known than those leading most corporations, do still exist, but the modern generation of chief executives have to be more concerned with tomorrow's balance sheet than history. All but the *Guardian/Observer* share this corporate structure.

Newspaper circulation

How does ownership translate into sales? The following tables show the proportions of newspaper sales attributable to the various publishers. Table 5.1 describes the daily market, aggregating the daily sales of all titles owned by each group. Table 5.2 describes the Sunday market, aggregating the Sunday sales of all titles owned by each group. Table 5.3 consolidates daily and Sunday sales, multiplying the average daily sale by six and adding the Sunday sale to produce a weekly sale of national newspapers for each owner. It gives the

Table 5.2   Sunday sales by publisher

Group	Titles	Sunday sales (000s) and % of market
News International (Murdoch)	Sunday Times, News of the World	4,378 41.0%
Associated Newspapers	Mail on Sunday	2,211 20.7%
Trinity Mirror	Sunday Mirror, People	1,851 17.3%
Express (Desmond)	Sunday Express, Daily Star Sunday	1,017 9.5%
Telegraph Media (Barclay Brothers)	Sunday Telegraph	622 5.8%
Guardian Media	Observer	444 4.2%
Independent News and Media (O'Reilly)	Independent on Sunday	166 1.6%
Total sales		10,689

Source: Computed from ABC headline circulation figures (November 2008)

Table 5.3   Weekly sales by publisher

Group	Titles	Copies over week – six dailies, plus one Sunday (000s)	% of market by weekly circulation
News International (Murdoch)	Times, Sun, Sunday Times, News of the World	22,008 plus 4,378 26,386	35.6
Associated Newspapers	Daily Mail, Mail on Sunday	13,164 plus 2,211, 15,375	20.7
Trinity Mirror	Daily Mirror, Sunday Mirror, People	8,400 plus 1,851, 10,251	13.8
Express (Desmond)	Daily Express, Daily Star, Sunday Express, Daily Star Sunday	8,796 plus 1,017, 9,813	13.2
Telegraph Media (Barclay Brothers)	Daily Telegraph, Sunday Telegraph	5,010 plus 622, 5,632	7.6
Pearson – weekday only	Financial Times	2,694 (no Sunday)	3.6
Guardian Media	Guardian, Observer	2,148 plus 462, 2,592	3.5
Independent News and Media (O'Reilly)	Independent, Independent on Sunday	1,206 plus 166, 1,372	1.9
Total copies sold in week		74,115	100.0

Source: Computed from ABC headline circulation figures (November 2008)

most accurate representation of the newspaper market as a whole. It shows that Rupert Murdoch's News International delivers 36 per cent of all national newspapers sold in Britain, with Lord Rothermere's Associated Newspapers responsible for 21 per cent. More than half, then, of the 76 million national papers sold each week come from two publishers. Of the rest, only Trinity Mirror and Northern and Shell (Express) sell more than 10 per cent. It should be remembered too, that of these national publishers Trinity Mirror and Associated Newspapers have substantial ownership of the regional press, and Guardian Media also has a significant regional stake. Internationally Rupert Murdoch is a major player and Tony O'Reilly a significant one.

Newspaper advertising

Revenue from selling advertising is an essential component of the economic model on which newspaper businesses are based. In paid-for newspapers it is the only major source of revenue apart from that derived from the price to the buyer of the paper. With free newspapers it is the sole source. This is why advertising departments are a central part of any newspaper company, with large sales teams, incentivised by performance bonuses, constantly on the telephone selling space. The amount that newspapers can charge for advertising is determined by the sale of the newspaper and the demographic 'quality' of the readership. Newspaper pagination is determined by the amount and value of advertising generated, and since Wapping gave managements the freedom to increase pagination at will pagination has risen vastly. Franklin (1997: 90) records the changes in pagination pre- and post-Wapping, with the *Sun*, for example, moving from an average 32 pages per issue in 1984 to 52 in 1994. Corresponding figures for the *Guardian* are 28 and 72, for the *Sunday Times* 178 and 362, and for the *Mail on Sunday* 64 and 220. Newspapers have added new sections and magazines, expanded sports coverage not only to provide better value for readers and more reasons to buy, but to also make room for more advertising thus bringing in more revenue. It is why publishers are investing in new printing presses, not only to provide higher quality, not only to generate the extra income from the contract printing of other publishers' products (this is increasingly important to regional publishers who often have contracts to print national newspapers around the country), but also to increase dramatically the use of colour throughout a newspaper. Colour advertising costs the advertiser more than black and white, and many advertisers are prepared to pay the extra for the additional impact that colour brings. Newspaper publishers provide rate cards giving the cost of advertising in their titles. These are all subject to much negotiation by media buyers, the intermediaries between the advertiser and the publisher, but the following illustrative rate card figures give some idea of what advertisers pay to advertise:

- *Daily Mail*: £36,000 black and white; £48,000 colour.
- *Sun*: £42,000 black and white; £54,000 colour.
- *Telegraph*: £27,000 black and white; £58,000 colour.
- *Guardian*: £11,000 black and white; £18,000 colour.
- *Independent*: £9,000 black and white; £14,000 colour.

All the above figures relate to a full page in the stated publication in September 2008 (Newspaper Marketing Association).

However, advertising revenues are closely dependent on the prevailing economic conditions in the wider economy, and a downturn in the economy will be quickly and closely related to companies' spend on advertising. The tabloid market is less dependent on advertising than the quality sector, drawing more of their income from sales revenue. The proportion of revenue attributable to advertising is around 30 per cent for the redtop end of the market and nearer 70 per cent for the quality sector (Seymour Ure, 1991, cited in Franklin, 1997: 92). One reason for this is of course the quantities of copies sold (the *Sun* sells nearly ten times as many copies per day as the *Guardian*); the other is that the quality press provides the target audience the advertisers want to reach, the affluent consumer. It is why the readership demographic data provided by the National Readership Survey (see Chapter 2) are so important to advertisers. It tells the proportion and number of readers from the AB upper social demographic occupational classifications as well as the age and sex of the readers of each newspaper. The redtop tabloids draw advertising mainly from supermarkets, retailers of white goods and mobile telephone companies, while the quality press can draw on more expensive consumer goods like cars, expensive holidays and financial services. Classified advertising is different, and important to the regional press which historically has drawn much of its revenue from the property, jobs and motors sectors which are by their nature localised. Some of the current difficulties of the regional and local press stem from the migration of classified advertising from print to online. National newspapers have less dependence on classified advertising, although employment, particularly at the senior managerial level, is important to the *Sunday Times* and the *Guardian* has developed a lucrative business in public-sector, education and media jobs advertising.

Concerns are expressed in some quarters about the influence advertising might have over editorial. According to McNair (2003b: 58):

> Further commercial pressure is exerted, according to some variants of the economic approach, by the constraints placed on journalistic content because of the need to attract and retain advertising revenue. There is evidence that such pressures exist. Companies do on occasion withdraw, or threaten to withdraw, advertisements from publications of which they disapprove.

Table 5.4 *Monthly advertising spend in the national press (all figures £000s)*

Category	Sept. 08	Dec. 07	Dec. 06	Dec. 05	Dec. 04
Popular dailies display	32,800	51,300	49,400	50,200	47,100
Popular dailies classified (exc. online recruitment)	9,300	5,800	7,100	7,000	6,400
Quality dailies display	35,600	34,000	28,800	26,100	23,800
Quality dailies classified (exc. online recruitment)	13,500	9,800	7,500	8,300	9,800
Popular Sundays display	9,100	9,700	9,500	7,700	10,500
Popular Sundays classified (exc. online recruitment)	2,200	1,500	1,500	1,400	1,700
Quality Sundays display	10,400	6,800	5,300	4,600	6,000
Quality Sundays classified (exc. online recruitment)	4,400	1,800	2,000	2,100	3,100
Popular supplements	11,400	11,000	11,700	9,700	10,200
Quality supplements	11,600	10,300	9,600	8,500	10,300
Online recruitment	2,600	900	700	600	500
Total (£000)	142,900	142,900	133,200	126,300	129,400

Popular dailies: *Sun, Mirror, Star, Mail, Express, Evening Standard*
Quality dailies: *Telegraph, Times, Guardian, Independent, Financial Times*
Popular Sundays: *News of the World, Mirror, People, Mail, Express, Star*
Quality Sundays: *Times, Telegraph, Observer, Independent*
Popular supplements: *ES, Express on Saturday, M Celebs, Star Magazine, The Look, We Love Telly, Weekend (Mail), Sunday Express Magazine, Hot Celebs, Night and Day, S2 Magazine, Star Magazine, Sunday, Sunday People Magazine, You*
Quality supplements: *Independent Magazine, Telegraph Magazine, The Times Magazine, Weekend (Guardian), Culture, Observer Magazine, Style, Sunday Review, Sunday Times Magazine, Telegraph Sunday Magazine*

Source: Newspaper Marketing Agency

This is most likely to happen in the consumer service editorial content, such as travel advertising in travel sections. But in the main national newspapers and their editors are resistant to interference from the advertising department, arguing that the credibility of editorial and the increasingly important trust of readers would be severely damaged if advertisers were seen to exert influence over a newspaper's journalism. In the regional press the dangers are greater, with 'advertorial' features – editorial copy written by journalists and paid for by advertisers – commonplace. Although usually labelled as an 'advertising feature' the presentation is often barely distinguishable from other editorial content.

Table 5.4 gives the advertising income of the national press, which collectively benefited from a spend of £1.9 billion in 2007. It shows the income of the popular press (including what is referred to throughout this book as the mid-market) and the quality press separately, also distinguishing between daily and Sunday sectors. The separate figures for the newspaper supplements and magazines which have proliferated over the last twenty years show how important these have been to advertising revenue.

As the UK economy moved into recession in 2008 advertising revenues dipped seriously, always one of the first effects of an economic downturn as companies find this a relatively easy cut to make. The combination of falling sales and falling revenues, compounded by the (albeit slow) movement of advertising to the internet, where growth is under way but revenues are far from competitive with those achieved from the print medium, put most publishers under pressure. Few of the newspaper publishers now developing their online news sites are achieving more than 5 per cent of total advertising revenues from the web.

Political economy of the regional press

The story of the regional press over the last twenty years has been one of concentration and change of ownership and the highly profitable management of decline. Technological change has brought dramatic falls in production costs. New owners, usually large conglomerates, have exploited economies of scale and engaged in successive rounds of cost cutting that have driven up share prices and reduced editorial staffs. A range of strategies and experiments has been adopted, from free newspapers, to local editionalising within local or regional circulation areas, to converting traditional evening newspapers into mornings and even daily titles into weeklies. After a decade of (profitable) complacency over the threat of online publishing, the regional press is now developing that area, recognising that their main source of advertising revenue – classified advertising of property, jobs and cars – is migrating faster than expected to the web, which is a more appropriate and user-friendly medium for it.

In the United States, where almost all newspaper journalism is regional – the size of the country prohibiting, for both distribution and cultural reasons, the existence of a dominant national press such as that found in the UK – the term 'corporate newspapering' is in widespread use. Gene Roberts, former managing editor of the *New York Times* and executive editor of the *Philadelphia Inquirer*, reflecting on the change affecting newspapers all over the USA, writes:

> In early 2000 a tremor out of Southern California was too big to be ignored. This was the takeover of the mighty Times Mirror Co – publishers of the *L.A. Times, Newsday*, the *Baltimore Sun* and other respected newspapers – by Chicago's Tribune Co. ... The Times Mirror acquisition really represented the absolute triumph of corporate newspapering. Simply put, it was the biggest, baddest deal in a world that has become a deal-maker's paradise. This is a world where conglomerates now rule unchallenged. Where independent papers, once as ubiquitous on the American landscape as water towers, are nearly

extinct. Where small hometown dailies in particular are being bought and sold like hog futures. (Roberts, 2001: 2–3)

The same process has taken place in the UK. As Franklin (1997: 108) observes: 'It is fast becoming a cliché to observe that local newspapers are local in name only, since large sections of the local press are owned and controlled by a handful of large companies. Behind the parish pump lies corporate power'. The declining sales of daily and weekly paid newspapers, Franklin says, have led to the virtual elimination of competition and the creation of monopolies in many local press markets (ibid.: 105).

It has been a gradual change, and the modern history of the regional press in Britain is littered with acquisitions and consolidation. A more recent feature has been the interest of venture capital or private equity in regional newspapers, sometimes through supporting management buy-outs. Since the purpose of these interventions is to acquire, to increase value by cutting costs, and then to sell on, taking a large profit, this has had a significant impact on the political economy of the regional press.

Corporate newspapering: from United to Johnston

This trend can be illustrated by looking in detail at what has happened to the ownership of one group: United Newspapers, a regional newspaper company formed in 1918, and including in its stable such famous morning titles as the *Yorkshire Post* (founded in 1754) and the *Sheffield Telegraph* and evening newspapers in Leeds, Sheffield, Preston, Blackpool, Northampton, Wigan and Doncaster. The group's historian Guy Schofield (1975: 112) recorded that 'every weekday 700,000 copies of evening newspapers owned by United are bought by the people of some 50 busy cities and towns, and clusters of villages'. But this was after the first round of consolidation, taking place in the 1960s and early 1970s. As Schofield recounts:

In the past two decades the position of the provincial evening paper has been greatly strengthened, thanks to the far-sighted resolution of managers in general. There used to be two, and sometimes three, evenings competing with each other in the larger towns and cities. This was a healthy state of affairs until rocketing costs, the advent of television and other factors turned it into a precarious one. This danger has been averted by a process of rationalisation. Agreements for mergers were carried through. In some cases the weaker paper was closed down. Today there is no provincial city or town in England where more than one evening newspaper is published. Frankly this is a form of local monopoly, but unless the industry had taken such steps some towns would have found themselves without an evening paper at all, with a loss to communal life, and shrinkage of media for information, comment and advertising that would have been nationally serious. (Schofield, 1975: 112)

Schofield saw the danger of monopoly in somewhat narrow terms, an important duty for editors to keep staffs 'on their toes to ensure the maintenance of that efficiency which competition formerly stimulated' (ibid.: 113).

United went from strength to strength, one of the leading players in the regional market, so profitable that in 1985, after a Monopolies Commission inquiry, it acquired the *Express* national newspapers. The regionals formed a separate part of United, called United Provincial Newspapers, or UPN. As it transpired the merger with a national newspaper group, particularly one going through such bad times as the *Express*, did not turn out well for United. Television magnate (Lord) Clive Hollick merged with (namely, effectively took over) United in 1996. He had some interest in the national titles but none in the regionals (apart from their profits, which were falling anyway); his real interest was television. In 1998 UPN was put up for sale in two parts: the smaller, United Southern Publications, going to Southcom, later Newscom, for £47.5 million; the much larger, UPN Yorkshire and Lancashire, to Candover, a venture capital company, for £360 million.

The key player in the latter process was Chris Oakley, a journalist with an unusual entrepreneurial flair, who had edited the *Lancashire Evening Post, Liverpool Echo* and *Birmingham Evening Mail*. After a successful editorship of the latter, for the American owner Ralph Ingersoll, Oakley, with five Birmingham colleagues, planned a management buy-out. Oakley's group, which became Midland Independent Newspapers, bought the company for £125 million in 1991. They sold to Mirror Group in 1997 for £297 million, a profit of £172m (or 138 per cent) in six years.

Oakley, now a multi-millionaire, joined the Mirror Group board but was soon frustrated and became the dominant figure in the UPN bid, suddenly in a position to buy the group owning three papers he had worked for: the *Yorkshire Post,* the *Yorkshire Evening Post* and the *Lancashire Evening Post.* The successful takeover resulted in Regional Independent Media (RIM), with Oakley as chief executive and Norman Fowler, a former member of Margaret Thatcher's cabinet, as chairman. Venture capitalists are never in it for the long term; that is not the nature of their activity. So RIM was sold to Johnston Press in 2002 for £560 million, a profit of £200 million in four years, or 56 per cent. Chris Oakley now works for Candover, seeking potential acquisitions.

The UPN case is a classic British example of corporate newspapering in action, more about leverage than journalism, with cost cutting to increase value and with huge profits being made, and taken out of companies, rather than re-invested. True, the current owner of the newspapers happens to be primarily a newspaper company, but along the way vast profits have been taken out of the newspapers by the financial community.

And while Johnston Press is indeed a newspaper company, it is also no stranger to the extraction of a high rate of profit from its titles. Johnston is a public company listed on the stock market like many other media companies whose share price is influenced by the bottom line, which is in turn influenced by revenues from circulation and advertising and efficiencies within the newspapers it controls. It was originally a family business in Scotland with a growing number of weekly titles, and it has now broken into the big time through a continuing process of acquisition. Before buying the UPN titles it acquired the East Midlands Allied Press (EMAP)'s 65 titles in 1996. It also bought Portsmouth and Sunderland Newspapers in 1999 as well as titles in Ireland, and it now owns the *Scotsman, Scotland on Sunday* and the *Edinburgh Evening News*. In 1998 it owned 142 titles and circulated 4.5 million copies a week; in July 2008 it owned 294 with a total circulation of 9.1 million copies a week (Newspaper Society figures). It is increasingly concerned with developing the websites of its newspapers. And it is probably best known for setting the trend, and expectation, for remarkable figures for profit on turnover. This has moved steadily upwards and was well over 30 per cent when the 2008 recession began. Other publishers seek and achieve the same order of return, figures undreamt of before the era of corporate newspapering. All this throughout a period of continuous circulation decline.

The era of takeovers

The succession of takeovers that dominated the last five years of the twentieth century started with Thomson Regional Newspapers (TRN) deciding, to get out of regional publishing in Britain. The major group owned by Lord (Roy) Thomson, who had also owned *The Times* and *Sunday Times*, was split up between Northcliffe (who paid £82 million for the Aberdeen titles) and the Barclay Brothers (£90 million for the Edinburgh titles) in Scotland, and Trinity, who paid £327.5 million for the remaining titles in England, Wales and Northern Ireland. Trinity thus became the largest regional publisher, with famous titles in Cardiff and Newcastle. Johnston Press acquired the EMAP titles for £211 million in 1996. Westminster Press decided, like TRN, to move out of regional newspapers and was sold to Newsquest later in 1996 for £305 million. In 1999 came the biggest deal of all, when Newsquest was bought for £904 million by the giant American publisher Gannett, and is now the third biggest regional publisher. (All takeover data from the Newspaper Society.) The shake-up was complete. Trinity had become the biggest, Johnston the boldest, and Gannett the invader from across the Atlantic. All had considered it worthwhile to spend millions in the industry they were told was in irreversible decline. Associated/Northcliffe represented the old guard, and they had greatly improved their position through the success of the free *Metro*.

There was to be one more massively significant merger/takeover. Two months after Gannett's arrival, Trinity, the largest regional publisher, invested £1,300 million in taking control of the Mirror Group. Just as United had

Table 5.5   *Top five regional publishers, July 2008*

Rank	Group	Titles	Weekly circulation (million)
1	Trinity Mirror	182	12.3
2	Johnston Press	294	9.1
3	Newsquest Media	210	9.0
4	Northcliffe Media	131	7.8
5	Associated Newspapers	3	7.2
	Total of top five publishers	820	45.4
	Total of top 20 publishers	1,147	61.1
	Total of all publishers (85)	1,290	62.8

Source: Newspaper Society

taken on a series of problems by buying the *Express*, so Trinity's relatively smooth success in the regions was not repeated in the national market. Only Northcliffe/Associated, it seems, can cope with both ends of the market with ease, but then they have a long history of doing just that. Even Northcliffe indicated that it was prepared to sell some or all of its titles for the right bid, but disagreed with the value being put on the company and abandoned the idea of selling.

Falling sales

The figures in Table 5.5 cover daily, weekly and Sunday paid-for and free titles, aggregating the total number of copies sold or distributed by a publisher in the course of a week. The figures for Associated Newspapers, in fifth place, are solely for the free *Metro* distributed in London (although it owns *Metro* titles in other big cities their numbers are included in the distribution figures of the other regional publishers responsible for that distribution and the collection of advertising revenues), the paid-for London *Evening Standard* acquired in January 2009, reportedly for £1 by the Russian oligarch Alexander Lebedev, and the free afternoon *London Lite*. Northcliffe Media, in fourth place, is wholly owned by Associated Newspapers, which is also the publisher of the *Daily Mail* and *Mail on Sunday*.

The regional newspaper paradox is that falling sales over a long period did not lead – at least until the recession following the credit crunch of 2008 – to falling profits nor a lack of interest by investors in entering the market or building their stake through acquisition. As has been demonstrated, there is still a lot of money to be made, particularly if costs are constantly pared down. But advertising revenues are closely linked to the economic cycle, and the downward trend of sales continues year on year. The audited ABC figures for the second half of 2007 tell the same story about all sectors of the market. Evening sales, down 5.2 per cent year on year; mornings, down 3.6 per cent; weeklies, down 1.6 per cent; Sundays, down 6.5 per cent. These figures cannot be regarded as other than poor, and the fact that they are repeated year after year provides little hope for optimism. Franklin (2008a: 9) notes that 'the city-based daily evening, but especially morning, titles have suffered dramatic losses, with papers like the *Birmingham Mail* losing 54% of readership across the decade 1995–2005'. There have been similar dramatic falls over the period by the Sheffield *Star* (down 38 per cent), *Birmingham Post* (down 49 per cent) and the *Yorkshire Post* (down 27 per cent). Temple (2008: 98) notes that 'the data clearly indicate that fewer people are reading local papers'. Cover price rises have been regular, so that 60p for a local weekly is common, and sits uncomfortably beside a much fatter national daily like the *Daily Mail* at 50p.

Free newspapers

On the face of it the answer to circulation decline and falling revenues would seem unlikely to be giving the paper away. Yet that has been the route taken by a number of regional publishers over the past few years. The national press has yet to take the same route, preferring to keep to price cutting, price wars and disguised frees. These are called bulks and are used to increase audited circulation figures, and thus advertising revenues, by doing deals with the airlines, train operators and hotels who provide newspapers free to their customers, having paid the publishers a nominal sum for these bulks. These count towards the headline circulation figures, although they appear in the detail as 'bulk' sales.

In the regions, however, frees really are free. That goes for London too, but as a distinct region, not as the centre of national publishing. The paper that is pressed into your hand or appears unsolicited through the letterbox at home really is free. This form of newspaper publishing has grown in recent years to become a significant component of mainstream publishing. First there were the scruffy, poorly designed local frees that consisted almost entirely of advertising with just a spot of editorial. They were more junk mail than newspapers and were ignored by the traditional local weeklies which remained popular and profitable. As Franklin (1997: 103) put it, they 'rely on non journalistic sources of news and derive their income wholly from advertising revenues'. The frees were not so much editorial competitors with the paid for titles – they had so little of the local community news that attracts readers – as an addition to the market. However, their success drew the traditional publishers into this form of free-newspaper publishing, and the number of such titles, mostly weeklies, grew from 185 in 1975, to 822 in 1987, and 1156 in 1990 (Franklin 1997: 104). But this represented a peak and by 2004 the figure was down to 650 and in 2008 there were 623 free weeklies (Newspaper Society figures, November 2008). A change in the nature of the free regional newspaper was coming about.

It was the advent of free 'real' newspapers that had such an impact on the market and the biggest initial influence was Swedish. Metro International had been born in Sweden and had invented the free morning newspaper distributed by hand or through public transport and strategically placed bins. In twelve years they developed the concept across the world, and now 70 editions are published in 23 countries with 8.7 million copies distributed every week. *Metro* claims 42 million readers a week, 40 per cent aged 18–35, 74 per cent under 49 (www.metro.lu).

Just as the Swedes were about to invade Britain, Associated Newspapers, publishers of the *Daily Mail*, entered the market with its own (and unrelated) *Metro*, and have also enjoyed great success. From a standing start in London in 1999, it now distributes around 1.4 million copies (ABC figures, January 2008) in 16 cities in Britain, and makes a profit of around £10 million a year. It describes itself as Britain's fourth largest morning paper, and by aggregating the various editions around the country that appears to be true. It is popular with young and AB readers, and thus appeals to advertisers. This is crucial since advertisers are its only source of revenue. Steve Auckland, *Metro*'s managing director, says that the difference between a modern free newspaper like *Metro* and the old uninvited free is that they require a decision on the part of the reader to take the copy from the person handing them out, or from the station or tram bin. They are 'actively acquired'. Measurement of distribution is as rigorous as that of sales, in that 'unacquired' copies are counted and subtracted from the numbers put out, and the figures are independently audited. Auckland believes that mornings are the best time for free newspaper distribution, providing the 'first media hit of the day'. And he stresses the number of 18–34, ABC1 readers of *Metro*. 'Right place, right time, right audience' is the mantra for the frees (Auckland, interview with Cole, September 2006.)

The traditional regional press, suffering like the nationals from declining sales, moved into the free market, usually supplementing the paid for titles. Of the 1,278 regional mornings, evenings, Sundays and weekly titles published in the UK at the end of 2008, just over half were distributed free. These 649 free newspapers were mostly weekly titles (623) but also included 13 morning newspapers, eight evenings and five Sundays (Newspaper Society database, November 2008). Nobody would claim they are as profitable as the paid for titles, but costs are low for publishers already selling newspapers so they can improve the bottom line. The top two free titles outside London, excluding *Metro*, are both in Nottingham. The *Topper* distributes 209,000 copies and the *Recorder* 152,000. With *Metro* distributing 44,000 in the East Midlands (where Nottingham is one of its main areas of activity) the city has become a centre of free reading.

After the success of *Metro* in London the battle of the evening frees was joined in the capital. Rupert Murdoch's News International, with no regional or London titles, let it be known that it was planning an evening free. Associated Newspapers, then publisher not only of *Metro* but also of the *Evening Standard* (the one surviving, but declining, paid for evening) refused to let its great rival enter its territory unchallenged. So in the autumn of 2006 the streets of London were awash with rival groups of tee-shirted distributors pressing a *London Lite* (Associated free) or *thelondonpaper* (Murdoch free) into the hands of city workers. In 1970 London sustained two paid-for evening papers selling around 2 million copies. In 2006 it was down to one, selling around 280,000. By the end of 2008 Londoners were if not buying at least taking possession of an additional 900,000 and more free evenings, 747,000 *Metros* and just under 100,000 copies of a business free, *City AM* (ABC, November 2008). It hardly suggested newspapers were going out of style, although paying for them may be. Associated's (and Murdoch's) success with free newspapers in the capital did extensive damage to the *Evening Standard* which suffered great losses in sale and revenues, becoming an ever greater drain on its owners. With expressed reluctance they decided to sell, and keep *London Lite*. An unlikely and unexpected buyer emerged in January 2009 in the form of a Russian millionaire called Alexander Lebedev.

The Manchester model

The *Manchester Evening News* has been a special case. Like most big city evening newspapers it had been suffering from a circulation decline for many years, for all the reasons listed earlier – changing patterns of work, transport, demographics and life-style. Once selling more than 400,000 copies in Greater Manchester and surrounding towns, by 2003 it was selling 153,000 and in 2006 the figure was around 130,000. In that year the paper's editor, Paul Horrocks, and new chief executive, Mark Dodson, came up with a different strategy. They had examined the success of free newspapers around the country, the morning *Metro* in Manchester itself and their own free weekly, the *Manchester Weekly Metro*, which they believed had to some extent competed with the *MEN* at the end of the week. They had spent a period selling the Friday edition of the *MEN* at a lower price than other publishing days, and it had boosted sales on that day. They had looked at the performance of the *MEN* in the centre of Manchester and found the circulation decline there had been much more rapid than elsewhere in the circulation area, to the extent that one of the most respected evening newspapers (owned, like the *Guardian*, by the Scott Trust) in England's traditional second newspaper city was selling only 7,000 or so copies in the heart of the city.

So they decided to give it away in this central area. They briefed the advertisers, recruited teams of distributors, and printed a lot more copies. Initially 50,000 were distributed, then 80,000, and then 100,000, in the city centre and at the airport. What was different about the *MEN*'s strategy from that pursued by other publishers was that this was not a new free newspaper; it was the same *MEN* that was being paid for in other parts of the city and surrounding areas. Today it allows the *MEN* to record a circulation of 162,000, although only 77,000 are paid for (down another 50,000 since 2006), with the remainder free (ABC audited figures February 2008 and June 2008). Clearly revenue from sales has suffered greatly. The strategy is to maintain or raise advertising revenue through increasing the number of copies read, and particularly to boost readership in the centre of the city where readers in the professional and managerial demographic groups and those who will take advantage of the shopping and leisure activities offered are more likely to be found. The Manchester model is also part of a broader strategy by MEN Media to integrate their print and digital offerings, which will be discussed further in Chapter 10.

In this chapter we have sketched out the changing political economy of the UK press as an industry. Whether such ownership structures have had, or continue to have, an ideological effect on newspaper output is something that will be explored when we turn to discuss competing theories about journalism, in Chapter 9. But first, in the next chapter, we will examine how the work of newspaper journalists themselves has changed, along with looking at the changes in newspaper content and the debates surrounding such changes.

6

FROM TELLING STORIES TO PROVIDING CONTENT: JOURNALISM IN THE DIGITAL AGE

Three words dominate the current discourse on newspaper practice, used by the editors and managements who control the press. They were not in common usage twenty, or even ten, years ago. They are brand, trust and content. They are a product of media convergence, and they are, or are used as, approximate but not precise synonyms for the traditional words newspaper, accuracy and stories. They are also usually prefaced by the expression 'the importance of …' and they represent an invasion of the editorial space by marketing departments and the ready adoption of this 'speak' by editors explaining their visions and plans for their 'products', another word that has drifted down from the management and onto the editorial floor. One could add 'bottom line' and 'profit' to this list, but neither is as new – newspapers have always been businesses and profits have always been linked directly to survival – and anyway 'margin' is the preferred word these days.

'Brand' is directly linked to new media and to media convergence. There is nothing axiomatic about success in print leading to success online, but the editors of the *Guardian, Telegraph, Sun* and *Mail* will frequently describe their success online as a reflection of the strength of their brands. By this they mean that the number of unique users they gain for their websites is a result of the reputation and profile of the print products, the newspapers, out of which their websites have developed. 'The quality of these sites should ensure a healthy future for these brand names whatever the future of their printed editions' (Temple, 2008: 211). They will claim that they are 'exploiting' a brand and 'reinforcing' it, and that therefore the online offering must be true to the print product. They will go on to associate the second of the three words with the first and talk about a 'trusted brand'. When the website is freely (literally) and globally available, then the choice of users as to which online news source to make their preferred option will, it is argued, depend on their familiarity with the authorship, or brand, and respect for its reliability, agenda, range and accuracy, or trust in it. *Guardian* editor Alan Rusbridger (1999a: 38), in a lecture on trust in newspapers, said that if he were a press baron he would care very much about whether or not his newspapers were trusted. 'I think that the whole issue of trust will become more, not less, important and also that it will have commercial implications for everyone working in the media'. He also said (1999a: 44) that he thought the internet was a revolution in communications to rival Caxton and Baird. But ultimately all that mattered was 'the simple question: is it true? Can I trust this source? If you can be trusted you will win in the end'.

Content, which used, in purely newspaper application, to be plural, takes on a new and refined meaning when used by media companies as opposed to newspaper publishers. 'We are now content providers', they proclaim, which of course they always were, only they were providing this content to consumers through one medium – print. The realisation that they were (expensively) gathering a huge amount of information, and publishing only a small fraction of it, coupled with the availability of a new technology (at a relatively small oncost) which allowed them to publish much more of it online, and possibly broadcast it as well, on or offline, encouraged them to think as they had not thought before, to separate intellectually the gathering and publishing of this content. The only problem was and is – and this adds another 'new' word to the original list of three – how to 'monetise' (make money from) the new publishing platform.

All of this is relevant to a consideration of contemporary practices and debates in newspaper journalism. But so are a number of other changes: societal and audience interests, news emphasis and agenda, the organisation of news gathering for new, converged media and the concerns in some quarters about journalism standards in the reporting of politics, the influence of public relations and news agencies and the popularisation of serious journalism. There are also much discussed issues concerning the range of newspaper content, irrespective of where else it is published. Have standards been maintained, if they were high in the first place? Have newspapers 'dumbed down'? Opinions diverge greatly. We discuss the multi-media future, and its consequences for newspapers, in detail in Chapter 10. The emphasis here is on newspapers in particular, rather than on the web sites they have spawned; however, some contemporary practices such as the organisation of the newsroom have already been affected, and will therefore be dealt with in this chapter.

Contemporary practices: new newsrooms for new media

The shift of emphasis by print publishers from the traditional newspaper product to content for publication on a variety of platforms has brought about a substantial rethink on the organisation and structure of the news gathering process. Changes still evolving are more radical than the last newspaper revolution, the post-1986, post-Wapping restructuring brought about by the new computer technologies that saw the end of hot metal and traditional printing. That changed the way words and pictures were translated onto the printed page. Today's revolution is about translating information from gatherers onto a variety of publication platforms. This has meant change not only in the end products but also in the means of gathering and delivering content to these. It has also meant upheaval in newsrooms, in the roles of many journalists and in the organisational methods employed to deliver converged journalism. It has required changes to the physical environment in which such changes are being put into practice. And all this has developed in a climate of gathering economic gloom, too much pessimism about the future of newspapers, and cuts in editorial staffs at precisely the time when journalists are required to do so much more.

Traditional newspaper publication has been dominated by deadlines, crucial times that had to be met in order for the newspaper to come out. Reporters had to deliver copy in time for sub-editors to prepare it for publication. Pictures had to be ready for pages to be designed. Pre-Wapping, stories had to be re-typed by printers and turned into slugs of metal, which had to be arranged and fitted into frames, with headlines, pictures and advertisements. These would be turned into papier mache 'flongs' from which metal plates would be made and attached to printing presses. Post-Wapping, first columns of type on thick paper were pasted on to page templates – this was called 'paste-up' – together with headlines and pictures also on paper, and then later full pages were made up on computer screens before they were sent to the printing presses. These presses had to be running at specified times to produce the required number of copies in time for their distribution around the country, first by rail and later by road. A break in this chain of events meant lost copies or late delivery to points of sale. The controlling influence of newspaper journalism was the clock, and for the daily press the cycle lasted all of 24 hours before it had to be repeated. All deadlines were directed at the single goal of having the newspaper on sale at a pre-ordained time, first thing in the morning or, in the case of the evening newspapers, at specified times throughout the day.

In the new media world such deadlines do still exist for the publication of a newspaper. But now that publishers are producing much more than newspapers, drawing on the same pool of information gathered by journalists, such deadlines no longer exist for much of a publisher's output. Hall (2008: 216) points out that online publishing by newspapers demanded a complete rethink of the values and processes through which newspaper journalists understood their work, as a result of which 'the publication or news cycle became redundant'. Web publication is 'rapidly changing the basic forms of news writing in terms of how it is read, how it looks, and how it works' (ibid.: 219). Stories have become shorter and must meet the demands of search engines. Greenslade (2008b) sees story length differently, finding much more fulfilment for journalists in writing stories and discovering there is no longer any need to cut something to ribbons to fit a space. Now it can be accommodated (on the website) without any loss of detail, through links from a story to further information or background or related stories.

The time-consuming processes of manufacture (printing) and distribution (lorry journeys) are not required by electronic media such as the website which can transmit information instantaneously. All that is required is that the information be deemed 'ready' for publication – and that it can be updated frequently – and that a decision can be taken as to where, how and when it is published. This has major implications for former 'newspaper only' journalists, for the organisation of their work patterns, and for the structure of editorial management and decision-taking within newsrooms. Initially, as a result of a newspaper culture which put maximum emphasis on being 'first' with the news, there was great reluctance to put stories on the website before the newspaper version was on sale. This was soon overcome, with the realisation that audiences were to a certain extent different and that for some readers a story on the website represented a 'trail' for the newspaper version. In any event, a popular story on the website could be good for the brand even if nobody had paid to read it.

Traditional newspaper organisation has changed little over the decades, with variations between newspapers much less significant than the commonalities. The structure has been based on 'desks' or departments, effectively nation states within the federation that comprises the newspaper as a whole. Home and foreign news desks, business, sport, features, leaders and comment, all with a distinct geographical or territorial space within an office, all with their own editors, will commission and receive material from reporters, columnists and leader writers, who are answerable to their department editor and will identify with their section of the newspaper. Only the most senior editorial executives, the editor and his or her senior colleagues, will take the more holistic view of the newspaper, and regular conferences are the mechanism by which the whole newspaper is brought together. Departmental editors have tended to know very little about what is going on elsewhere on a paper and have also tended to fight for their own contributions at conferences, with the editor or his or her representative arbitrating on the prominence given to stories in the newspaper as a whole. In a traditional newspaper structure with the set deadlines outlined above there will be a clear routine with the main decisions taken at the same time every day. This does not fit with multi-media publishing.

Thus the newspaper publishers now acting as media companies, and often calling themselves that, are working out new organisational structures. It helps to have the opportunity for a redesign of editorial space, and it helps even more to have new offices in which a fresh start can be made. That, however, is the relatively easy part. Changing the culture, changing the roles of individuals, shaking up working practices established and developed over many years are all much harder. To take two examples, Will Lewis, editor-in-chief of Telegraph Media (daily newspaper, Sunday newspaper, website incorporating Telegraph TV and numerous subsites) and Alan Rusbridger, editor-in-chief of Guardian Media (daily newspaper, Sunday newspaper (*Observer*), website dominant for more than a decade among those based in newspapers) are both taking advantage of new offices to restructure their operations to fit the demands of new media. Lewis had a head start, moving the *Telegraph* operation into new offices as he became editor in late 2006. Rusbridger, the driving force behind the *Guardian* website throughout his editorship which started in 1995, shifted his operation to new offices at the end of 2008. For both, cultural change represented the biggest challenge.

Lewis was in charge of the development of the new *Telegraph* offices before he became editor, and was thus able to impose his vision for the group, or at least its physical manifestation, on a clean sheet of paper. But he had to do it while the *Telegraph* was in upheaval, with new owners and an unsettled staff with very traditional views. There were redundancies, and more departures as Lewis's radical ideas for the development of a multimedia publishing group began to be implemented. The process was not without pain, and the new management came in for much criticism of the way they had handled the redefinition of roles within editorial. Many journalists who had been with the *Telegraph* for a long time left or were made redundant. There were accusations that Lewis was taking the heart out of the paper and eroding its traditional standards. His response was to draw attention to the problems that had brought about the sale of the paper.

The new *Telegraph* newsroom is designed to integrate a variety of publishing functions. It is configured as a hub for executives representing both print and online, with its associated video and audio content, to share decisions about what is published when and where, with spokes radiating from the hub where the providers of this content, the reporters, work. Thus distinctions between what is aimed at the papers and what goes online are broken down, specialists are used to discuss and analyse issues for *Telegraph* web TV, and the nature, scope and scale of the story for the different platforms are planned. Lewis claims it is already working well. He sees a 'virtuous circle' between print and web (Greenslade, 2008b).

The *Guardian* culture, although very different from that of the *Telegraph*, is also a deeply embedded one. Staff turnover is very low and it is a newspaper on which most of the journalists have a sense of its history and values while interpreting them in a variety of ways. Despite the success of Guardian Unlimited, the website, over a number of years, it was far from integrated with the newspaper, was physically separate and was largely ignored by the more traditional of the newspaper staff. The move to new offices was the one-off opportunity to change all that, and Rusbridger seized it.

'Within 10 years a generation of people who thought they would be working in a print medium suddenly have to think about how you do stuff on screen', he told *Press Gazette* (23 May 2008). That meant a radical restructuring with single news, business and sports teams of reporters serving the *Guardian*, the *Observer* and the website, all run by what Rusbridger describes as 'platform neutral' heads of national news, international news, business and sport. The traditional news editors become, effectively, news editors for two newspapers and the website, with the deputy editor in overall charge of news, business and sport. There are also groupings, or 'pods', of specialist writers concentrating on a particular area and having direct access to the website. Inevitably there are complaints about a lack of identity with one particular publishing outlet, and fears for the separate identity of the *Observer*. There are concerns also for the futures of executives who had specific responsibility for coverage on one paper or the website being replaced by one person with responsibility for it all. Rusbridger admits it is a radically different structure, beyond anything he has faced in his long term as editor. But he says it will 'release creativity. The jargon is now, I'm told, we're a "matrix" organisation' (*Press Gazette*, 2008).

Although such structural matters are internal to the media organisation and not of concern to audiences for the various publishing platforms, the present unknown is the effect on the content. Will it become more uniform as writers work for all platforms rather than one, perhaps not knowing the destination of their words when they write them? Will the difference in character of a daily and a Sunday newspaper be eroded by having the same writers working for both? Will the integration of those who have worked for the website exclusively influence the print content?

There are implications as well for reporters in terms of the time spent researching stories when publication is possible at any time and any frequency compared with once a day or once a week. Comparisons with rolling news and 'breaking news' on television and radio suggest the risk of immediacy taking precedence over depth or authority, with so much broadcast reporter time taken up on air that little is left over for the business of finding out. The experience of the regional press has been that expanding the amount of content required from reporters in order to service the website has happened at the same time as reductions in editorial staff. Increasing the volume of content must make greater demands on reporters and would not seem to be consistent with cost cutting unless journalists have considerable spare capacity (see the section on 'churnalism' below).

The newspaper agenda

If one role of a newspaper is to reflect society then the newspaper agenda will change as society changes, to reflect current interests, preoccupations and concerns. Politicians are often accused of being cut off from the electorate; newspapers cannot afford to be cut off from their readers because the consequence is losing them. In the 1960s the national press was slow to react to, and report, the cultural revolution that was taking place, to recognise youth culture and protest. The serious press ignored what it did not take to be serious – in cultural as well political terms – and did not realise that its younger 'upmarket' traditional readers had interests and concerns that the newspapers were not recognising. There was high culture and there was low culture, in their eyes, and they failed to acknowledge popular culture. TV was downmarket and opera was upmarket. Football was for the masses, who read other newspapers; cricket was for the readers of serious newspapers. The change in the agenda of newspapers has partly, and only partly, been about reflecting society as it is rather than as it was. The *Telegraph*, until recently, was one example of a newspaper that had clung to the old order.

Alan Rusbridger (1999b) described the changing broadsheet agenda this way:

> You can't put your head in the sand and talk just to graduates from the older universities. And you can't just shove in columns of text these days and expect people to read it. There are too many other media competing for people's attention. This is not C.P. Snow land, where there's high culture and there's low culture and you're interested in one or the other. Most of our readers have the capacity to think more broadly than that. They want to know about the single currency and they would feel cheated if the *Guardian* didn't give them that. But they also want to know about Liam Gallagher and Patsy Kensit. It's very dangerous to get into the mindset that there are broadsheet subjects and tabloid subjects. What there has to be is a unity of tone, and that's how you define broadsheet values.

The serious press has changed greatly since the mid-twentieth century era, viewed nostalgically by many of those who talk of 'dumbing down'. There is less word-by-word coverage of parliamentary debate but as much politics (see below); there is more sport and popular culture; there is more health, fitness and lifestyle; there is more comment and opinion; there are more celebrities; there is less about unknown aristocracy, and less deferential royal coverage (but still a lot); arguably, there is as much international coverage; and as much crime.

The press is more democratic in the sense that, whether they like it or not (and some don't), readers of serious papers are less likely than they were to be left ignorant of the talking points of the public at large. They know of the existence of TV talent shows drawing huge audiences, of reality TV shows like *Big Brother*, of Posh and Becks and the relationships of the heir to the throne. Sometimes it will be presented with lofty detachment and references to 'the tabloids', but it will be there nonetheless. To that extent there has been an homogenising of the news agenda with the serious and mid-market press having more in common than they did. The redtop tabloid end of the market is now the most distinct (and losing sales fastest), often living a vicarious editorial existence by, for example, giving over pages to 'inside' gossip about *Big Brother* contestants.

Examples of significant change in the newspaper agenda across all market sectors include the rise of the columnist and the growth in health, celebrity and sports coverage.

Columnists

The late Hugo Young (2004: xv) wrote that since he had been writing for newspapers 'the absence of columnists has been comprehensively made good – or possibly the reverse'. He had encountered an acquaintance working for the government who had been asked by Prime Minister Blair's office to compile a list of all the national newspaper columnists to whom Downing Street might want to get a political message across. He had so far counted 221. It included Sunday as well as daily newspaper columnists, political, arts, women's and sports columnists. 'But the transition from zero to 221-plus registers a change in the priorities of journalism for which there is only one good thing to be said. At least, with so many, we cancel each other out' (ibid.).

McNair (2008: 116) identifies three species of column. First there is the 'polemical column', which addresses the reader in tones ranging from the counter-intuitive and the sceptical to the indignant and even the outraged. Then there is the 'analytical/advisory column', which applies the authority of the journalist to an in-depth consideration of a topic in the news, and usually offers advice. Finally there is the 'satirical column, which with more or less cruelty mocks those in the news'. The journalist, according to McNair, citing the parliamentary sketch writers, becomes a 'court jester, poking fun at the powerful'.

The late Anthony Sampson (1996: 45) bemoaned the proliferation of columnists, particularly in the serious press, seeing it as evidence of a deterioration in standards. 'There has been an explosion of columns providing comment without facts, discussing friends, parties or other journalists. Columnists tell us what happened on the way to Sainsbury's, what their children did at school, how they enjoyed holidays. One wonders what there is left for these people to talk about at home'. Greenslade (2003a: 627–628) considered the proliferation of columnists as 'the most visible difference' between the papers of the past and those of the 1990s. 'Both broadsheets and tabloids published scores of writers every day, usually offering their opinions on the news'. He is dismissive of Sampson's views, saying they were informed by 'a misguided nostalgia about a non-existent golden age of journalism'.

Young's figure of 221 has surely grown, partly as a result of the proliferation of newspaper sections all demanding their columnists. There is, post-Wapping and the advent of greatly increased pagination, a need for more words to fill more space – it does not necessarily represent a diminution in the amount of news in a paper. Publishing columns is cheaper than gathering news, which makes them attractive to cost-cutting publishers. Only the most celebrated columnists, the celebrities of journalism, command the high fees of legend; Richard Littlejohn of the *Daily Mail* reputedly earns around £1million a year.

Such newspaper columnists, whether writing about politics or their personal lives ('me' columns), commenting on the England football team or the media, are the best known of journalists, many appearing on radio and television debate shows like *Question Time*, on Radio 5 discussions of sport or phone-ins, or simply pontificating as 'experts' on current events. Inevitably the most outspoken will command the highest fees, and in their columns are able to be more extreme or provocative than the anonymous leader writers who are constrained by speaking for a paper. So, in the area of political comment, the *Daily Mail* and *Daily Telegraph* have Melanie Phillips and Simon Heffer respectively speaking for the radical right, the *Guardian* has Polly Toynbee, Martin Kettle and Jackie Ashley reflecting left-of-centre opinions, as well as Simon Jenkins of a more 'one nation Tory' persuasion. The *Independent* publishes right-wing views from Bruce Anderson and left-wing views from Yasmin Alibhai-Brown.

Collectively they have become known as the 'commentariat', and the more famous political columnists are sought out by senior politicians for briefing. They are said to be influential. According to Julia Hobsbawm and John Lloyd (2008: 7) 'most of those within political life see political columns as of fundamental importance to the conduct of their public lives'. They describe British newspaper commentary as 'among the liveliest, most combative and sharpest in the world' and say that 'it is now seen by editors and owners of newspapers as more important than reporting'. Hobsbawm and Lloyd conducted a poll among a 'small group of interested individuals from politics, business, media, public life and academia' to determine the top ten most influential commentators. These included bloggers, the rapidly growing online equivalent of the newspaper columnist. These were the top five (ibid.: 16):

Polly Toynbee – *Guardian*
Trevor Kavanagh – *Sun*
Irwin Stelzer – *Sunday Times*
Nick Robinson – BBC (blog)
Anatole Kaletsky – *Times*

Hobsbawm and Lloyd refer, sceptically, to the columnists' tendency to self-denigration, their admission that they are 'an overwhelmingly London-based elite', and their denial of any great influence. That is not the view of senior politicians. Former Labour cabinet minister Charles Clarke told

Hobsbawm and Lloyd (2008: 11) 'of course the commentariat is powerful. Any government committed to change needs to understand that the case for change can only be sustained through strong argument. Commentators' reflect the strength of that argument. They give intellectual underpinning and create intellectual fashion'.

Health and fitness

The increase in health journalism and related lifestyle and fitness stories has been exponential over the last decade as the national obsession with our physical condition has risen as fast as our life expectancy. Exploiting anxiety and the search for everlasting life, entire pages of the national press are given to dedicated sections on the subject while health-related stories litter the news pages. It may appear that hypochondria is rife, but it certainly absorbs newspaper audiences. The health or medical correspondent is much in demand. The coverage ranges from 'miracle cures' to dietary and behavioural advice. It explores 'problems' from controlling weight to sexual performance. It draws on research published in medical journals, the claims of the pharmaceutical industry, the 'theories' of fitness gurus and the personal stories of the sufferers and those who have triumphed over physical or mental adversity.

The *Daily Mail* leads the way with a weekly Good Health supplement often 16 pages in length. It draws advertising for pills, snoring and thinning hair cures, losing weight, facial and pelvic muscle control, and hearing aids. Peter Wilby (2008c), former *Independent on Sunday* editor and now press commentator in the *Guardian*, examined one issue of the *Mail*, on a Good Health day, and found news stories about cocoa being good for your heart, a diet pill to make you feel full as soon as you start eating, gum disease increasing the risk of cancer, and that a third of babies whose parents smoke at home will end up in hospital. In Good Health Wilby also found underpants to control blood pressure, tree bark to ease arthritis, a herb that could relieve ear infection and peanut butter to stops hiccups.

The medical profession is deeply suspicious of health journalism, worried about the creation of false hopes for the seriously ill, the raising of expectations for new drugs or treatments and the exaggeration of reported 'breakthroughs'. It is the most visible area showing the imperfections in the reporting of science, in which scientists as well as journalists have played their part. The need for funding may play a part in the hyping of medical research papers, the need for a story the exaggerations of journalists. Crucial here are the different time scales to which medical researchers and journalists work. Searching for a cure may take many years and research papers are often no more than interim reports. Journalists might use the word 'may' but it will often be swamped by the phrase 'miracle cure'. Medical scientists do not use the word 'miracle'.

Celebrity

Celebrity – some call it celebrity culture – is now, for better or worse, part of the national agenda and this is reflected in the coverage given in the press, not only the popular press. Cole (2005: 33) describes 'the rise and rise of celebrity journalism, where the lives and times of the rich and famous and not so famous have seemingly engrossed the nation'. This has meant that newspapers, particularly at the popular end of the market, have had to borrow ideas and often material from magazines. The relationships between the *Mail* and *Hello!* and between the *Express* and *OK!* are obvious examples. But more subtly the human-interest approach of women's weekly magazines like *Take a Break* and *Woman* have been increasingly copied by newspapers.

Temple (2008: 176) accepts that the amount of celebrity coverage has expanded and multiplied in recent years and contributed to redefining the news values of all newspapers, but says that the widespread belief that this is a recent phenomenon does not stand up to critical examination. He cites Williams (1958: 284) saying that entertainment had always been, and always would be, a strong characteristic of any decent newspaper.

The *Mirror* and *Sun* now have daily spreads – 3 AM Girls and Bizarre – where their reporters frequent clubs late at night gathering title tattle and (hopefully compromising) pictures of (usually B and C list) celebrities. The more famous tend to feature on the news pages, particularly if it involves bad behaviour or relationship problems. Celebrity coverage has been helped by user-generated material, with photographs taken on mobile telephones challenging the paparazzi and tip-offs and information regularly given to newspapers. It has become an industry, with both celebrities and journalists sharing an interest. It is only when the celebrity climbs to, or is already at, the highest level that tensions and conflict develop. Celebrities who have welcomed exposure on the way up usually seek privacy when they have got there. There is a love–hate relationship between celebrities and the redtop tabloids whose editors are often celebrities themselves, none more than Piers Morgan who edited the *Mirror* from 1996 until 2004. He basked in his proximity to celebrities and later interviewed them about their experiences with the tabloid press for his *Tabloid Tales* television programme, prompting this reflection in Morgan's best-selling 'diaries' (2005: 378):

Interviewed Anthea Turner today for *Tabloid Tales*, and it turned out to be quite an emotional experience for her. As we analysed how the media had built her up and destroyed her, tears started flooding down her face. And I felt genuinely sorry for her. She's not Adolf Hitler; she's just a nice, bit cheesy, TV presenter who had an affair. And for that we collectively dragged her through the mill until she was effectively dead. She looked a broken hearted woman in front of me today, and I felt bad about that.

Celebrity journalism at the redtop end of the market requires relationships. Agents, public-relations people, television producers, record companies, publishers, all seek mutually beneficial relationships with the newspapers. Some aspiring celebrities simply promote themselves, often ignorant about what their claim to celebrity is. Television talent and reality shows promote celebrity, *Big Brother* making public faces of the unknown who sometimes go on to uncertain careers exploiting their short period of 'fame'.

The serious press does not ignore celebrity culture, sometimes deriding it at length, sometimes playing it straight in recognition that there are certain people, programmes and incidents 'everybody' is talking about. Editors of such papers know that this is one route to attracting the young readers they seek, including university students, and they also see the celebrity magazines their children are reading.

Sport

In terms of volume no area of newspaper coverage has grown more than sport, and that applies most to the serious press. The Premier League and Nick Hornby (author of *Fever Pitch*, an account of being an Arsenal fan) should probably take most responsibility, together with Rupert Murdoch, both for Sky TV and for Wapping which brought an end to constraints on pagination. Football, and in its wake sport in general, became fashionable, classless and a national obsession. Sky Sports is televised around the clock from around the world. Nick Hornby gave it intellectual credibility. BBC Radio 5 Live devote most of its weekends, evenings and phone-ins to it. No politician could afford not to have a football team that he or she 'supported' and the default conversation in all sections of society became sport. The newspapers could hardly opt out, despite the failure of sports pages to attract much advertising to offset the travel costs of sending sports reporters around the globe. They opted in.

Formerly it was match reports and results, the football pools and 'rattling the woodwork'. Now it is analysis, graphics, profiles, data and opinion. It is interviewing stars who have little to say, speculating about transfers and managerial changes, and seriously high-quality photography. Sport has earned its own supplements, often with 16 or 24 pages. It has its own star columnists and TV critics. And it has created a new breed of retired sportsman turned sports writer (in which area cricketers tend to do better than footballers). Among journalism students more seem to aspire to writing about sport than about politics or wars, and courses in sports journalism are now being offered.

Sports writing often represents some of the best writing in newspapers. Some of it is deeply cerebral, indeed sometimes pretentiously so. Quality sports coverage is now vital to success, and that means big-name writers and very comprehensive coverage. Because sport is about fantasy and dreams, and these days at least half the population are having them.

Current debates about the press

For those within the newspaper industry, editorial and management, there is only one current debate: media convergence, digital media, multi-platform publishing. It is all about the future of newspapers and their place in a digital future. It is about changing business models to deal with decreasing revenues from traditional print publishing, to develop a range of publishing off the back of the newspaper business, and to find ways of making money out of online publishing.

But even if they are not preoccupying those within the newspaper world there are issues that concern the rest of us. They are about the future too, but also relate to the present. They are about standards, about the quality of journalism, about the role of journalism and about the future form of journalism. Three important issues are considered here: the relationship between politics and the media and the relevance of this to a healthy and engaged democracy; standards of reporting in a period where costs are being cut and, partly as a result of media diversification, journalists are being asked to do more; and the journalists of today and the recruitment and training of the future journalists who will have to deal with all of the above.

Politics and the press

One of Tony Blair's last acts as prime minister before standing down in 2007 was to attack the media over their coverage of politics. In a public lecture at Reuters in London he said that the media, increasingly and dangerously because of competition, were being driven by 'impact'. Accuracy was secondary to impact; something interesting was less powerful than something shocking; and scandal or controversy beat reporting hands down (Blair, 2007).

In his most reported passage, the outgoing prime minister said: 'The fear of missing out means today's media, more than ever before, hunts in a pack. In these modes it is like a feral beast, just tearing people and reputations to bits'. He said that attacking motive was more important than attacking judgement. It was not enough to have made an error; it had to be venal. Blair believed that commentary on the news had become as or more important than the news itself, and that the confusion of news and commentary was routine. There was as much interpretation of what a politician was saying as coverage of them actually saying it. He believed 'this relationship between public life and media is now damaged in a manner that requires repair. The damage saps the country's confidence and self-belief; it undermines its assessment of itself, its institutions; and above all it reduces our capacity to take the right decisions, in the right spirit for our future'.

Tony Blair was perhaps an unlikely person to be making such a critique of political reporting. He had, with the help of his close colleagues and friends Peter Mandelson and Alastair Campbell, demonstrated the art of news management, or spin, as never before, and his handling of the 'evidence' leading to the invasion of Iraq had damaged his premiership. But there was no doubting the passion of this one of a series of valedictory speeches. In making it he was joining a wider and ongoing debate, started by the *Financial Times* journalist John Lloyd (2004a, 2004b).

The press response to Blair was mostly negative. The *Telegraph* found his argument 'deeply disturbing, founded on false premises and worthy of strongest refutation'. The *Financial Times* said: 'The media has many faults. But responsibility for spin, cronyism, sofa government and the fatal, mis-judgement over Iraq lies with Mr Blair and his government'. The *Express* pointed out that 'in the animal kingdom, the opposite of feral is tame. Presumably that is the sort of press Mr Blair would prefer'. But there was support too for Blair. Michael White, then the *Guardian*'s political editor, said Blair's diagnosis of how the modern media were driven by instant tech-nologies and 24/7 global markets was hard to dispute. White continued: 'The tricky bit is how society responds to the problems thereby created, notably the fast-declining levels of public trust in public institutions, by no means confined to politics and politicians, in an information-rich age where the boundaries between facts and comment – and between both and enter-tainment – have all but collapsed'. White said that in our different ways we were all in the same lifeboat where scandal, impact and commentary were what kept us competitive.

Roger Alton (2007), then *Observer* editor, described Blair's speech as highly perceptive and said that it could be used as a memo to newsdesks. However Emily Bell (2007), the *Guardian*'s director of digital content, speaking from a website perspective, took issue with Blair. Parliament, she said in her blog, was one of the most impossible institutions to report on in Britain. To go there as a lobby correspondent you had to have a pass, and for years she had tried to obtain one for her web reporter. Parliament was 'fusty and obscure, some-thing the politicians and correspondents actually rather like'.

John Lloyd (2004a: 12) portrays the relationship between political jour-nalists and politicians as a 'struggle for power':

> The struggle between politicians and the media is critical because this conflict, which has usually been presented as a healthy clash of independent institutions in a democratic polity, has for some time assumed the character of a zero-sum-game

struggle for power. This is not necessarily healthy, because it diminishes, rather than aerates or increases, freedom, and it increases the anomie and distrust within civil society.

Lloyd (2004b) argues that too much cynicism is bad for democracy, that journalism risks damaging the democratic fabric that we need to support us. In his Reuters Memorial Lecture he said:

> There is, the media tell us, a crisis in society: a crisis of withdrawal of engagement and of trust. Implicitly and explicitly, we in the media put the responsibility for that on public figures; usually politicians. We should, in the pursuit of our own ideals, look at ourselves as actors, as well as continue to act as investigators.

Politicians had long criticised the press, particularly the serious press, for the nature and quantity of the political coverage. They missed the pages of parliamentary debate in the serious newspapers, seemingly unaware that first the broadcasting and then the televising of parliament made it accessible to the general public unparaphrased. They disliked the way that 'performances' by MPs in the chamber were left to the parliamentary sketch writers with their irreverent approach, unaware that it was the bypassing of parliament by increasingly presidential prime ministers that made the chamber less important. They bemoaned what they saw as a concentration on personalities rather than policies, ignoring the fact that they were contributing to this in their off-record conversations with journalists. Jack Straw (1993: 46), then an opposition MP, produced a report on *The Decline in Press Reporting of Parliament*. 'The stereotyped newsroom view of parliament has been that it is boring and irrelevant', he wrote, 'with the result that the number of journalists in the press gallery has been cut and the coverage of debates scaled down. At the same time, the number of lobby correspondents, reporting gossip, briefings, and background has greatly increased'. He argued that this continuing process of downgrading parliament was in danger of seriously weakening the general public's understanding of, and confidence in, the democratic system.

Churnalism: life in the news factory

Nothing so preoccupies journalists as journalism. They love gossip about their colleagues, damaging anecdotes about their editors, and, at a higher level, debates about journalism and journalists. So when *Flat Earth News* was published at the beginning of 2008 it was bound to get media attention because not only was it about the media but also so harsh. It made good copy; it was reviewed everywhere; it was the subject of argument and debate among journalists. And it was very negative about contemporary journalistic practices. The book's author, Nick Davies, is a *Guardian* writer who produces long, carefully researched reportage on current social issues, which are well promoted and projected in the paper. He decided to focus his reporting skills on his own trade of reporting, and was supported in this by his editor Alan Rusbridger. The intention was that the *Guardian* would serialise the book, but this plan was abandoned when Davies included some damaging allegations against a senior *Observer* journalist. Rusbridger is editor in chief of the *Observer*.

Davies's judgement of contemporary journalism is savage. He claims that 'almost all journalists across the whole developed world now work within a kind of professional cage which distorts their work and crushes their spirit'. He feels forced to admit 'that I work in a corrupted profession' (Davies, 2008: 3). He blames modern corporate ownership of newspapers, and particularly Rupert Murdoch:

> The whole story of modern media failure is complicated and subtle. It involves all kinds of manipulation, occasional conspiracy, lying, cheating, stupidity, gullibility, a collapse of skill and a new wave of deliberate propaganda. But the story begins with journalists who tell you the Earth is flat, because genuinely they think it might be. The scale of it is terrifying. (2008: 28)

Although such hyperbole is reflective of the tone of Davies's book, and the attitudes of the usually unnamed reporters he quotes, it is underpinned by empirical work carried out by a team of researchers at Cardiff University's School of Journalism, Media and Cultural Studies. It is this more sober material, contained in a report – *The Quality and Independence of British Journalism* (2008), by Professor Justin Lewis, Dr Andrew Williams, Professor Bob Franklin, Dr James Thomas and Nick Mosdell – and two journal articles – in *Journalism Studies* and *Journalism Practice* – that will be considered here. The thesis, in essence, is that journalists today are required to produce many more stories in any given period than ever before, and that these stories do not provide 'independent journalism' because they draw heavily on public-relations and agency material.

Nick Davies calls the increased demand for reporters to produce more copy 'churnalism' – a term coined by Waseem Zakir, a BBC journalist (Harcup, 2004: 3) – and cites a young (unnamed) graduate reporter working on a regional daily tabloid. She provided these data for one week's work:

- Number of stories covered: 48
- People spoken to: 26
- People seen face to face: 4 out of 26
- Total hours out of the office: 3 out of 45.5

Davies comments:

> This is life in the news factory. No reporter who is turning out nearly 10 stories every shift can possibly do his or her job properly. No reporter who spends only three hours out of the office in an entire working week can possibly develop enough good leads or build enough good contacts. No reporter who speaks to only 26 people in researching 48 stories can possibly be checking their truth. This is churnalism. (2008: 59)

Lewis et al. examined the influence of public-relations and news agencies on news stories in the serious national press. They analysed two weeks of domestic-news coverage in the *Guardian, Times, Telegraph, Independent* and *Daily Mail* in March/April 2006, a total of 2,207 items. They found 72 per cent were written by named journalists, the rest unattributed to a named writer apart from one attributed to the Press Association, the national news agency. However, comparing the original agency copy to the content of the stories in the newspapers they found 30 per cent replicating the PA original copy and a further 19 per cent largely dependent on such copy, in both cases without attribution (Lewis et al., 2008: 5).

The Cardiff researchers also examined public-relations influence on the sample of news stories, finding 'nearly one in five newspaper stories were verifiably derived mainly or wholly from PR material or activity' (ibid.: 7). They concluded that

> even in a sample based on the UK's most prestigious news outlets, journalists are heavily reliant on pre-packaged information, either from the PR industry or other media (notably agency services) ... 60% of press stories rely wholly or mainly on pre-packaged information, a further 20% are reliant to varying degrees on PR and agency materials. Of the remaining 20% only 12% are without any discernible pre-packaged content and in 8% of cases the presence of PR content was unclear. (ibid.: 14)

Following the publication of Davies's book and the Cardiff research the Press Association reacted strongly to the linking of its own news service with material produced by PR agencies, stressing that its reputation is based on providing a news service to various clients, including newspapers, which is fast, fair and accurate. PA editor Jonathan Grun (2008) wrote that the Cardiff researchers considered an all-party House of Commons Public Accounts Committee report as a government press release. Grun also identified other inaccuracies. The head of the research team, Justin Lewis, told him that a section of the report was being withdrawn because it had always been regarded as the most speculative and the least robust. Because the PA service is taken by most national and regional newspapers it is hardly surprising that similar copy appears in a variety of outlets. No newspapers have reporters all over the country, and while it is true that the number of district reporters employed by national newspapers has fallen dramatically over the years there is nothing new in newspapers relying on PA for much of their content. There is also nothing new in PA copy being taken into a reporter's copy without attribution, although the practice is perhaps questionable. Much court reporting is sourced from PA as well as crime stories, accidents and disasters around the country. It is no different from international agencies like Reuters providing copy from around the world.

In another journal article based on the same research (Lewis et al., 2008b: 27–28) the Cardiff team cite four aspects of what they describe as 'marked changes in journalists' newsgathering and reporting practices'. These are:

- The increasingly influential role for public-relations professionals and news agencies
- Fewer journalists required to write more stories – an increasingly pressurised and low-paid work force
- No time to check stories, to be sure that the claims they make are true
- Less editorial independence than twenty years ago (ibid.: 27–28)

Lewis et al. conclude that there is evidence of 'an increasing reliance on pre-packaged material at all levels of British journalism'. This, they say, makes it possible to produce a 'quality' newspaper on cheap, if not free, second-hand material. The 'heavy price' for this is that 'the quality of information in a democratic society is steadily impoverished' (ibid.: 42–43).

The Cardiff findings would be contested by editors, with national-newspaper editors separating their practice from the regional and local press. Certainly, so-called 'churnalism' is more evident in the chronically understaffed newsrooms of the provincial press, where researchers Deirdre O'Neill and Catherine O'Connor found that a majority of published stories appeared to rely on a single source, most frequently resource-rich organisations, leading them to conclude:

> [J]ournalists are becoming more passive, often merely passing on information to the public that they have been given ... Too frequently the result is bland, banal copy at best; or free advertising and propaganda at worst. All these trends are a serious threat to local democracy, the public interest, public trust, the local public sphere, and the standards of journalism. (O'Neill and O'Connor, 2008: 498)

When discussing the influence of public relations it is important to distinguish between the rewriting of press releases – accepting what they say rather than recognising the partiality of their provenance – and the use of press releases to alert newspapers to information. This might be a ministerial speech or the visit of an internationally famous pop star, the autumn schedules for a TV broadcaster or the launch of the iPhone, a royal visit to China or the publication of a controversial new book on journalism. The important question is whether news organisations use PR material as a basis for their own reporters to develop stories, or whether the material is used as provided, unchecked. Record companies, for example, have always alerted the news media to concerts or new CDs, and press releases from the government are an important form of political communication. There is legitimate public interest in the information.

For all its gloom and hyperbole – and if Nick Davies had produced a more measured book, with more caveats, it would not have had half the impact – *Flat Earth News* and its Cardiff supporters stand as a challenge to the press to defend its practices, or change them. As Temple (2008: 170) argues, newspapers, especially those in the quality sector, 'need to be more open and transparent about their sources and less willing to run PR blurb or political spin without seeking alternative perspectives ... If British print journalism is to improve its dreadful public image, it must be more rigorous in serving the public sphere'.

Journalists: background and training

Journalism, including newspaper journalism, has become almost exclusively a graduate occupation over the past decade. There has been a dramatic change in the way in which journalists are trained, with further and higher education taking over the basic training from the publishers which used to carry out their own training on the apprenticeship model. Trainee journalists, usually school-leavers rather than graduates, would be 'indentured' to a newspaper – effectively employed on a training contract – and trained on the job by experienced journalists, sent to a neighbouring college for one day a week – 'day release' – or for a sustained period of a month or so – 'block release' – to learn their law, public affairs and shorthand. They would take exams set by the National Council for the Training of Journalists (NCTJ) and eventually acquire its Proficiency Certificate, whereupon they were described as 'seniors' and paid a bit more. At that time most young and aspiring journalists would begin their careers on local or regional newspapers, and for one time the National Union of Journalists (NUJ) barred national newspapers from hiring new entrants to journalism. A few graduates found their way round this restriction, usually by being hired as leader writers or joining London evening newspapers.

In the 1980s, with the arrival of postgraduate journalism courses in further and higher education, followed in the 1990s by undergraduate courses, journalism training began the shift to universities and colleges. This was greeted with suspicion by many of the newspaper editors until they realised the kinds of cost savings 'pre-entry' training could provide. Training budgets could be cut, as could the time senior journalists spent mentoring young recruits, who would have learned the basic journalism skills and knowledge in an educational environment, paid for by the taxpayer or the students (or their families) themselves. The rapid increase in participation in higher education, from 10 per cent of school leavers in the 1970s to 40 per cent and rising today, encouraged this trend. Young journalists in the regional and local press would still take the NCTJ exams for the Proficiency Test, now called the National Certificate, but typically they would take the first stage of this, the Preliminary Certificate, during college and university courses accredited by the NCTJ, and the students themselves would pay for these exams.

So today journalism has become a graduate career and often a career for those with a higher degree or diploma in journalism. Hanna and Sanders (2007), in a longitudinal survey of undergraduates studying journalism, note that the number of such students in British universities rose fivefold between 1994/5 and 2004/5, from 415 to 2035. By early 2006 there were such courses in 38 British universities (2007: 406). Students were asked at the beginning and end of their courses whether they intended to pursue a career in journalism. Those 'sure' that they would fell from 75 per cent to 53 per cent. Hanna and Sanders (2007: 415) also noted the high proportion of male graduates who wanted to engage in sports journalism, and the number whose motivation for entering journalism was 'the chance to help people'. This figure was 26 per cent in Britain, as compared with 44 per cent in Australia and 61 per cent in the United States.

The most comprehensive recent survey of journalists, undertaken by the Journalism Training Forum and published in 2002 (*Journalists at Work*, NTO/Skillset) recorded that there were 60–70,000 journalists in the UK and predicted that this figure would rise by a further 20,000 by 2010:

> Journalism is now, in effect, a graduate only occupation. 98% of all journalists have a degree or a postgraduate degree qualification. The only journalists who do not have these high level qualifications are older journalists who have been in the profession for a long time. (ibid.: 8)

The survey also found that 70 per cent of journalists were under 40, that 55 per cent worked in London and the south-east, that 96 per cent were white and just 3 per cent came from families headed by a semi-skilled or unskilled worker. This uniformity of social and ethnic background causes concern to many in journalism and is, if anything, increasing. It leads to a greater detachment of journalists from the social issues they are reporting and commenting on at a time when such issues are high on the political agenda.

Another survey, carried out by the Society of Editors which represents senior journalists in the print and broadcast media, concentrated on ethnic diversity in newsrooms of newspapers in areas of high ethnic-minority population. Table 6.1 shows how few ethnic-minority journalists were working in regional newsrooms when the Society of Editors' report *Diversity in the Newsroom* was published in 2004.

Table 6.1   *Numbers of ethnic minority journalists (and the ethnic minority population)*

Newspaper title	Ethnic minority journalists	Ethnic minority proportion of population
Birmingham Evening Mail	seven out of 93	30%
Bradford Telegraph and Argus	two out of 65	22%
Harrow Observer	one out of 12	43%
Burnley Express	one out of 38	11%
Leicester Mercury	four out of 120	38%
Manchester Evening News	six out of 112	circulation area consists of 10 towns, with ethnic minority populations ranging from 1–11%
Oldham Evening Chronicle	one out of 34	14%
Sentinel (Stoke)	five out of 92	7%
Uxbridge Gazette	one out of 10	14%
Yorkshire Evening Post	none out of 68	8.7%

The figures in Table 6.1 represent a snapshot taken in 2004, and some efforts have been made to deal with these imbalances, mainly through bursaries to fund pre-entry journalism course fees, targeted at ethnic-minority and socially deprived aspiring entrants. But so far the picture has changed little. As the media commentator Peter Wilby (2008b) put it:

> Journalism's narrow social and ethnic base – which, one media company executive told me, is not reflected in advertising and circulation departments – matters more than it does in other elite occupations. Faced with trying to understand, say, the grievances of the Muslim community or what drives inner-city youth to violence, or what it's like to have children attending a 'sink school', most journalists are lost. They have no contacts and no inside information.

The lack of social and ethnic diversity is most pronounced at the top, where the educational diversity of national newspaper editors and leading columnists shows considerable uniformity. This was researched by the independent Sutton Trust (*The Educational Backgrounds of Leading Journalists*, 2006), repeating a similar survey twenty years earlier. Its chairman, Sir Peter Lampl, said in his introduction to the latest report:

> We have found that leading news and current affairs journalists – those figures so central in shaping public opinion and national debate – are more likely than not to have been to independent schools which educate just 7% of the population. Of the top 100 journalists in 2006, 54% were independently educated, an increase from 49% in 1986. Not only

does this say something about the state of our education system, but it also raises questions about the nature of the media's relationship with society: is it healthy that those who are most influential in determining and interpreting the news agenda have educational backgrounds that are so fundamentally different to the vast majority of the population?

The Sutton Trust defines, somewhat arbitrarily, the leading newspaper journalists as the editors of national newspapers and news weeklies, and the top national newspaper columnists, 'the elite and hugely influential opinion formers who set the agenda and tone for national debates'. The survey showed that of 26 editors of national newspapers and political weeklies 17 had gone to independent schools and nine to Oxford or Cambridge universities. Of the 23 top columnists, 10 had attended independent schools and 17 Oxford or Cambridge universities (the latter figure was 15 out of 22 in 1986).

Dumbing down: a final word

While describing modern newspaper editorial trends, such as the increase in columns, celebrity and sports coverage, and current debates about the state of political coverage, the increased use of public relations and news agency material (wrongly linked in some quarters), this chapter has essentially been addressing what has become known as 'dumbing down'. There is an influential conventional wisdom, promoted by many academics and writers, from Franklin to Allan and Sampson, and some journalists, most notably Davies, that the phenomenon is incontestable, that corporate owners, market forces, capitalism, Murdoch, journalists themselves have driven down standards, and with them sales of newspapers. But there are contrary voices, every bit as worthy of respect, who take a different view, who see positive good in a less elitist, less male-dominated press. They point to the changes in society that have brought about a changed rather than a diminished editorial agenda. While accepting that staff- and cost-cutting have been the enemy of some good traditional forms of journalism, particularly in the regional and local press, it could hardly be argued that the national press has been craven in its approach to politicians or their policies, or reluctant to expose the ill-treatment of some groups in society or unacceptable standards in public or private services. Sometimes these critiques of modern newspaper journalism appear to be based on a misplaced nostalgia for a mythical golden age or sniffiness about the interests of younger generations.

Greenslade (2003a: 628) believes the whole dumbing down debate is 'underpinned by snobbery'. Critics of current journalism ignore the demographic, sociological and cultural changes wrought as a result of growing affluence and greater educational attainment. 'The notion that there were serious people who only wanted to read serious news was untenable. A rounded human being of the 1990s could appreciate reading about domestic political in-fighting, developments in rock music, the state of British football and the problems of Third World debt'.

Temple (2008: 180) points to research that shows that while there is no correlation between interest in celebrity culture and the likelihood of not voting, there is a negative correlation between interest in politics and interest in celebrity culture. 'It may well be the case that for those who dislike politics, celebrity programmes and magazines will be their major doorway into the public sphere'. Temple suggests that criticisms of dumbing down could be viewed as 'a response to the feminisation of journalism, a move away from a male dominated news agenda. The rise in consumer and lifestyle coverage could be interpreted as reflecting a new visibility for what was often derogatively referred to as "women's issues"'. He cites McNair (2003a: 50), suggesting that a previously male-dominated news agenda has become 'less pompous, less pedagogic, less male, more human, more vivacious, more demotic'. Greenslade (2003a: 629) quotes columnist India Knight writing in the *Sunday Times* (24 September 2000), making the point more assertively. She felt that increasingly 'dumbing down' referred to 'stuff that women might like'. She asked: 'Why should a woman's choice of editorial content be of less intellectual value than a man's? Why should it be less relevant for women to read about relationships than for men to read about a football match?'

McNair (2003b: 223) regards the critics of dumbing down as providing

> at best contestable opinions as to what newspapers should be writing about, and at worst rather elitist responses to such welcome developments as the feminisation of journalism (by which I mean the changing role of women as producers and consumers of the media) and the consequent blurring of the personal/private, political/public distinctions which have traditionally structured the public sphere.

Despite the vehemence with which both sides of the debate express themselves, the reality may well be that trends labelled as 'dumbing down' and those labelled as 'media democratisation' are both happening simultaneously, with consequences that might be both negative and positive for the role of the press within the public sphere. Life has a tendency to be messy like that.

Alan Rusbridger (1999b), responsible for a newspaper in the firing line of the dumbing-down critics, dismisses the concept as

> a plausible way of describing the disenchantment of the people who either were, or missed out on being, the old elite, with this new difficult world in which high culture and so-called low culture meet, in which classes blur and different voices are heard. Dumbing down is a dumb term to describe something far more complex at work in society today, and every alarm bell ought to ring every time you hear it.

7

THE PRESS UNDER SCRUTINY:
SELF-REGULATION AND ETHICS

Sexual intercourse began in 1963, we are told in Philip Larkin's celebrated poem 'Annus Mirabilis', which is Latin for wonderful year. We can be equally precise about the genesis of newspaper ethics. The UK press had its *Annus Horribilis*, or year of misfortune, between April 1989 – when the *Sun* outraged Merseyside by defaming the victims of the Hillsborough disaster – and February 1990 – when the *Sunday Sport* invaded the hospital room of a popular TV actor who was recovering from a car accident caused by a hurricane. National newspaper editors of the time were famously warned by culture minister David Mellor that they were 'drinking in the Last Chance Saloon', and the issue of newspaper ethics – or the lack thereof – shot up the political agenda (Sanders, 2003: 80). So the government did what governments tend to do in such circumstances: set up a committee chaired by a lawyer, in this case David Calcutt.

It is odd that a watershed moment for the British press should have been provoked by a publication that many journalists do not even regard as a newspaper: the *Sunday Sport*. An actor by the name of Gordon Kaye starred in this particular drama, although he was scarcely aware of it at the time. It happened when Kaye, famous for the television comedy series *'Allo 'Allo*, was on a life-support machine suffering from a serious head injury. Two *Sport* journalists entered Charing Cross Hospital in London and, ignoring conventions and notices about visiting, found their way to Kaye's room. There they took pictures and attempted an interview with the very sick man, who was in a state of semi-consciousness (Keeble, 2009: 135). A nurse discovered them and they were ushered out. But they had their 'scoop', and critics of press intrusion had a cause celebre. There was a massive row. The actor's agent went to court in an unsuccessful attempt at preventing publication, with Lord Justice Glidewell ruling: 'It is well known in English law there is no right of privacy, and accordingly there is no right of action for breach of a person's privacy'. He added that parliament might like to consider whether such a law protecting an individual's privacy should be introduced. The story and pictures were duly published in the *Sunday Sport* and, when the paper was subsequently criticised by the self-regulator of the newspaper industry, it retorted with the headline: 'BOLLOCKS TO THE PRESS COUNCIL' (Greenslade, 2004: 540).

Suddenly press standards became the talk of the town and, thanks to the actions of a semi-pornographic rag with a tiny circulation, there was now a head of steam behind calls for privacy legislation. Peter Cole was among those who gathered at the Tower Hotel in London when the *Independent* editor, Andreas Whittam Smith, chaired a meeting of all national newspaper editors to decide how to deal with the threat. Cole recalls: 'There were the tabloid editors defending their right to publish stories of scandal and celebrity. Then there were the broadsheet editors, loftily listening to their distasteful colleagues and having to accept that, for the moment at least, they were engaged in a common fight'. The editors continued to meet while, simultaneously, the Calcutt committee deliberated. And out of all this came a new body to replace the seemingly ineffectual Press Council: the Press Complaints Commission, or PCC, of which more below.

It may have seemed as if the topic of press standards had emerged from nowhere in the period 1989–1990, but in reality such issues had been there all along, mostly lurking in the shadows. It was just that, a bit like sex before the publication of *Lady Chatterley's Lover*, journalistic ethics were not normally considered a suitable topic of conversation in polite society. Today, in contrast, just as the media thrust sex in your face whether you wanted it or not, it is hard to avoid the discussion of ethics in the media. Curiously for a trade that has never been renowned for an ability to be intelligently self-reflective, media punditry is now one of the fastest growing sectors of newspaper and online journalism; each week, the ex-editors' club and their fellow travellers churn out several thousand words examining the industry's entrails.

When she was the wife of the serving prime minister, Cherie Blair told a group of students that there was 'no professional morality in journalism' (quoted in Dico and Elliott, 2006). That remains a popular view, yet we have come a long way from the days when *Sun* editor Kelvin MacKenzie could be celebrated for dismissing ethics as 'that place to the east of London where people wear white socks'. If MacKenzie's comment appeared crass to many people even in the 1980s, it looks positively prehistoric from the perspective of today's world of ethical institutes, university courses on media ethics, a rapidly expanding literature on the ethics of journalism, and even debates about the ethics of ethics. One journalist who has ploughed an ethical furrow for many years is Mike Jempson, director of the Mediawise Trust, who observes:

Journalism is under scrutiny as never before. The field of media ethics is being picked over by a veritable land army of quasi-academic and professional institutions churning over the issues that have dogged journalists for generations, and chewing over how we can do our job better ... Journalists and the public now have a veritable farmers' market from which to select their ethics. (Jempson, 2007: 22–23)

He lists the following organisations that exist to scrutinise journalists' ethics: Mediawise (www.mediawise.org.uk); the Institute of Communication Ethics (www.communication-ethics.org.uk); the International Communications Forum (www.icforum.org); the Institute for Global Ethics UK Trust (www.globalethics.org); the Media Corporate Social Responsibility Forum (www.mediacsrforum.org); the Media Ethics Institute (http://ncfmedia. blogspot.com); the Media Standards Trust (http://www.mediastandards trust.org); Polis (www.lse.ac.uk/collections/polis); and the Reuters Institute for the Study of Journalism (http://reutersinstitute.politics.ox.ac.uk). More seem to be springing up all the time, mostly sharing the common characteristic that relatively few working journalists are likely to be involved in their day-to-day activities. Yet it would be wrong to conclude from all this that journalistic ethics are either a new or a passing concern.

Although the word 'ethics' may not have been found in many of the contents or index pages of journalism tomes published during most of the twentieth century – books such as *The Press* by Henry Wickham Steed (1938) or *A Close Look at Newspapers* by EW Hildick (1966), to give just two examples – in reality ethical considerations have been a constitutive element of journalism since newspapers began. In *The Complete Journalist*, Frederick Mansfield (1936) discusses issues that remain contentious more than seventy years later, including sensationalism, invasion of privacy, coverage of suicide and the distortion of facts to fit pre-conceived agendas. Similarly, *Times* editor Wickham Steed was clearly writing about what we would think of as ethical issues, although he did not use the phrase, when he described the responsibility of newspapers in the following terms:

The underlying principle that governs, or should govern, the Press is that the gathering and selling of news and views is essentially a public trust. It is based upon a tacit contract with the public that the news shall be true to the best of the knowledge and belief of those who offer it for sale ... The same kind of trust is implied in the relationship between a doctor and his patients, though medical men work under the discipline of a professional code and are obliged to hold medical degrees, whereas journalism is a 'free' profession subject only to the external restrictions which the law of the land may place upon it. But the dishonest doctor can harm, at worst, only a few dozen or a few score patients, while a dishonest journalist may poison the minds of hundreds of thousands or millions of his fellow men. (Steed, 1938: 14)

Ethical considerations may have been implicit in journalistic practice all along, but it would be fair to say that an open discussion of what are now termed ethical issues remained the exception rather than the rule within the UK's mainstream newspaper industry at least until the 1980s, and arguably well into the 1990s.

Hillsborough disaster: the truth?

It is the 'tacit contract' of trust, as identified by Steed above, that lies at the heart of journalism: trust between journalist and source no less than trust between journalist and audience. Yet 'trust does not sell newspapers', argues Jon Grubb, former editor of the *Scunthorpe Telegraph* and now editing the *Lincolnshire Echo*. He says that 'death, shock, horror' are what readers appear to prefer (quoted in Keeble, 2006: 11). When trust is broken the consequences can be severe, which is why the *Sun* – easily the biggest-selling daily newspaper in the UK – has never regained the sales it lost on Merseyside as a consequence of its front-page splash just four days after 96 Liverpool football supporters were killed in a crush at the Hillsborough football stadium in Sheffield. Under the definitive banner headline 'THE TRUTH', the paper stated:

- Some fans picked the pockets of victims
- Some fans urinated on the brave cops
- Some fans beat up a PC giving the kiss of life (*Sun*, 19 April 1989)

Copies of the offending edition were publicly burned in the streets of Liverpool, many city landlords banned the *Sun* from their pubs, and newsagents either refused to stock it or kept it under the counter for fear of offending customers. As the newspaper's unofficial biographers Peter Chippindale and Chris Horrie (1992: 289–292) note: '*Sun* readers in Liverpool had voted spontaneously with their feet and sales of the paper had collapsed'. Editor Kelvin MacKenzie made a grudging apology on BBC radio but the damage had been done.

Twenty years later circulation of the *Sun* on Merseyside had not recovered, and it has been estimated that around 50,000 sales are still lost in the area every day as a direct result of that single headline back in 1989 (Conlan, 2006). Although many of today's potential readers were not even born when the tragedy occurred, the ghosts of Hillsborough periodically return to haunt the paper's editorial and circulation departments alike. In 1992, for example, the former Liverpool player and manager Graham Souness was widely criticised for choosing to sell his story to the *Sun* (Cozens, 2004). And in 2004 footballer Wayne Rooney (then playing for Merseyside club Everton) was vilified after signing a deal to sell his story to the *Sun* and its stablemate the *News of the World* for a reported £250,000. This time the backlash was so vehement that it prompted the *Sun* to run a belated full-page apology for its 'carelessness and thoughtlessness following that blackest of days' at Hillsborough (Ponsford, 2004). Then, towards the end of 2006, ex-editor Kelvin MacKenzie reportedly told a private business lunch that he stuck by the offending 1989 story: 'All I did wrong there was tell the truth … I went on the *World at One* the next day and apologised. I only did that because Rupert Murdoch told me to. I wasn't sorry then and I'm not sorry now because we told the truth' (quoted in Lister, 2006). After his remarks were reported in the local media old wounds were reopened, prompting 40,000 Liverpool supporters to ensure their feelings were heard loud and clear during the BBC's live television coverage of the club's FA Cup match against Arsenal in January 2007. For six minutes – the precise time the 1989 match at Hillsborough had lasted before being abandoned – they made their hostility to the *Sun* obvious by non-stop chants of 'Justice for the 96', and by holding up red and white cards spelling out, 'The truth' (Lister, 2007). The twentieth anniversary of the tragedy was marked at the Albert pub, next to Liverpool's Anfield ground, with a mocked-up poster of the notorious front page, its masthead dripping with blood, reading: 'The truth, 96 dead. Hillsborough 15th April 1989. Don't buy the *Sun*' (Gibson and Carter, 2009). Who says that it doesn't matter what's in the papers because today's news is merely tomorrow's fish-and-chip wrapping?

It was its original labelling of unsubstantiated claims as 'the truth' that turned out to be such a hugely embarrassing own goal for the *Sun*. Not only did it present an allegation as fact but, in doing so, the paper was in effect attacking its own core readership: sport-loving, largely working class, mostly white and male. In contrast to many of the stories they would read in the *Sun*, readers on Merseyside this time had access to alternative versions of the truth from personal experience and/or friends and family, in addition to more measured reporting by the regional media; this led to a breakdown of trust between the *Sun* and its readers, the consequences of which are still being felt by Murdoch's News International.

The *Sun* is on far firmer ground when it trains its fire not on 'its own' but on those perceived to be 'other': paedophiles, gays, feminists, trade unionists, lefties, social workers, anyone who finds its Page Three soft-porn distasteful, people who are too fat, too thin, too Muslim, too whatever, and of course asylum seekers – indeed, all foreigners with the exception of Australian-turned-American squillionaires called Rupert. By labelling groups of people as 'them' – in effect, the evil outsiders – the UK's popular tabloids can be seen as establishing an imagined community of 'us', their own readers, who are presented as the norm from which everything else is a deviation (Conboy, 2006: 104). This process of simplification, which reduces complex realities to the 'binary opposition' of good versus evil (Jewkes, 2004: 45), is as much a question of newspaper ethics as is invasion of privacy or the protection of confidential sources, because it boils down to a betrayal of trust – the trust that a society's citizens place in journalists to report accurately, fairly and honestly.

The *Sun* is at the sharp end of daily tabloid journalism, so it should come as no shock that it turns out to be the most complained about newspaper in the history of the Press Complaints Commission. However, just 18 of those complaints against the *Sun* were upheld in ten years because the vast majority of all complaints to the PCC are either rejected or 'resolved' informally (Frost, 2004: 109). Depending on your point of view, that is either a glowing success story for press self-regulation (Shannon, 2001), or a sign that the PCC is a watchdog with too little bark, let alone bite, to which the press pay mere lip service (Temple, 2008: 140). Subscribing to the former view is, unsurprisingly, *Sun* editor Rebekah Wade, who has praised the PCC for 'raising press standards … higher and higher and higher' (Select Committee, 2003). Less convinced is former *Daily Telegraph* editor Max Hastings (2002: 282), who believes the PCC is sometimes guilty of providing 'figleaves of justification for "redtop" excesses'. It is an argument that, like the best newspaper stories, will run and run.

City Slickers: a licence to print money

One case in which the PCC has been accused of being a particularly tooth-less watchdog is the City Slickers one, which cast a shadow over the UK press during the early years of this century. As with the *Sun*'s coverage of Hillsborough, it again involved a breach of trust between a newspaper – this time the *Daily Mirror* – and its millions of readers. But it was more personal, as it involved some of the paper's journalists fleecing readers for financial gain. The Slickers story is a far cry from the days when, with some justification, the *Daily Mirror* could pride itself on being 'the voice of the people … on the side of the underdog', as its historian Maurice Edelman (1966: 1; 141) put it four decades ago. It does, however, have echoes of the infamous occasion on which one-time *Mirror* proprietor Robert Maxwell launched a Spot-the-Ball com-petition to attract readers, only to instruct his editor to fix the judging process to ensure that nobody could win the promised £1 million prize money (Greenslade, 1992: 112–115). Fiddling a readers' competition in this way was a brazen breach of trust – which only came to light subsequently because the editor in question, Roy Greenslade, decided to make it public following Maxwell's death – but at least it did not masquerade as journalism. Because the Slickers sailed under the flag of reporting rather than that of entertain-ment, their case is an even more salutary reminder of what can happen if we forget what newspapers – indeed, journalism – are supposed to be for.

The Slickers story dates back to the brief but much hyped 'dotcom boom' of the late 1990s, which followed the widening of share ownership that had been a policy of the Thatcher and Major governments. This was the climate in which the *Mirror* – formerly self-consciously a paper of the working class, albeit one dismissed as 'the navvies' comic' by genuine class warriors such as trade-union activist Jack Dash (1970: 154) – launched a column to discuss personal financial investments in general and, in particular, to advise readers on what stocks and shares to buy and sell. The City Slickers column was a departure for a mass-circulation popular newspaper, and its impact indicated the potential power of the press both to inform and to manipulate. The journalists who wrote it, Anil Bhoyrul and James Hipwell, quickly came to realise that by producing favourable copy about a company they could persuade a large number of readers to buy certain shares. As Anil Bhoyrul put it: 'We had created a monster that was out of control. Every time I tipped a share the price shot up between 30 per cent and 100 per cent the next morning. Suddenly, the *Mirror* was engulfed in the Slickers craze – and it was getting scary' (quoted in PCC, 2000). The journalists involved had been granted a licence to print money.

Aware of the column's impact, Bhoyrul and Hipwell – known collectively as the Slickers – themselves began to buy and sell some of the shares about which they were writing. They soon developed a simple and lucrative method of operation:

- First, identify a share that could become the 'tip of the day' in the following day's City Slickers column
- Then, buy a number of those shares at their current value
- Next day the tip would be published in the *Mirror*
- Then, sit back and watch the share price rocket
- Finally, sell the shares at a handsome profit later that day.

Between them, in just seven months, the Slickers made at least £55,000 from such deals (Slattery, 2006). For many observers, *Mirror* journalists' manipulation of the financial markets for personal gain was one of the most aggravated breaches of trust in the history of newspaper journalism, because the cash taken by the journalists did not come out of thin air; it came from the pockets of those readers who followed the paper's share tips in good faith.

It was too good to last, and the scam was brought to light by rather more honest journalism when the *Daily Telegraph* published an item concerning the share dealings of *Mirror* editor Piers Morgan. One thing led to another, the story was picked up and picked over by other sections of the media before, with grim inevitability, the whole business was dubbed 'Mirrorgate' (Greenslade, 2004: 659–660). In February 2000, Bhoyrul and Hipwell were sacked for gross misconduct following an investigation by the newspaper's publishers. The Press Complaints Commission subsequently ruled that the Slickers column had involved 'flagrant, multiple breaches' of the PCC code of practice, which forbids journalists to deal in shares about which they have recently written or are about to write (PCC, 2000).

The Slickers eventually ended up in the law courts where both were convicted of conspiring to breach the Financial Services Act. The judge, Mr Justice Beatson, condemned what he described as 'a culture of advanced information about tips and share dealing' at the *Mirror* (Ponsford, 2006), and he took into consideration that the pair had received little or no guidance from their superiors on the newspaper (Slattery, 2006). Hipwell was jailed for six months and Bhoyrul was sentenced to a 180-hour community service order (Howe, 2006). *Mirror* editor Piers Morgan did not find himself in the dock, nor was he sacked over the Slickers case; that ignominy was to come later, after he continued to defend the publication of apparently faked photographs purporting to show British soldiers abusing prisoners in Iraq. Morgan was, however, criticised by the PCC in relation to the Slickers, for failing to ensure that his staff observed the self-regulatory code of practice with sufficient rigour. Morgan had profited personally from dealing in shares that had featured in the City Slickers column, and the PCC judged that his conduct had 'fallen short of the high professional standards demanded by the code' (PCC, 2000). However, the PCC added that it did 'not find it necessary to choose between the conflicting versions' as to whether Morgan had known in advance – i.e. before he bought the shares – that certain shares were to be tipped in his newspaper (PCC, 2000). Morgan insisted he was a totally innocent victim of a coincidence that, he conceded, did not look good. He added: 'I might have been a rogue when it came to my journalistic behaviour, but I was an honest rogue' (Morgan, 2008: 23).

Although the PCC can tick off newspapers and newspaper journalists, it cannot strike them off in the way that misbehaving doctors, lawyers and other professionals can be struck off a register and denied permission to ply their trade. In fact, Hipwell (2006) continued to practise as a journalist even while he was in a prison cell, from where he contributed a prison diary for the *Guardian*. The newspaper pointed out that it was not paying Hipwell for the column, thereby avoiding possible censure for breaching Clause 16 of the PCC code of practice, which bans payment to criminals or their associates 'for stories, pictures or information, which seek to exploit a particular crime or to glorify or glamorise crime in general'.

Freedom of the press?

In the UK, then, although journalists may be sacked if they fall foul of or embarrass their employers, and they can be sued for libel or jailed for contempt of court, they cannot be denied the right to call themselves journalists or to practise journalism. That is because, following failed attempts at more formal regulation in the seventeenth century, we enjoy what is essentially a 'free press' (Shannon, 2001: 3). Journalists in democratic societies have habitually resisted the idea of an official 'register' of approved journalists, on the grounds that journalists are merely citizens armed with notebooks and/or microphones; who should have the right to say who is allowed to ask questions of the powers-that-be and publish the answers?

Newspaper journalism in Britain emerged from a print culture that proved resistant to restrictions and which was itself a democratising social force from the seventeenth century onwards, enabling print journalists to carve out for themselves a relatively unregulated space (Harcup, 2007). This is in marked contrast to the much more strict regulatory regime under which broadcast journalists in the UK work, which reflects both the different technologies involved in the development of such journalism (radio and television depended on the limited number of wavebands available, which led to a system of licensing) and the fact that, by the time broadcasting arrived on the scene, the state had got its act together and realised the potential power of the media. So TV and radio journalists work under a system of statutory regulation backed up by the force of the law. And while broadcast journalists cannot be struck off any official register, they can cause their employers to be heavily fined or even to lose their licence to broadcast; punishments that go a long way to explain why claims of unethical excesses are far more likely to be directed at the press than at broadcast journalism (Harcup, 2009a). As Temple observes:

> The reluctance of governments to bring the press under statutory control demonstrates both the strength and the mythology of a 'free press' and government's fear of the 'free press' – and perhaps even a realisation that a press free from direct governmental interference is a prerequisite for a democracy. (Temple, 2008: 84–85)

This relative freedom of the press – the freedom to be irresponsible, as many critics would put it – means that there have long been concerns about the ethics of journalists in general and newspaper journalists in particular. Back in 1930 the poet Humbert Wolfe articulated a popular feeling that journalists were not to be trusted, when he wrote in his verse novel *The Uncelestial City*:

> You cannot hope to bribe or twist,
> thank God! the British journalist.
> But, seeing what the man will do
> unbribed, there's no occasion to.

In the same period, Conservative party leader Stanley Baldwin bitterly condemned the ethics of press barons Beaverbrook and Rothermere, owners of the then hugely influential *Daily Express* and *Daily Mail* respectively:

> The newspapers attacking me are not newspapers in the ordinary sense. They are engines of propaganda for the constantly changing policies, desires, personal wishes,

personal dislikes of two men. What are their methods? Their methods are direct falsehood, misrepresentations, half-truths, the alteration of the speaker's meaning by publishing a sentence apart from the context ... What the proprietorship of these papers is
aiming at is power, and power without responsibility – the prerogative of the harlot
throughout the ages. (Quoted in Griffiths, 2006: 251–252)

Many journalists of the time were themselves expressing disquiet at
proprietors' political bias as well as the 'distasteful and unseemly manner' in which journalists were expected to intrude upon people's private
lives for the purpose of increasing the circulation of their newspapers and
the profit of their employers (Mansfield, 1936: 372). Such concerns
resulted in the National Union of Journalists establishing, in 1936, the
UK's first code of ethical conduct for journalists (Bundock, 1957: 128–
129). The code promised union backing for journalists who refused to do
work 'incompatible with the honour and interests of the profession', and
declared: 'In obtaining news or pictures, reporters and press photographers should do nothing that will cause pain or humiliation to innocent,
bereaved, or otherwise distressed persons. News, pictures and documents
should be acquired by honest methods only' (quoted in O'Malley and
Soley, 2000: 43). The code – which has since been updated and amended
according to votes at the union's conference, most recently in 2007 – was
incorporated into the union's rules. Members found guilty of breaking it
run the risk of being reprimanded, fined, or even expelled, though such
punishments have been extremely few and far between. Since 1986
union members have elected an Ethics Council to promote higher ethical standards by raising awareness of the code, and to hear complaints
against members alleged to have breached it (Frost, 2000: 224). This
'policing' role has proved to be controversial, as one leading member of
the NUJ pointed out: 'Journalists say they want a union to represent
them, not to tell them how to do their jobs' (quoted in Snoddy, 1992: 197).
In recent years, therefore, the Ethics Council has focused more on con-
sciousness-raising about ethical issues than on dealing with complaints,
with an NUJ spokesperson describing the union's code of conduct as 'a
beacon for journalists to aim for rather than a means to punish' (quoted
in Keeble, 2001: 15).

Self-regulation of the press

Journalists' own concerns about ethics also contributed to the creation of
the aforementioned Press Council – forerunner of the PCC – following the
Second World War (Griffiths, 2006: 304–309). It was the NUJ that lobbied
the post-war Labour government into setting up a Royal Commission on

the Press in 1947, and when the commission reported two years later it proposed the establishment of a General Council of the Press:

[T]o safeguard the freedom of the press; to encourage the growth of the sense of public responsibility and public service amongst all those engaged in the profession of journalism – that is, in the editorial production of newspapers – whether as directors, editors, or other journalists; and to further the efficiency of the profession and the well-being of those who practise it. (Quoted in Shannon, 2001: 10)

Such a council was duly established in 1953; dominated by newspaper editors and proprietors, it was described as 'informal, part-time, and cosy', with the right to deal with complaints but no power to punish (Shannon, 2001: 12). Its name was changed to the Press Council ten years later and, although its balance of membership was gradually tipped in favour of non-newspaper representatives, it eventually came to be regarded as a 'wholly ineffective' organisation that was treated with barely concealed contempt by many of the newspapers that it was meant to be leading towards the moral high ground (O'Malley and Soley, 2000: 79).

Such was the sorry state of press self-regulation when the lawyer David Calcutt QC was invited to peer through the opaque windows of the Last Chance Saloon and give his opinion on whether or not it was time for last orders to be called. His answer was: almost, but not quite. When the report of the Calcutt committee was published in 1990, in the wake of the Gordon Kaye affair discussed earlier, it recommended that a new self-regulatory complaints body be set up and given a probationary period of 18 months; if press excesses had not stopped by then, there should be statutory regulation (Griffiths, 2006: 387). Interestingly, one of the members of the Calcutt committee was a barrister by the name of David Eady who went on to become a judge – of whom more later (Campbell, 2008).

So the Press Council was disbanded and replaced by the Press Complaints Commission in 1991 with the task of warding off the danger – as the proprietors saw it – of a tougher regulatory regime and privacy legislation (Keeble, 2001: 16). Media lawyer Geoffrey Robertson (2008) has written that, if the old Press Council was 'toothless', the new PCC could be described as 'gumless'. The PCC covers both newspapers and magazines, plus the online content of websites run by newspaper and magazine publishers. It is paid for by a levy of the newspaper and periodical industries, collected by the Press Standards Board of Finance (Pressbof). The centrepiece of the PCC is a Code of Practice drawn up by a committee of editors under the chairmanship for many years of Les Hinton, executive chairman of Rupert Murdoch's News International. Since 2008 the committee has been chaired by Paul Dacre, editor of the *Daily Mail* – of whom, also more later.

Since its inception in 1991 the PCC has operated, essentially, as a form of customer complaints organisation. However, the 'customers' with a right to complain are not a newspaper's readers; rather, because the PCC will only rarely consider a complaint from a 'third party', the customers who can complain are those whose lives have been *personally* touched in some way by a reporter, a photographer or a sub. If, following a complaint, the PCC finds that a newspaper or magazine has breached its code, then that publication must publish an adjudication. Ian Beales, a former regional newspaper editor who helped draw up the code and now secretary to the code committee, explains the rationale behind the lack of any system of punishment:

> There are no fines or compensation, since these would inevitably involve lawyers, making the system legalistic, slow and expensive … Adverse adjudications are effective. Editors dislike having to publish them. It means their mistakes are exposed to their own readers, and often to criticism and ridicule in the columns of their commercial rivals, which is doubly damaging. (2005: 8)

Adjudications, however, are relatively scarce. A study of the PCC's first decade of operation shows that, of almost 23,000 complaints received, fewer than one in 25 were even adjudicated on (3.8 per cent), and just one complaint out of every 60 (1.6 per cent) was actually upheld (Frost, 2004: 106). That is a sure sign of a watchdog with no teeth, argue the PCC's critics, who range from journalist Nick Davies (2008) to Lord Justice of Appeal Stephen Sedley (2006). Not so, counter the PCC's supporters, who argue that, although adjudication is a last resort, the very existence of the code helps guide journalists through the ethical minefield they face every day. Its chairman, until 2009, Christopher Meyer, describes the PCC as offering 'flexible, mature regulation whose main aim is the delivery of practical and common-sense results' (PCC, 2007a: 1).

The PCC code in action

We will now examine how this system of self-regulation operates in practice, with all percentages of complaints taken from the PCC's annual report; the full PCC code is printed in the Appendix to this book; check www.pcc. org.uk for any updates. The very first of the code's 16 clauses concerns *accuracy*, which is the issue that invariably attracts most complaints to the PCC. Almost three-quarters (72.6 per cent) concern this clause, in which the press are exhorted to 'take care not to publish inaccurate, misleading or distorted information'; to distinguish between comment and fact; and to correct significant inaccuracies.

Anyone closely connected to a story that appears in the press will know from experience that inaccurate information can find its way into print disturbingly often. This happens for all sorts of reasons, only a few of them having anything to do with deliberate deception by journalists; more usually, the reasons are a combination of shortage of time, sources not yet knowing the full story, a failure to check assumptions, a misreading of notes, and simple misunderstandings. Some inaccuracies may cause mere annoyance while others will prompt outrage, but they all need to be taken seriously because the press is supposed to be in the business of providing information rather than misinformation. There are countless examples of such complaints in the PCC's archives. Take the following report – reprinted in its entirety – concerning an article in a local newspaper, the *Birstall News*:

COMPLAINT

Mr G George Demetriou, proprietor of a sandwich shop in Birstall called Bon Appetite, complained that the newspaper had inaccurately reported the following: that a dead rat and open holes had been found on his premises; and that his shop would remain permanently closed.

RESOLUTION

The complaint was resolved when the newspaper published the complainant's version of events which made the following clear: that a mouse, rather than a rat, was found on his premises; that the shop was closed for less than two days; that officers were satisfied that the shop was not a risk; that no holes were found in the shop; and that the pipes had now been sealed correctly. The complainant emphasised that Bon Appetite had been given the all clear and was open for business as usual. (PCC, 2006a: 29)

The above is an example of a complaint being resolved on the basis of conciliation, of the PCC 'breaking the deadlock between complainant and editor', as Ian Beales (2005: 10) puts it. But this does not always work. The *Burton Mail*, for example, ran a headline about a 'coach crash' over a report about traffic delays following a collision between a coach and a car. The coach firm, which was named in the story, complained on the grounds that the coach had not in fact hit anything and was stationary when it was itself hit by a car. The newspaper accepted this error of fact and pointed out in mitigation that the misleading information had been supplied by police. The editor subsequently reminded reporters to be especially careful when describing collisions but did not run an apology on the grounds that by that stage it had become an old story. With the door shut on its favourite tactic of conciliation, the PCC upheld a complaint against the *Burton Mail* for a failure to comply with Clause One of the code which requires significant inaccuracies to be corrected 'promptly and with due prominence' (PCC, 2006a: 5). As Ian Beales (2005: 16) observes: 'Care must be taken to minimise both errors and their impact. Mistakes may be inevitable, but it is important that they are put right swiftly and clearly'.

If mistakes did not occur there would be no need for Clause Two of the code to exist. This clause requires the press to provide a fair *opportunity for reply* to inaccuracies that have been published, and it accounted for 0.9 per cent of the complaints submitted in 2006. Typically, those who complain under this clause will also complain under Clause One, and that was the scenario for this case against the free newspaper *Metro*:

COMPLAINT

Mr Maxwell Rumney, Director of Legal & Business Affairs at September Films, complained that an article on the television programme *It's Now or Never,* which was produced by the company, contained inaccuracies and no right to reply had been afforded.

RESOLUTION

The complaint was resolved when the newspaper published the following letter from the complainant: 'Your article of July 27 ('Was this the worst idea for a TV show ever?') claimed that September Films – producers of the programme *It's Now or Never* – procured the commission for the show from ITV during 'boozy media executive lunches'. This is sheer fabrication. In fact, the show took over a year of development work and numerous sober meetings with ITV. In addition, the allegation that the show was 'not ... surprisingly ... one of the biggest flops ever seen on TV ... and was axed' was entirely inaccurate. An audience peaking at 1.9 million is hardly insignificant and the show and its format have sold throughout the world. In addition, ITV have announced that the show is to be rescheduled and are currently working with us on it. We have been attempting to correct these inaccuracies since the original article was published and you have now allowed us to make these points clear. (PCC, 2006a: 54)

The PCC code does not guarantee a *right* of reply; instead, it places an obligation on editors to provide an opportunity to reply when it is 'reasonably' called for and when an adequate opportunity to reply has not already been offered. Rather than an entitlement, the opportunity to reply to inaccuracies 'relies on what is reasonable in the circumstances, which is decided by the PCC' (Beales, 2005: 32).

Clause Three of the code, concerning *privacy*, attracted just over a tenth (10.8 per cent) of complaints in 2006. Although privacy complaints are always far fewer than ones about inaccurate reporting, privacy is one of the most controversial areas of the PCC's activities, not least because it is difficult for the press to *un*intrude once it has placed private information in the public domain. In 2007, for example, the *News of the World* ran a story headlined 'YOU LOVE BORAT', which concerned a man caught by his partner engaging in 'secret internet sexychat with a string of Kazakhstani beauties'. The story quoted emails sent by the man and obtained without his consent by his partner; the paper also published a picture of him semi-naked, taken from a webcam. In upholding the man's complaint under Clause Three, the PCC ruled:

This sort of intrusion would normally require a very strong public interest justification, something that was not a feature in this case. While the woman had a right to discuss their relationship, and clearly had strong views about the complainant and his behaviour, this was not sufficient to warrant publishing information taken from private emails to which the woman was not a party. In deciding how to balance the woman's right to free expression with the complainant's right to privacy, the editor had made an error of judgement. (PCC, 2007b: 14)

The paper may have had to publish the PCC's eventual critical ruling in the above case, but it had still enjoyed the commercial benefit of having run the story in the first place; the complainant may have won, but millions of people had already had the opportunity to read his 'sexychat' with little or nothing in the way of public interest to justify it. It is such cases that led critics of the PCC to argue that the most intrusive newspapers are the real winners even when they lose.

Clause Four covers *harassment* and concerns 4.3 per cent of complaints to the PCC. This was the clause used by Kate Middleton, currently the girl-friend of Prince William, to complain about the scrums of photographers following her down the street as she was simply going about her daily life. Her complaint to the PCC about the *Daily Mirror* was resolved after the newspaper published the following statement:

The *Daily Mirror* yesterday said 'we got it wrong' after Kate Middleton complained to the press watchdog about alleged harassment. Lawyers for Prince William's 25-year-old girlfriend contacted the Press Complaints Commission about a photograph. Editor Richard Wallace said: 'On Thursday we published an innocuous picture of Ms Middleton walking down the street with a cup of coffee. It was taken by a freelance photographer in circumstances where we were later told she felt harassed. We got it wrong and we sincerely regret that'. The PCC said it was still investigating. (PCC, 2007b: 35)

Its investigation in fact ceased as soon as Middleton's lawyers accepted the paper's expression of regret; the PCC then issued a statement reminding all editors of the need to comply with Clause Four of its code. The media scrums around Middleton certainly got smaller following this, but it was not clear if that was because of the PCC's warning or because her anticipated engagement to Prince William had failed to materialise.

Clause Five of the code requires enquiries into a person's *grief or shock* to be handled sensitively and for care to be taken not to include excessive detail when reporting suicides. It accounts for 4.7 per cent of complaints. Complaints were upheld against the *Wigan Evening Post* and the *Wigan Observer* when a widow alleged that articles about the inquest into her husband's suicide had contained too much detail of precisely how he had electrocuted himself. The PCC ruled:

The Commission agreed with the complainant that the newspapers had included too much detail in describing how the suicide happened. Inquests are held in public and newspapers are free to report their proceedings, but to abide by the terms of the code

... the papers should on this occasion have been less specific about the method used. By going into such detail, there was a danger that sufficient information was included to spell out to others how to carry out such a suicide. (PCC, 2007b: 21–22)

That was the first case to be adjudicated under the suicide element of the clause, which was added to the code during 2006, and the PCC took the opportunity 'to underline to all editors the importance of taking care over the reporting of suicide'.

The first five clauses of the PCC code discussed above accounted for 93.3 per cent of all complaints during 2006, which was a fairly typical year. The remaining 11 clauses were cited in just 6.7 per cent of complaints. The figures break down as follows: *Children* 2.1 per cent; *Children in sex cases* 0 per cent; *Hospitals* 0.6 per cent; *Reporting of crime* 0 per cent; *Clandestine devices and subterfuge* 0.5 per cent; *Victims of sexual assault* 0.1 per cent; *Discrimination* 2.6 per cent; *Financial journalism* 0.1 per cent; *Confidential sources* 0.5 per cent; *Witness payments* 0.1 per cent; *Payment to criminals* 0.1 per cent (PCC, 2007a: 5).

As we saw earlier, however, the PCC adjudicates on only a tiny number of the complaints it receives, which is one of the sticks with which it is habitually beaten by critics. Another is that, even when it upholds a complaint, publishing a PCC ruling is a mere 'pinprick' to the offending newspaper, in the words of Peter Wilby (2008a), another former editor now plying his trade as a media commentator. It is certainly a pinprick compared to the huge front-page 'sorry' to Kate and Gerry McCann in March 2008 over numerous stories suggesting they caused the death of their daughter Madeleine and then covered up their involvement; the grovelling apologies in the *Daily Express*, *Daily Star*, *Sunday Express* and *Daily Star Sunday* were accompanied by the payment of a reported £550,000 into the family's Madeleine Fund. Yet the PCC was a mere bystander in this case as the McCanns bypassed it to initiate legal proceedings for a defamation against the newspapers; the apologies and the payment were the result of an out-of-court settlement between the family and the Express Group. Former tabloid editor David Banks commented on the case:

> Everybody's calling for the heads of the editors, but when you get a group apology it strikes me that there's a group conspiracy. You don't get four editors on their own making the same mistake for 11 months. I don't think it's a terrible day for the press. It's a terrible day for the Press Complaints Commission – they've been left behind. (Quoted in *Press Gazette*, 2008)

The PCC has also been a bystander in the increasing number of cases in which people in the public eye have gone to court and argued that their privacy had been breached under the Human Rights Act of 1998 without any countervailing public interest justification. Many such cases – including one that went in favour of Formula One boss Max Mosley against the *News of the World*, which had revealed his involvement in a sado-masochistic orgy – have been heard by Mr Justice Eady. When still a barrister David Eady had been a member of the Calcutt committee that was critical of newspapers' ethical standards back in 1989–1990. As a High Court judge who presides over many privacy cases, he was famously accused by *Daily Mail* editor Paul Dacre of bringing in a privacy law by the backdoor because of his 'animus against the popular press'. Dacre, who had only recently become chairman of the PCC's code committee, told the Society of Editors' conference at the end of 2008:

> [I]nexorably, and insidiously, the British press is having a privacy law imposed on it, which – apart from allowing the corrupt and the crooked to sleep easily in their beds – is, I would argue, undermining the ability of mass-circulation newspapers to sell newspapers in an ever more difficult market. This law is not coming from parliament … but from the arrogant and amoral judgements – words I use very deliberately – of one man. I am referring, of course, to Justice David Eady who has, again and again, under the privacy clause of the Human Rights Act, found against newspapers and their age-old freedom to expose the moral short-comings of those in high places … Since time immemorial public shaming has been a vital element in defending the parameters of what are considered acceptable standards of social behaviour, helping ensure that citizens – rich and poor – adhere to them for the good of the greater community. For hundreds of years, the press has played a role in that process. It has the freedom to identify those who have offended public standards of decency – the very standards its readers believe in – and hold the transgressors up to public condemnation. If their readers don't agree with the defence of such values, they would not buy those papers in such huge numbers. Put another way, if mass-circulation newspapers … don't have the freedom to write about scandal, I doubt whether they will retain their mass circulations with the obvious worrying implications for the democratic process. Now some revile a moralis-ing media. Others, such as myself, believe it is the duty of the media to take an ethical stand. Either way, it is a choice but Justice Eady – with his awesome powers – has taken away our freedom of expression to make that choice. (Dacre, 2008)

Predictably, Dacre's 'ethical stand' attracted hostility not only from those lawyers who claimed he had misunderstood human-rights legislation (Robertson, 2008), but also from journalistic commentators who dismissed the claims of the *Daily Mail* or *News of the World* to occupy the moral high ground. For the *Guardian*'s Polly Toynbee, Dacre's brand of journalism is far more unethical and unsavoury than anything Max Mosley had been revealed to be doing in his spare time:

> The *Mail*'s mishmash of lurid scandal, bitching about women and random moralising zigzags all over the place, dishing out pain and praise often according to who it has suc-ceeded in buying with its limitless chequebook, or who has infuriated it by selling their wares to another bidder … Dacre – along with Rupert Murdoch in his different way – probably does more damage to the nation's happiness and wellbeing than any other sin-gle person, stirring up hatred, anger, fear, paranoia and cynicism with his daily images of a nation going to hell in a downward spiral of crime and depravity. (Toynbee, 2008)

We can be assured that the feeling is mutual. But the vehemence and resonance of such arguments demonstrate the continuing role that newspapers continue to play in the civic life of the UK, declining sales notwithstanding.

Taming the feral beast or vice versa?

Although it has been largely bypassed in the privacy cases that so irked Paul Dacre, the PCC seems to be here to stay for the foreseeable future. That is despite the fact that when Calcutt was invited to review its performance during its probationary period he concluded the PCC was so ineffective that it should be replaced by some kind of statutory complaints tribunal. The then Tory government rejected his call, and 'the light touch of self-regulation had triumphed over the heavy hand of legislation as the guiding principle for encouraging ethical press behaviour' (Sanders, 2003: 81–82). Since then various politicians have made occasional noises about toughening up the regulation of newspapers, and one of the last things Labour Prime Minister Tony Blair did before leaving Downing Street was to attack the press as behaving 'like a feral beast, just tearing people and reputations to bits' (quoted in *Press Gazette*, 2007a). When he was in power, however, Blair seemed much happier to wine, dine and woo powerful editors and proprietors than to challenge their behaviour. The passing on of power to Gordon Brown coincided with the publication of the results of a House of Commons Culture, Media and Sport Select Committee probe into the PCC and press self-regulation. The report concluded that there was no case for a broadcast-style statutory regulation of the press, and Prime Minister Brown speedily offered his endorsement of this hands-off approach. After all, unlike owners or editors, prime ministers have to stand for election; why would they choose to antagonise the very section of the media that has no requirement to be politically impartial and which, at the very least, helps to set the political agenda for the country?

For all the recurrent criticisms of the PCC as a toothless and even gumless watchdog, it has clearly played some role in helping to change the ethical climate in newsrooms. Even if editors approach the code with an attitude of 'What can we get away with?', that will still stop some of the worst excesses of the press happening quite so often. Awareness of the PCC code gives journalists a series of reference points by which they can measure – even change – their behaviour. This is highlighted by former crime reporter Steve Panter, who admits he used to get up to some pretty dodgy 'tricks of the trade' in the years before the PCC's code of practice began to be taken seriously in newsrooms. Tricks such as not showing a press card when knocking on the door of a victim or a relative, and allowing them to think he was a police officer; or using 'emotional blackmail' to persuade bereaved parents to talk by telling them it would be their fault if the paper got the story wrong: 'It was disgraceful behaviour, looking back. That's why the code is a good thing because, on reflection, I'm ashamed of that. But I was doing a job, my only instruction was to get the story' (quoted in Harcup, 2007: 96). Although such antics still go on at times, the PCC has helped make them less common. Yet to date the PCC has been unwilling to support those journalists who feel under pressure from editors to behave unethically, as we shall see below.

Not just cogs in the machine?

The deliberations of the PCC are not the only way in which the press is regulated. There is the law: most obviously the laws of defamation and of contempt of court in addition to the Human Rights Act. Then there is the phenomenon of the readers' editor, of which more below. And very, very occasionally a newspaper's own journalists may raise their voices – and risk their jobs – in a defence of ethics. For Mick Temple (2008: 138–139), this amounts to 'censorship by journalists'.

Such an incident occurred one night in the autumn of 2006, when ethical concerns suddenly emerged in what many regard as one of the least likely of locations: the editorial floor of the downmarket *Daily Star* newspaper, where staff journalists took a collective stand against what many saw as 'deliberately offensive' copy that made fun of Muslims. The cause for concern was a spoof version of a supposed Islamic *Daily Fatwah*, which claimed to demonstrate 'how Britain's fave newspaper would look under Muslim rule', promising a 'page three burka babes picture special' and offering a 'free beard for every bomber' (Burrell, 2006). Steve Usher, Father of the NUJ chapel at the *Daily Star*, later explained that he had been approached by concerned members of staff during the evening of 17 October 2006, as the page was about to be put to bed for the following morning's newspaper: 'They were very much against it because it would offend the Muslim community and affect the future of the paper. There could have been copies burnt, newsagents refusing to take the *Star* and many lost sales' (quoted in *Journalist*, 2006). Members of the NUJ in the newsroom at the time held an emergency chapel meeting and voted to express their concern at the 'deliberately offensive' copy. After news of the journalists' opposition was passed up the editorial chain, the page was pulled at the last minute. 'It was as if a light had suddenly come on and they saw what they were doing', said Usher. 'The guys who raised it did the company a huge favour' (quoted in *Journalist*, 2006).

Media commentator Stephen Glover (2006) felt that the newspaper's proprietor Richard Desmond 'should be grateful to have been saved by a bunch of NUJ rebels'. Not everyone agreed, as Temple notes:

> While a minority of staff felt that such interference by the NUJ went against principles of free speech, the NUJ responded that while the union would not ordinarily attempt to influence a paper's editorial stance, the content of the *Star*'s Fatwa Special was 'beyond the pale' and 'appalling' ... The down-market weekly lads magazine *Zoo* ran a similar feature – headlined 'Your all-new veil-friendly *Zoo*' – with no problems, perhaps illustrating the special power newspapers are assumed to have in influencing the public sphere. (Temple, 2008: 139)

That even a tits-and-bums newspaper such as the *Daily Star* can be discussed in terms of the public sphere, and be regarded as higher up the food chain than a tits-and-bums magazine such as *Zoo*, does indeed point to the continuing power of newspapers in the UK.

The episode prompted a *Press Gazette* columnist to ask rhetorically: '[W]hat was the NUJ chapel doing lobbying to get the page pulled? What the fuck has it got to do with them? ... The editor lives or dies by his or her own decisions. We are merely there to carry out the editor's wishes' (Grey Cardigan, 2006). But is that really all that journalists are there for, to obey orders whatever the wishes of the editor, or proprietor, might be? That is a common perception, notes Richard Keeble:

> Most newspaper operations are hierarchically organised with power to those (usually white men) at the top. Many lower down the pecking order often see themselves as impotent (and largely dispensable) cogs in a much larger machine. There is much talk of press freedom but little of the journalists' freedom to influence the organisation for which they work. (Keeble, 2006: 26–27)

Yet journalists on the *Daily Express* did exactly that – try to influence their own newspaper – when, through their NUJ chapel in 2001 and again in 2004, they publicly disassociated themselves from a series of 'inflammatory' headlines about asylum seekers and gypsies. The journalists had demonstrated that, as one put it, 'we are not the proprietors' stenographers' (quoted in Morgan, 2001). They also wrote to the PCC asking it to insert a 'conscience clause' into its code of practice, whereby journalists who refused unethical assignments would be protected from disciplinary action or dismissal (Harcup, 2007). The request was rejected because, in the words of the PCC's Professor Robert Pinker, 'it is not our job to become involved in disputes between employers and their staff' (quoted in Bayley and Macaskill, 2004: 17). The debate about such a clause continues.

A civilised conversation

Since 1997, the *Guardian* newspaper has pioneered the idea of a readers' editor (first Ian Mayes, now Siobhain Butterworth), who deals with complaints independent of the editor and who has a regular space in the paper to correct inaccuracies and discuss wider journalistic issues. Although the *Guardian* was not the first – the *Irish Times*, for example, has had a readers' representative in the editorial department since 1989 – it has arguably done the most to champion the role of a truly independent arbiter who cannot by sacked by the editor nor have his or her copy vetoed. More newspapers have since established corrections and clarifications columns and/or appointed people to deal with readers' complaints – the *Guardian* model has been adopted by the Danish daily *Politiken* and by the *Hindu* in India – but many are pale imitations struggling with newspapers' traditional reluctance to admit mistakes publicly.

The *Guardian*'s own research suggests that four out of five readers feel the existence of the readers' editor makes the paper more responsive to their views and opinions (Guardian News and Media, 2007: 24). Alan Rusbridger told the Society of Editors conference that appointing an independent readers' editor was 'the single most liberating thing I've done' during his lengthy stint as *Guardian* editor. That was partly because 'one of the most depressing things about being an editor is dealing with irate readers or people who think we have perpetuated some atrocity against them ... it's by and large better to hand it over to someone neutral who has nothing to defend'. But, if a desire to avoid such 'sticky conversations' was part of the motivation, it was only a minor part. The major motivation was because it seemed to be a way for the newspaper to win (back) the trust of readers:

> We exist as newspapers to get things right, to tell the truth as best we can. It's generally a bad thing to print things that are wrong, or which turn out to be wrong. We have great power. The havoc we can cause by getting things even slightly wrong is something we rarely admit, but we know we have it. So I came to the conclusion that we had some sort of obligation to have a daily and prominent space which would become part of the toolkit we use to get at – and report – the truth. (Rusbridger, 2002)

As Ian Mayes put it when addressing journalism students at the University of Sheffield, the existence of an independent readers' editor and a prominent corrections column increases rather than diminishes that lifeblood of journalism – trust:

> It is the only form of self-regulation that has the effect of increasing trust between readers and a specific publication. It is a conversation in civilised tones. Why should a newspaper that is constantly calling on others to be accountable not be accountable itself? (Mayes, 2006)

A civilised conversation is a fine thing, although it is often noticeable by its absence on some of the threads discussing ethical and other issues on newspaper blogs – where you are as likely to find personal abuse and accusations of hypocrisy as you are critical engagement or enlightenment. There is certainly plenty of scope for hypocrisy whenever newspaper ethics are discussed, as Ken Morgan, the last director of the old Press Council, reminds us:

> There is the hypocrisy of public figures, of course, presenting one face to their electorate and the world, but another in private; then there is the hypocrisy of editors claiming hand on heart that their invasion of privacy was executed solely in the serious public interest, never just to satisfy prurient appetites and boost circulations. And finally there is the hypocrisy of offended members of the public who will roundly condemn newspaper excesses and intrusions each night but still go out in millions next morning to buy and read avidly more of the same. (Morgan, 2007: 11)

Morgan's words prompt the question: does society get the press it deserves? When some of the lowest forms of journalism are rewarded with some of the highest circulation figures, it does appear that bottom line economics result in the ethics of the bottom line. This potential conflict between that which is in the public interest and that which merely interests the public is seen most sharply when so-called investigative journalists start poking their noses into other people's affairs – as will be examined in the next chapter.

8

DIGGING DEEPER: INVESTIGATIVE
JOURNALISM IN NEWSPAPERS

It was a clash of the Titans – a rumble in the Fleet Street jungle. In the red corner was 'Gorgeous' George Galloway, the tough-talking political street fighter from Dundee. In the blue corner was Mazher 'Fake Sheikh' Mahmood, a man said to be capable of smooth talking everyone from minor royals to millionaire football managers. Galloway, the left-wing Member of Parliament for Bethnal Green and Bow in London, had been invited to dine with two Muslim businessmen at the Dorchester; afterwards he claimed they had made anti-semitic remarks and had offered secret funds to his political party. He smelled a rat and within days was boasting to anyone who would listen that he had foiled a *News of the World* sting operation. For its part, the newspaper confirmed that Mahmood had indeed been one of the fake businessmen at the meal, but also argued that its star investigator had been carrying out 'wholly legitimate inquiries'. Galloway then turned the tables on the secretive Mahmood by posting photographs of him on the internet, prompting the *News of the World* to rush to court in an ultimately futile attempt at preventing publication of his image (Silver, 2006).

Although Mahmood (2008: 294) denied the accusations about anti-semitic comments and later explained that the outspoken MP had not even been the prime target of the investigation, it was Round 1 to Galloway. Despite his earlier apparently bizarre decision to expose himself to ridicule on the TV programme *Celebrity Big Brother*, Galloway now appeared to be winning the battle of public opinion. He was cheered on from a ringside seat by one of those dismissed by Mahmood (2008: 9) as 'media commentators who sit in their armchairs and pontificate on our investigations'. That would be Roy Greenslade, one-time tabloid journalist and briefly editor of the *Daily Mirror*, now the media commentator's media commentator and in his spare time a Professor of Journalism at City University in London. Greenslade accused the *News of the World* in general and Mahmood in particular of using methods that 'debase journalism'. He described subterfuge as 'the most controversial weapon in journalism's armoury ... that should be used sparingly because it can too easily be abused', and continued:

> Though the *News of the World* consistently points to the (alleged) fact that Mahmood has been responsible for the jailing of 130 people, defence lawyers have regularly sought to show that their clients have been victims of elaborate sting operations ... It encourages bad journalistic behaviour. It's hardly any wonder that journalists are held in such low esteem by the people they purport to represent and that the sales of the scandalous redtops appear to be in free-fall. (Greenslade, 2006)

In free-fall their circulation figures may be, but newspapers that specialise in exposing scandals connected to sex and drugs and rock'n'roll still sell millions more copies than do those whose investigative journalism is restricted to more mundane matters of political or financial impropriety. As Greenslade (2008: 335) later noted, Mahmood 'set the investigative standard for Britain's popular papers from the mid-1990s onwards'. Scandal-mongering titles are often honoured by their peers, with shagging and snorting stories frequently picking up Scoop of the Year gongs at journalism awards. And, over the years, Mazher Mahmood has given the *News of the World* some of its proudest moments, such as when a TV actor was jailed for supplying illegal drugs to an Arabian prince who turned out to be you-know-who. He defends his work as being in the public interest:

> Subterfuge is a legitimate and basic tool of investigative journalism, and the Fake Sheikh is just one of a whole range of personas that I adopt to infiltrate targets; I am just as likely to turn up as an asylum seeker, a taxi driver, or worker from a building site ... Without going undercover my colleagues and I would have no hope of exposing drug dealers, paedophiles and the like. After all, nobody would offer to sell me drugs or weapons if I proudly announced that I am a reporter from the *News of the World*. (Mahmood, 2008: 8)

Whether or not his investigations are always in the public interest, they frequently seem to interest large numbers of the public. Who could forget the 'Toongate tapes' of 1998 when Newcastle United directors were secretly recorded in a Spanish brothel as they boasted of their sexploits, disparaged their own club's supporters, mocked their star footballer as acting like Mary Poppins and dismissed all Geordie women as 'dogs'? Three years later Mahmood recorded the Countess of Wessex apparently using her royal connections for the benefit of her public-relations firm and describing the prime minister's wife as 'horrid, horrid, horrid'. Then in January 2006 Mahmood posed as an Arab businessman and lured England football coach Sven-Goran Eriksson to Dubai to discuss a supposed multi-million pound deal; once again the conversation was taped and once again it included indiscretions about the players then under Eriksson's charge, which made for entertaining if hardly earth-shattering Sunday morning reading (MacDonald, 2006).

Things do not always go to plan, however. Five alleged plotters were arrested and charged after Mahmood wrote about a 2002 plot to kidnap the Beckhams' children, but the case was later thrown out when a court found the newspaper's informant to be unreliable (Greenslade, 2006; MacDonald, 2006). And in the summer of 2006, not long after his spat with Galloway, Mahmood's methods were subjected to further public scrutiny when a jury cleared three men of plotting to buy radioactive material for a 'dirty bomb' (Vasagar, 2006). This time the *News of the World*'s man posed as a potential seller of 'red mercury', which was described by the paper as 'a deadly substance developed by cold war Russian scientists for making briefcase nuclear bombs' (Vasagar, 2006). Mahmood worked closely with the police to investigate whether the alleged plotters might be interested in buying the material, but the subsequent court case saw the three men acquited on charges of conspiring to fund terrorism and conspiring to possess an article for terrorist purposes. After a three-month trial, costing an estimated £1 million, the trio's defence solicitors said in a victory statement: 'This is a great tribute to the jury system and English justice and a dark day for the *News of the World*' (Vasagar, 2006).

Coming so soon after the Eriksson and Galloway escapades, this dark day prompted some soul-searching among those concerned with ethical journalism. But there was little evidence of soul-searching from Mahmood (2008: 97–101) – who 'took orders' from police who 'even read my story, and made minor amendments' – when he rejected the criticism of 'media commentators-cum-vultures … who have never undertaken an investigation in their lives'. Journalism studies professor Peter Cole was one of those unimpressed by the story at the time:

> The words 'red mercury' set alarm bells ringing. In the 1980s, the *Sunday Times* spent much time and effort investigating claims about this allegedly fearsome chemical. The paper found no evidence of its existence, nor has any other reliable authority since. Yet tales of 'red mercury' continue to be hawked around by snake-oil salesmen and 'investigative reporters' … The crux of the debate, it seems to me, is what comes first – the story or the fake sheikh? Journalism should be asking the questions and exposing the corruption of those who want things kept quiet. Journalism should investigate the tip-offs of whistle-blowers. It should not lead targets into temptation. Journalism is not about entrapment, about setting up the sting and hoping the target walks into the trap. That way, the journalist is a player in the story, not a reporter. Nor, I think, is it about working on joint ventures with the police. It is about working independently and then, if appropriate, presenting the police with the results of that probe. (Cole, 2006)

It is true that such qualms tend to be uttered by those with a background in broadsheet or 'quality' newspapers – the papers dismissed by many tabloid hacks as the unpopulars, the ones that nobody reads – rather than by people with personal experience of executing tabloid-style sting operations. Does that fact indicate that such concerns can simply be dismissed as newspaper snobbery by armchair critics, or does it reveal the problematic and contested nature of investigative journalism itself? That is among the questions to which we now turn.

Prurience or revelation?

Judging by the tone of his book *Confessions of a Fake Sheikh*, Mazher Mahmood (2008) has few if any doubts about either his job or his methodology, and it cannot be denied that he has exposed some real villains and lowlifes in his time. Despite expressions of disquiet from editors whose newspapers have only a fraction of its circulation, the *News of the World* has continued to stand by its star man. Editor Colin Myler boasted to the 2007 Society of Editors conference that Mahmood's investigations had resulted in 230 criminal convictions to date. Intriguingly, he added that in future there would be fewer stories about celebrities taking drugs or engaging in other forms of misbehaviour because 'I think there are other issues out there he should be looking at – issues that affect our daily life and society' (quoted in *Press Gazette*, 2007b). Yet less than two weeks later Mahmood's byline appeared beneath the headline: 'SNORTY, SNORTY SOPHIE! CELEB STAR SOPHIE ANDERTON IS £10k HOOKER AND COKE DEALER' (*News of the World*, 18 November 2007). The story resulted from a classic redtop sting operation with the added bonus that, in this converged media age, users of the newspaper's website could watch secretly filmed video clips such as 'Model demands £15k a day for sex with her and another girl' and 'Celeb star Sophie strips for sex'. These clips attracted 'the largest number of hits since our website was launched', Mahmood (2008: 165) later boasted.

Elsewhere on the site, in relation to a not dissimilar tale, there is even a video clip knowingly entitled 'Our reporter makes his excuses and leaves' (http://www.newsoftheworld.co.uk/videoplayer/index.php). And, in evidence that user-generated content does not always enhance the quality of debate within the public sphere, there is the ubiquitous 'Your Comments' facility. Typical comments on a story about an alleged '£2,000-a-night hooker', who may or may not have had an on-off relationship with a footballer, included: 'I'd easy pay that 2 bang her, she's well fit' (http://www.newsoftheworld.co.uk/news/article30624.ece).

This is all good, not very clean, fun except for those being 'exposed' and their families, but is it what investigative journalism is supposed to be about? Can it really be called 'journalism at its most politically vigorous and methodologically rigorous', as investigative reporting has been characterised by US scholars James Ettema and Theodore Glasser (2007: 491)? Should it even be spoken of in the same breath as the work of Anna Politkovskaya, whose reports for a small-circulation Russian newspaper exposed human-rights abuses and attracted numerous death threats before she was shot dead in 2006? Hers was not an isolated death; Politkovskaya was one of an estimated 20 Russian journalists to have been killed or to have died in suspicious circumstances since the year 2000 (Osborn, 2007). She knew the risks but, whenever friends or family suggested she might stop making enemies with her investigative reporting, she replied: 'How could I live with myself if I didn't write the truth?' (quoted in Specter, 2007). Politkovskaya was 'marginalised at home but honoured internationally', writes David Finkelstein (2008: 130–132), who observes that: 'Holding political and corporate institutions to account in a complex world takes courage and dedication, particularly when vested interests use extreme measures to silence reporters'.

There are no doubt plenty of people who would like to silence – or at least take revenge on – the Fake Sheikh too, which is one of the reasons the *News of the World* gave for trying to prevent publication of photographs of him. And before we get too high and mighty about what qualifies for the term 'investigative journalism', we should remember that newspapers in particular have long operated at the edges of taste and decency. Some investigative journalists now exalted as role models were themselves once accused of sexual prurience; William Stead, for example, who began the long tradition of journalists going undercover. In 1885, when editor of the *Pall Mall Gazette*, Stead exposed the hitherto hidden existence of child prostitution in Victorian England by posing as a punter and 'buying' a 13-year-old virgin girl. The story, which he ran under the heading 'THE MAIDEN TRIBUTE OF MODERN BABYLON', scandalised polite society and boosted the paper's circulation (Snoddy, 1992: 46–49). Stead was arrested and served two months in prison before eventually helping to persuade parliament to increase the age of heterosexual consent from 13 to 16 years (Clarke, 2004: 259). But that didn't stop him being denounced by the rival *Standard* newspaper for publishing 'the most offensive, highly-coloured and disgusting details ... which appeals to the lascivious curiosity of every casual passer-by, and excites the latent pruriency of a half-educated crowd' (quoted in Clarke, 2004: 261).

The Maiden Tribute investigation set a pattern that would be followed in many subsequent exposes by the British press, according to Hugo de Burgh:

Stead changed the style of reporting by conjoining high moral tone with sensational description, the favoured style of many newspapers in Britain today. Stead got attention not only by prurience, but also by revelation. That this kind of trade existed was almost certainly news to most of his readers. His undercover, investigative style was premonitory ... His story was talked of everywhere and commented upon by innumerable other papers, circulation rose and touts sold copies at two hundred times the asking price. Investigative journalism had been invented ... (2008: 45)

The undercover tradition continues today not merely in the stings so beloved of the *News of the World* but also in ostensibly more serious investigations. Probably the most high-profile example of the past decade saw the *Daily Mirror* publish on its front page a photograph of its reporter Ryan Parry standing on the balcony of Buckingham Palace, with the headline: 'INTRUDER – AS BUSH ARRIVES, WE REVEAL MIRRORMAN HAS BEEN A PALACE FOOTMAN FOR TWO MONTHS IN THE BIGGEST ROYAL SECURITY SCANDAL EVER' (19 November 2003). Parry had tricked his way into the job by using a mixture of real and fake references while hiding his true occupation as a journalist, and he later explained the justification for such deception:

> We set out to test security. It was about testing security at the palace at a time of terrorist threat. Post 9/11 there is always a terrorist threat and there is clearly a fear in the royal household. All we did was test out their recruitment system, which should be airtight and which should have checked my friends, my family and my finances ... At the end of the day it was a security issue. Any terrorist wanting to plant a bomb in the palace wouldn't think twice about lying to a personnel officer. It was a security issue, so it was hugely in the public interest. (Quoted in Harcup, 2007: 35–36.)

Not so, according to critics such as Greenslade (2008a: 337), who dismissed the *Mirror*'s palace coup as 'pseudo-investigative journalism, a cheap and easy substitute for the real thing'.

The public interest

The issue of the public interest arises time after time in the fall-out from investigative journalism. As former *News of the World* reporter Gerry Brown wrote in his entertaining, revealing and unreconstructed memoirs: 'Don't complain to me about invasion of privacy. If it's in the public interest, I prefer to call it invasion of secrecy' (Brown, 1995: 315). The Press Complaints Commission defines the public interest in the following terms:

1. The public interest includes, but is not confined to:
    i) Detecting or exposing crime or serious impropriety.
    ii) Protecting public health and safety.
    iii) Preventing the public from being misled by an action or statement of an individual or organisation.
2. There is a public interest in freedom of expression itself.
3. Whenever the public interest is invoked, the PCC will require editors to demonstrate fully how the public interest was served.

4. The PCC will consider the extent to which material is already in the public domain, or will become so.
5. In cases involving children under 16, editors must demonstrate an exceptional public interest to over-ride the normally paramount interest of the child. (www.pcc.org. uk/cop/practice.html)

Redtop editors often invoke the public-interest defence to justify exposing the alleged misbehaviour of celebrities – arguing that these people are supposed to be role models for impressionable youngsters, for example – but Piers Morgan later admitted that, during his editorship of the *News of the World*, 'most of the time the public interest defence was trumped-up nonsense' (quoted in Hattenstone, 2005). That may have been the case, but the concept of the public interest remains a useful yardstick by which to measure less frivolous newspaper investigations. And they don't get much less frivolous than the *Sunday Times*' coverage of the Thalidomide babies, which has passed into legend as a classic of the genre.

Around 450 children were born with missing limbs in 1960 and 1961 and the common factor was that their mothers had all taken the sleeping pill Thalidomide when pregnant (Greenslade, 2003a: 276–278). The drug was withdrawn from sale and the company that had marketed it in the UK, Distillers, quietly paid small amounts of compensation to families who dropped legal claims of negligence. There were a few newspaper stories about the episode during the 1960s but it was only in the early 1970s that the *Sunday Times*' Insight team, set up by editor Harold Evans, launched a major investigation into the whole affair. Because legal cases were still outstanding, the paper's campaign concentrated on the moral issues – 'the Thalidomide children shame Distillers' – rather than risk contempt of court by publishing too much about the legal complexities of specific cases, yet the drugs company succeeded in imposing injunctions that prevented the *Sunday Times* from telling the full story until years later. The paper stuck with the investigation as much as it could in such circumstances and its persistence gradually resulted in something of a public outcry against Distillers. Edward Heath's government decided to set up a trust fund for victims and to initiate a royal commission to consider the issue of damages for personal injuries, as Greenslade recalls:

> Then the *Sunday Times* published a list of the holders of Distillers shares, and scores of them, including insurance companies and merchant banks, added to the public pressure. Distillers finally agreed in January 1973 to pay £20 million, to compensate the families, almost ten times the original offer. Evans was not content to leave it there. He pursued the matter of the legal gags which had inhibited press freedom, eventually winning two historic judgements. The injunction was finally lifted in June 1976, and the *Sunday Times* immediately published the article it had prepared four years before. It wasn't until April 1979 that the European Court of Human Rights overturned a House of

Lords decision that to publish the original article would have been a contempt of court ...
In the following years, the successful outcome of the campaign, along with the legal vic-
tories, ensured that the *Sunday Times* and, most especially, Evans himself were crowned
with glory. It came to be viewed as a triumph for both investigative reporting and campaigning journalism, as powerful an incentive to would-be reporters as the 1970s
Watergate scandal was in the United States. (Greenslade, 2003a: 277)

However, some of the journalists involved later reflected on whether the
investigation really justified all the herograms and plaudits it attracted, as
Phillip Knightley records:

It has taken me twenty years to face up to the fact that the *Sunday Times* Thalidomide campaign was not the great success it was made out to be ... [When] some of us get together
and look back at the fight on behalf of the children we end up discussing two crucial questions: Did we do it right? Would it have been better to have kept out of the whole affair? ...
To start with, some of the parents found the exposure in the press a painful experience ...
Next, there was discontent over the way the compensation was paid ... Disturbing stories
of greed and envy began to emerge. (Knightley, 1998: 155–178)

Despite such soul-searching, most journalists who were around at the time
would undoubtedly agree with Greenslade (2003a: 278) in declaring the
investigation a 'journalistic triumph'. As the years have gone by, the episode
has seemingly gained rather than diminished in importance as journalists,
commentators and academics compare contemporary investigations with the
Thalidomide one, and frequently find that modern versions tend to pale in
comparison. That is partly because, in addition to the legal risks involved, pursuit of the Thalidomide story required a huge investment of both time and
resources. It was also a classic example of the team approach adopted by the
Sunday Times under Evans's editorship. Today Insight tends to be seen as an
example of a bygone age when '*Sunday Times* reporters could spend whatever
time and money they needed in order to get their story' (Davies, 2008: 295);
a time when serious newspapers were prepared to throw serious staff and
serious money at serious investigations, the likes of which we will probably
not see again. According to Stephen Dorril, investigative journalism enjoyed
'a brief bloom in the sixties, flowered for a short period in the seventies, badly
wilted in the eighties and is now effectively dead' (Dorril, 2000).

Not that everyone was quite so impressed by Insight in any event. Paul
Foot, for example, argued that, 'the legend of the old *Sunday Times*, its editor Harry Evans and its investigative Insight column is, like most legends,
hideously exaggerated' (Foot, 1999: 80). Foot himself became something of
a legendary figure as an investigative journalist for both *Private Eye* and the
Daily Mirror. Indeed, he was sacked by the latter for daring to investigate
goings-on at the paper itself; unsurprisingly, this was one story readers did
not see in the *Mirror*. However, although he clearly was one, Foot did not

approve of the term investigative journalist, as he explained: 'It's a complete fraud, the idea that there is race apart called investigative journalists. An ordinary reporter doing a perfectly ordinary story carries out these functions, the difference would be the enthusiasm and the scepticism with which you approach something' (quoted in Harcup, 2004: 77).

Foot became synonymous with investigations into alleged miscarriages of justice. He described how he went about probing the case of four men wrongly jailed for the murder of newspaper delivery boy Carl Bridgewater:

> I started writing about it in 1980. Ann Whelan, whose son was convicted, wrote to me at the *Mirror* a very moving letter. My initial feeling was, 'What mother wouldn't say that her son was innocent?' So it was some time before I went up there. But I went up to Birmingham and met her and her family. I wasn't convinced to begin with because it was a horrible murder and there was *some* evidence against them, there was a confession. It took quite a lot of time before I became in any way convinced, but I did become absolutely convinced, and as I did so I wrote with more and more certainty. Ann found witnesses who said, 'I told a pack of lies, I didn't realise how important it was'. But mostly it was just going over the evidence that had been presented in court against them, reading depositions, the judge's summing up and so on, talking to everyone involved. There were things showing they were somewhere else at the time, that somebody else had done the murder, it just went on and on. I must have written at least 30 articles in the *Mirror*. Eventually the men were released in 1997. The *Mirror* subs would joke, 'Here comes the man who supports the murder of newspaper boys', and occasionally the editor would say, 'Oh Christ, you're not doing this again are you?' But the repetition is absolutely crucial because it encourages other sources to come forward. (Quoted in Harcup, 2004: 77)

Paul Foot is no longer with us but, despite what the harshest critics of the press would have us believe, investigative journalism in the public interest has not vanished.

Investigative journalism in the press today

We saw earlier that the Fake Sheikh costume has not yet been hung up and that celeb stings remain a staple of the Sunday tabloids. We also heard claims that Thalidomide-style investigative reporting is now largely a thing of the past. So is that effectively it for serious investigative journalism in the press? Have the beancounters succeeded in killing it off, as feared by Nick Davies in his bleak (2008) assessment of the industry, *Flat Earth News*? Far from it, in fact. Following Foot's death in 2004, an annual award in his name was set up by *Private Eye*, the *Guardian* and the National Union of Journalists to help keep alive the spirit of investigative journalism within the UK press. In November 2008 the judges announced a record entry for the award and split the first prize between *Private Eye* journalist Richard Brooks, for a probe into government financial irregularities, and Camilla Cavendish of the *Times*, who investigated the workings of the Children Act 1989.

The previous year's award had also been shared between two investigations. One, by David Leigh and Rob Evans of the *Guardian*, concerned bribery and corruption in the British arms trade. The story included Swiss bank accounts, alleged cover-ups and one of the world's most powerful corporations, BAE. Leigh and Evans's story resulted in criminal investigations on three continents, an international probe into the UK under an anti-bribery treaty and the removal of an Attorney-General. In addition to a series of stories in the *Guardian* newspaper, which prompted several debates in parliament, the investigation was also the focus of an innovative area on the newspaper's website. The *BAE Files* site took several months to build and enables anyone to have access to hundreds of the original documents used by journalists to piece together events; it also includes video and audio clips of key players in the saga along with interactive maps, graphics, pictures of the weapons involved and an archive of all BAE stories, demonstrating how print and online journalism can be combined to great effect when the necessary time and resources are invested (http://www.guardian.co.uk/baefiles). For Charlie Beckett, a former journalist who now runs the Polis thinktank at the London School of Economics, the *BAE Files* website is a classic example of what he terms 'networked journalism'. He explains:

> It has the potential to reform the whole way investigative journalism works ... There is no substitute for giving investigative journalists more time and having faith in their ability to get results from digging deeper and researching more widely. But the internet and other new technology can help. Websites with the crowd-sourcing potential of the *BAE Files* can push the story along by encouraging other journalists or the public to feed back information into their newsroom about this or other similar stories of global corruption. (Beckett, 2008: 151–152)

Leigh and Evans are not the only ones keeping alive the flame of serious investigative reporting in our newspapers. This was demonstrated when the pair shared the 2007 award with a journalist from much lower down the media food chain: Deborah Wain of the *Doncaster Free Press*, one of the vast empire of local and regional newspapers owned by Johnston Press, a company not normally renowned for investing in investigative journalism. Wain showed what a tenacious and sceptical local journalist can achieve even without the backup of an investigative team, a big budget, or in-house lawyers, when she turned her attention to a multi-million pound project called Doncaster Education City. The award judges said that Wain's 18-month investigation revealed that the highest capita-spending education scheme in England and Wales had turned into 'a costly fiasco' involving 'a truly shocking story of self-interest, greed and ineptitude' (Hold the Front Page, 2007).

In the course of her investigation Wain made extensive use of the Freedom of Information (FOI) Act 2000, which only became fully operational on 1 January 2005. Since that date newspaper journalists have used it to uncover countless stories – from the trivial to the disturbing – that would otherwise have remained secret. Examples include:

- The *Lincolnshire Echo* revealed the fact that Lincolnshire police dealt with 3,399 incidents in a sample week yet told the media about just 23 incidents (Hold the Front Page, 2006).
- The *Guardian* exposed the way the Foreign Office sought to cover up evidence of handwritten mentions of Israel in the first draft of the UK government's notorious dossier on Iraq's supposed weapons of mass destruction (Norton-Taylor, 2008).
- The fraud trial of a former mayor and mayoress cost taxpayers almost £200,000 in court costs, discovered the *Crosby Herald* (Hold the Front Page, 2008).
- The *Sunday Times* found that an environment minister claimed a mileage allowance of more than £4,000 for driving his private car 10,852 miles around his constituency, even though he was a London MP with an official car and lived just 12 miles away (Ungoed-Thomas and Bessaoud, 2007).
- Ian Paisley Junior resigned as a minister in the Northern Ireland administration after the *Belfast Telegraph* revealed irregularities over his constituency office rental expenses (Gordon, 2008).
- The *Observer* obtained the list of people who were wined and dined by Tony Blair at public expense at Chequers, the prime minister's country retreat; they ranged from Spice Girl Geri Halliwell to journalism professor Ian Hargreaves (Barnett, 2005).
- The *Express and Star* newspaper uncovered the fact that 35 West Midlands police officers were arrested in just one year for offences including assault, shoplifting and drink driving (Hold the Front Page, 2008).

It is far too early to tell how press use of FOI will develop over time, although it is likely that, as journalists become more adept at making use of the legislation, public authorities will become more skilled at evading it. Even from its initial impact, however, two trends can be discerned: one positive, one negative. First the good news. Submitting FOI requests to public authorities is now increasingly seen as a part of 'normal' journalism and not just something for anoraks or investigative specialists; if this increases the quantity of fresh information uncovered and strengthens the idea that investigation can inform *all* reporting, then that can only be positive for journalism. The potential downside is that, because it can be relatively painless for an individual journalist to uncover information using FOI, it perhaps encourages the reliance on cheap and easy 'exclusives' at the expense of more sustained investigations. Not every document once labelled 'confidential' is necessarily interesting or important and not every story can be properly understood or analysed by obtaining a quick snapshot of information. If newspapers' enthusiasm for FOI stories discourages them from also investing time and resources into more painstaking work, then that would be a far from healthy development.

For the most part, newspaper investigations are less dramatic than the undercover exploits of Mahmood or Parry described earlier yet more time-consuming than banging in an FOI request and turning the results into a splash. More typical investigations involve the meticulous cross-referencing of information strands, poring over piles of documents or trawling computer databases, searching for the right people, and persuading them to talk; it can also be about nurturing and protecting confidential sources of information, also known as 'whistleblowers'. As experienced press investigator Jonathan Calvert puts it: 'Some stories you make five calls on, some twenty. When you are making a hundred, that's investigative journalism' (quoted in de Burgh, 2008: 17). Journalism educator Mark Hanna (2008: 163) adds that, 'however useful databases are, the crucial "intelligence" is more likely to come from speaking to someone'.

Investigative reporting, then, is about attitude and effort as much as it is about using specific skills. According to David Spark, it typically involves journalists taking the following steps:

- Get to the facts at the heart of an issue – don't be content with spokesmen's comments.
- Explain difficult concepts – don't write around them.
- Don't just echo the views of your main source – find other sources with other views.
- Speak to as many relevant people as possible.
- Ask the simple and obvious questions which open out the subject.
- Don't take everything and everyone at their face value.
- Remember that everyone, every organisation and every event has a history which may have a bearing on what is happening now. (Spark, 1999: xii)

Spark lays great stress on finding other sources rather than relying on just one, and academic research underlines the importance of this because, according to a study by Mark Feldstein (2007: 505), 'many investigative reporters end up serving essentially as publicists for their sources, figuratively embedded with them in much the same way as war correspondents are sheltered by protective soldiers in the midst of combat'.

Guerrilla tactics

With investigative journalism, as with so much of journalism, context is crucial. As we have seen earlier, the sort of reporting that might be greeted with an indifferent shrug in one country runs the risk of attracting an assassin's bullet in another. Yet there are journalists who continue to dig around, find things out, and publish the results to a wider public, even in the most unpromising of contexts. A study by Jingrong Tong (2007) has traced some of the ways in which Chinese journalists, led by the newspaper *Nanfang Dushi Bao* (the *Southern Metropolis Daily*), have developed an investigative tradition in recent years, 'reporting on social issues and dodgy doings by local officials'. She refers to journalists' use of 'guerrilla reporting tactics' to get around official censorship and other constraints in China. One of their key tactics is knowing how far to go and which elements are taboo: '[J]ournalists can subvert bans and circumvent minefields by avoiding the most sensitive aspects of banned events and seeking safer – but perhaps deeper – themes instead ... [This] does not mean that journalists must avoid all risky topics, but rather must exercise careful judgement in search of potentially success-ful strategies' (Tong, 2007: 531). Another tactic is careful 'writing between the lines', as she explains:

> The best way to keep a report safe is to avoid overt expressions of value or opinion and to weave the meaning of events into the presentation of facts. Nonetheless, journalists use a variety of discursive tactics such as the implication of causal agency and the description of meaningful detail to suggest viewpoints that would annoy the authorities if indicated fully and clearly. (Tong, 2007: 534)

Given the propensity of the authorities in China to lock up awkward journalists, the use of the word 'annoy' in the above passage is either a glo-rious understatement or itself an example of a guerrilla tactic at work. Similar guerrilla tactics have been adopted in Zimbabwe, Nigeria and other African countries in which journalists do their best to 'keep the adversarial, watchdog and agenda-setting roles alive in rather harsh conditions' (Mudhai, 2007: 541; also Ojo, 2007). And so it is in much of the world. Yet even in western democracies journalists can find such tactics useful. After all, didn't the *Sunday Times* try to circumvent the constraints of the law with its Thalidomide investigation? And, even at the height of his lengthy and lauded investigative stint at the *Daily Mirror*, Paul Foot pinned to the wall a list of the owner's friends – not so that he could avoid investigating them, but so he could ensure that any story about anyone on the list was already copper-bottomed before proprietor Robert Maxwell got to hear about it. Foot recalled: 'You have to have the story sewn up and prepared for when Maxwell says, 'Are you sure this is right?' But we got most of the stuff published' (quoted in Harcup, 2004: 14).

Tribune of the commoner

Foot did indeed get his investigations published and many newspaper jour-nalists around the world continue to do so today – sometimes ducking and diving, mostly metaphorically but some literally – despite the fact that many face far greater risks than the wrath of a bullying proprietor or an injunction from a judge roused from his slumbers. Anyone who glances at the front page splashes of the UK's popular newspapers on most Sunday mornings could be forgiven for despairing at the apparent pointlessness of so much of it. But, as the examples of Anna Politkovskaya and others have demonstrated, that's not the way it's got to be. Journalists can still 'act as the moral conscience of society' by 'exposing what others dare not' (Finkelstein, 2008: 130), and that which is typically labelled 'investigative journalism' remains one of the key ways in which that can be done. Therefore, notwithstanding its contested nature and despite the fact that it will mean different things in different contexts – geographically, over time, and across different media markets – investigative reporting remains central to the purpose of newspaper journalism.

As a job title or a self-description, 'the term "investigative journalist" smacks of pretension, and has few ardent adherents among practitioners', argues investigator-turned-journalism-lecturer Mark Hanna (2005: 122–123). He continues: 'But it helps denote the self-motivation, the experience and knowledge, the methodology and the set of skills which sustain a journalist through a complex, lengthy assignment … [I]nvestigations are expensive, because of staff time and research outlay, yet may not uncover anything to publish'. Whether or not we like the term investigative journalism, for journalists and academics alike it retains its currency and symbolic importance as an exemplar of what *all* good journalism ought to be about: a fourth estate, or watchdog, informing the public sphere. Such concepts, which will be discussed in more depth in the following chapter, should be at the heart of discussions about journalism. And, for Hugo de Burgh (2000: 315), the investigative journalist plays the most vital democratic role as 'the tribune of the commoner, exerting on her or his behalf the right to know, to examine and to criticise'. Such fine words might indeed smack of pretension, but that does not mean they have no validity; and if newspapers ever abandon their quest to find things out on behalf of their readers, then the press might just as well be dead.

Part III
Making Sense of Newspapers

9

HACKS AND THE ACADEMY:
THEORISING JOURNALISM

Studying the media is a Mickey Mouse subject, suitable only for wasters and charlatans. We know that because the media keep telling us so. The phrases 'media studies' and 'Mickey Mouse' are used together so frequently that it is a wonder the Disney corporation hasn't placed the matter in the hands of M'Learned Friends. For Tim Luckhurst (2008), a journalist turned academic, media studies is rightly thought of as 'a debased catch-all, ridiculed in newsrooms everywhere'. As veteran Fleet Street editor Richard Stott (2007: 78) admitted when faced with the latest published output from a university journalism department: 'It's difficult to stop a curl of the lip, a Roger Moore raised eyebrow'. Few editors even try to suppress this inclination to sneer, it seems. 'I'd be far more interested in seeing someone with a law degree', declared Veronica Wadley, when editor of the *Evening Standard*, adding with a hint of pride: 'As far as I know I've never interviewed anyone with a media studies degree' (quoted in Beckett, 2006). Perish the thought.

Sally Feldman of the University of Westminster – which claims to have been the first institution to offer a media studies degree and in 2008 became the first to drop the title, although not the subject – thinks that such critics simply don't like it up 'em:

> Journalists who spend so much of their professional lives intruding and probing don't much like it when they're the ones being scrutinised and assessed. They love to quote the story of the eminent media studies professor who was invited to spend a day at a national newspaper. He was bemused by the almost miraculous process whereby a flurry of agitated phone calls, barking editors, scurrying reporters and frantic subs finally resulted in the next day's edition pumping out of the presses in the early hours of the morning. 'Well, it works OK in practice,' he conceded. 'But it could never work in theory'. (Feldman, 2008)

Even the bookish-looking Andreas Whittam Smith, one of the founders of the highish-brow *Independent*, has joined the mob of angry media villagers carrying metaphorical flaming torches towards university journalism and media departments. After attacking the 'superficiality' of media studies, and the way it 'borrow[s] ways of thinking from other disciplines', he offered the following observation:

> Then there is the paradox that the people who actually work in the media, whose output is studied in sixth forms and universities, find it difficult to take the subject seriously. They cannot believe that what they do is worthy of academic consideration ... Journalism is just a trade where the gifted, the average and the incompetent sit side by side in the same office producing work of varying quality. Least of all is it an academic discipline ... (Smith, 2008)

Journalism may indeed be a trade rather than a formally constituted profession, but it is difficult to see what exactly that has that got to do with whether or not it is something worthy of study. Indeed, the paradox in the above statement is that, far from believing what they do to be unworthy of academic consideration, so many journalists seem to believe that academics are unworthy of studying journalism – and incapable of offering any insight into journalistic activities.

Viewed from outside the newsroom, the Andreas fault – shared by Stott, Wadley and many other senior journalists over the age of 30 – can look remarkably like kneejerk defensiveness. This is not a new phenomenon. Take this supremely narrow-minded leader column published in a quality newspaper more than a decade ago, which was headlined 'HOW NOT TO BE A JOURNALIST':

> Media studies is a trivial, minor field of research, spuriously created for jargon-spinners and academic makeweights. Students learn nothing of value because the subject doesn't know its own purpose, is unimportant, and because most people teaching it don't know what they're talking about. Yet it is the fastest-growing subject in higher education. Careers counsellors might wonder why they have failed to stop students applying to waste their time and taxpayers' money. Perhaps we can help: this paper regards a degree in media studies as a disqualification for the career of journalism. That might put a few of them off. (*Independent*, 31 October 1996)

There is a distinct whiff of book-burning about the attitude quoted above, which was published on Halloween – an appropriate day for launching a witch-hunt. The author of that leader was journalist David Walker (2000, 236–237), who later confessed his 'unselfreflexive' sins and recognised that 'there are strong reasons why journalists need the self-knowledge that comes from external norm and criterion referencing'; that is, from an engagement with ideas about journalism that have emerged from academia. Yet, he noted with regret, the work of sociologists and other academics in scrutinising the media 'nowadays goes almost entirely unread by journalists'.

Sometimes the dismissive attitude towards academic theory is fully justified, according to one media scholar who told researchers: 'I go to conferences and you see papers ... what was it? ... 'The lesbian iconography in Buffy the Vampire Slayer' ... I mean, you're asking for abuse' (quoted in Hujanen et al., 2008: 55). Whether or not the authors of such papers are asking for abuse, is it not a demeaning sight to see so many senior journalists – who insist on their right, nay duty, to hold other institutions and industries up to scrutiny – united in their contempt for the idea that journalism and media should be similarly scrutinised? As Francis Beckett observes:

> Media studies students examine the actions of editors and journalists, and sometimes find them wanting. Media folk, as a class, are not used to being examined. If there is to be examination, they prefer it to be done by their own kind, hence the explosion of 'media commentators' in the newspapers, the majority of them former editors. (Beckett, 2006)

The attitude among many experienced hacks, especially those who have emerged from the so-called school of hard knocks and climbed the greasy pole to become editors or editorial directors, is that 'practical-based training is tolerated but more theoretical studies are generally thought a waste of time ... [M]utual suspicion persists between the press and academia' (Keeble, 2006: 26, 260). As one journalism studies professor has observed: 'Journalists' responses to theoretical concerns voiced by academics vary within different organisational contexts. Usually, though, they regard their own professionalism and autonomy as proof against academic theories which speak of any overt economic or ideological domination of news and its content' (Harrison, 2006: 27).

If those who study – or teach – journalism are likely to be 'treated with disdain, ridicule and contempt by many working within the industries', they might not find themselves much better thought of within academia, where they might be 'looked down on by their colleagues in the more traditional and established disciplines' (Williams, 2003: 12). Jackie Errigo and Bob Franklin (2004: 47) note that many journalists-turned-lecturers, or 'hackademics' as they put it, have felt 'bruised by their experiences with more elitist academic colleagues, as well as confused by the sociologese in which some scholars theorise'. A recent survey of communication and media research in the UK found that 'media subjects are often traditionally frowned upon by the public, and therefore they also tend to be looked down on by traditional academia' (Hujanen et al., 2008: 54). And when a Cambridge University spokesperson was quoted dismissing media studies as 'not relevant to the sort of courses we offer' (Beckett, 2006), it was hard not to imagine the accompanying sniff, if not downright sneer.

Yet, despite – or perhaps because of – such hostility from traditional journalistic and academic quarters, the media in general, and journalism in particular, have long held a fascination for a school of academic thinkers who wish to engage with the world beyond the lecture theatre and the library. It cannot be denied that there may be a fair amount of hogwash published under the labels of 'media studies' and 'theory'; just as there is plenty of rubbish produced daily under the label of 'journalism'. But who are journalists to judge as worthless all academic scrutiny of their trade, more often than not without reading any of it? Surely journalists, whose fellow practitioners range from those who produce *Nuts* or the *Daily Sport* to those responsible for the *Financial Times* or the *London Review of Books* – and all points in between – should know better than to hurl the baby into the gutter along with the bathwater.

Tensions between theory and practice

By standing back to gain a little perspective, by asking questions from outside the hothouse atmosphere of the newsroom, and by not taking established practices for granted, the academic study of journalism can offer us different ways of thinking about the things we do and about what it all means. By abstracting individual behaviour, exploring trends and analysing tendencies, the process of theorising about journalism can help us to see beyond the end of our own noses. However, this process is more likely to be a fruitful one if there is some connection between those involved in theory and practice rather than the disengagement that is too often the norm (Kunelius, 2006: 672; Foley, 2007: 67–68). As a journalist who moved into higher education and tried to get to grips with more theoretical explanations of her craft, Barbie Zelizer's experience – in her case, in the United States – was far from unique:

> When I arrived at the university – 'freshly expert' from the world of journalism – I felt like I'd entered a parallel universe. Nothing I had read as a graduate student reflected the working world I had just left. Partial, often uncompromisingly authoritative, and reflective far more of the academic environments in which they'd been tendered than the journalistic settings they described, these views failed to capture the life I knew … And so a glaring disconnect taints the spaces between journalistic practice and journalistic inquiry. (Zelizer, 2004: 2, 7)

As more journalists make the move into the academy, on both sides of the Atlantic, there is evidence that it may be possible to bridge this disconnect. Sarah Niblock, another journalist-turned-academic, points to the potential of combining practitioner and theoretical perspectives to help us better understand journalism:

> Recent commentary on the development of journalism studies as a discrete academic discipline, separate from media studies, communications and sociology, has centred on questioning the efficacy of traditional scholarly methodologies for analysing journalistic practice. From a media studies and media sociology perspective it is argued that methods such as the textual analysis of news coverage can draw significant conclusions about editorial judgement. From another perspective, it is argued that looking primarily

at the products and practices of journalists from a position that is *outside* the daily pressures faced within the industry leaves many important contextual and practical questions unanswered ... There is certainly a tension between theoretical approaches to journalism and its everyday practice ... On the one hand, from the academic perspective, there is the notion that a body of knowledge is inherent in everyday practice, and that this corpus can be abstracted and unpacked. From the practitioner perspective, journalists season their editorial judgement by doing, by 'thinking on their feet', not through overt abstraction and application to theoretical models. (Niblock, 2007: 21–23; emphasis in original)

The existence of such a tension suggests the need for a 'new critical approach' to the study of journalism that recognises the importance of analysing journalistic practice from the *inside looking out* as well as – rather than solely from – the *outside looking in* (Niblock, 2007: 23). In this way, journalism studies within the academy requires 'the melding of theory and practice in a judicious mix of skills and experience along with scholarly study' (Errigo and Franklin, 2004: 46). Such an approach, in which practitioners and practitioners-turned-scholars can be both reflective and reflexive about journalistic practice, needs to take account of more theoretical perspectives because without such knowledge journalists 'may not possess the vocabulary to think critically about their industry's practices' (Niblock, 2007: 31).

It is wrong to think of theory as the opposite of practice, argues the cultural studies theorist Raymond Williams (1976: 317). Rather, theory should be 'in active relation to practice', involving 'an interaction between things done, things observed and (systematic) explanation of these'. So theory is in effect simply 'a scheme of ideas which explain practice' (Williams, 1976: 316). There is no need to be afraid of it. As media studies professor Kevin Williams points out, theory is simply 'part of an effort by scholars to make sense of what is happening around them'. He explains:

The purpose of theory is to explain, comprehend and interpret phenomena and put forward propositions suggesting why such phenomena occur in the manner they do ... [G]ood theory should ... help us to understand and make sense of our personal experience and the wider structures and processes of daily life, and how they shape our interaction with other people. The ultimate test, then, of any theory is the extent to which it furthers our understanding of the world in which we live. (Williams, 2003: 11, 15, 18)

Some key theories about journalism

As long as we keep in mind that no one theory can possibly explain everything, then theoretical concepts can be invaluable tools that are available for us to use when attempting to understand the roles, practices and meanings of journalism. A good example is the idea of the press as a fourth estate of the realm, operating in a semi-constitutional way alongside MPs, the aristocracy and the church and acting as 'a counterbalance and check to the other three estates'

(Harrison, 2006: 49). This conception of the press as a fourth estate – the other three being the House of Commons, the Lords Temporal, and the Lords Spiritual – originally referred specifically to the parliamentary press gallery in the eighteenth century, but subsequently became a more general label for the press as a whole. Today the concept has widespread currency as one that locates journalists in a watchdog role: as the eyes and ears of the public, ever watchful, prepared to bark and occasionally bite when danger approaches. Temple (2008: 19) may regard the fourth estate as an intoxicating and self-perpetuating myth, but reference to it now seems so natural among journalists that most do not even think of it as a theoretical concept at all.

Another useful concept – albeit one that is far more likely to be cited in university seminars than in bars frequented by hacks – is that of the public sphere. German academic Jurgen Habermas (1989) writes about the public sphere as the space in which informed citizens engage with each other in rational discussion and critical reflection. Although the public sphere is a conceptual space, it also has physical manifestations; for example, in the coffee houses of Paris and London in the late seventeenth and early eighteenth centuries, where 'reasoned discourse' could take place independent of the state, albeit among a fairly limited section of the population (Allan, 1997: 298). As a self-confessed intellectual – not to mention being foreign – Habermas may have been unqualified to be a UK newspaperman; but his thinking can still help us to understand what we do and why. His concept of the public sphere as a space in which informed citizens can engage in critical reflection is relevant to discussions about the media because it is an ideal against which journalism may be measured, as Brian McNair (2000: 1) notes: 'Analysts and critics may dispute the extent to which Britain has a properly functioning "public sphere" ... but all agree that such a space should exist, and that the media are at its core'.

Arguably, then, the healthy functioning of a public sphere depends on a diversity of people having access to the media; not in the heavily controlled environment of a newspaper letters' page or a moderated comments function on a newspaper website, but access on a more equal basis: '[P]ersons become citizens when they participate in an institutionalised public sphere backed by institutions that make it possible for them to make claims upon each other only if they stand as equals to those who may make the same claims upon them' (Bohman, 2004: 152–153).

Yet, in the Habermasian view, increasing commercialisation has seen the decline of the press as a public space that had once enabled 'the people to reflect critically upon itself and on the practices of the state' (Stevenson, 2002: 49). For Habermas, the public sphere became corrupted with the increasing commercialisation of the media, which became more concerned with 'making profit for their owners rather than acting as information providers for their readers' (Williams, 2003: 68–69). Today, according to this analysis, reasoned public discussion has been replaced by 'the progressive privatisation of the citizenry and the trivialisation ... of questions of public concern' (Stevenson, 2002: 50). Habermas decries the way in which a formerly critical public sphere has not only lost its edge but has also become a means of political and social manipulation:

> The ever more densely strung communications network of the electronic mass media today is organised in such a manner that it controls the loyalty of a depoliticised population, rather than serving to make the social and state controls in turn subject to a decentralised and uninhibited discursive formation of the public will, channelled in such a way as to be of consequence – and this in spite of the technical potential for liberation which this technology represents. (Habermas, 1974: 4)

This does not refer to the sort of control that we might associate with a totalitarian state, perhaps best symbolised by the omnipresent Big Brother in George Orwell's novel *1984*; rather, it is the less total but nonetheless effective control of a media marketplace dominated by the likes of *Celebrity Big Brother*. However, Habermas has been accused of idealising 'a bygone and elitist form of political life' (McQuail, 2000: 158), and the recent market-led blurring of boundaries between popular and serious culture has been praised for producing less deferential and more 'demystificatory' forms of journalism than existed in the supposedly good old days (McNair, 2000: 60).

It is not necessary to go all the way with either argument to recognise that the theoretical concept of the public sphere can be a useful tool – or model – to help us think more deeply about journalism. As with the fourth estate, the idea of the public sphere helps us to understand the social importance of journalism and, therefore, why striving to be an entertainer should never be enough for a good, reflective journalist. And, again as with the fourth estate, it is intimately connected to ideas – and ideals – of democracy (Temple, 2008: 10).

Democracy is another much theorised idea. With particular relevance to journalism, four theoretical models of democracy have been identified by Jesper Stromback (2005): Procedural Democracy (free and fair elections); Competitive Democracy (competitive elections); Participatory Democracy (citizen participation); and Deliberative Democracy (discussions among the public and their representatives). The first two models are based on the election of representatives and the second two depend on more direct forms of citizen participation. The representative models require journalists to act as watchdogs on behalf of citizens; that is, journalism as a form of fourth estate as discussed above. In the participatory models, citizens have more room to speak for themselves, but journalists retain a key role because 'democracy can never become more deliberative without the active participation of media and journalism' (Stromback, 2005: 340).

At first glance, such weighty considerations may seem entirely divorced from the contents of page three of the *Sun* – even from page three of the *Daily Telegraph* – yet it is only by thinking about democracy that we can hope to understand the role(s) of the press in a country such as the UK.

Journalism and democracy cannot even exist without each other, according to James Carey (cited in Stromback, 2005: 332), while Bill Kovach and Tom Rosenstiel (2003: 12–18) argue that journalism owes its first loyalty to citizens and has as its primary purpose providing those citizens 'with the information they need to be free and self-governing'. The extent to which page three of the *Sun* contributes towards such an end is surely as important an area for debate as are media coverage of more obviously heavyweight topics such as politics (McNair, 2000; Franklin, 2004) or the repercussions of the Hutton Report (Lloyd, 2004a; Harcup, 2007).

Academic studies suggest that many of the least powerful sections of society face severe structural obstacles in gaining access to mainstream media, creating within journalism what has been described as a 'democratic deficit' (Manning, 2001: 137, 226–227; Hackett, 2005: 95). It is this tendency of the media to marginalise the tired, the poor and the huddled masses that has prompted some journalists and others to establish forms of alternative or citizens' media with more open and participatory structures (Downing et al., 2001; Rodriguez, 2001; Atton, 2002; Harcup, 2003; Atton and Hamilton, 2009). In this sense, ideas of democracy have not only helped us to understand journalism in theory but have also helped inform different forms of journalism in practice; forms of alternative journalism that have in turn had an influence on mainstream journalism (Harcup, 2005).

The very existence of journalism that labels itself 'alternative' suggests dissatisfaction with the range of products on offer in the mainstream marketplace. Yet both mainstream and alternative publications operate under what is called the 'free press' model, whereby anyone in the UK is free to publish a newspaper or magazine without having to be licensed by anyone in authority. Under this system, although publishers need to be mindful of the laws of defamation, contempt and obscenity – and the fact that occasionally a judge might be woken in the middle of the night and asked to halt the presses with a temporary injunction – publishers do not have to submit to censorship in advance. Therefore, according to what tends to be referred to as the liberal theory of press freedom, the public gets the press it both desires and deserves. In other words, newspapers stand or fall in the democracy of the free market, and 'press freedom is a property right exercised by publishers on behalf of society' (Curran and Seaton, 2003: 346).

Yet a political economy approach to theorising about journalism points out that newspaper journalism within the UK operates within a capitalist economy in which commercial decisions inevitably impact upon the production of journalism itself; commercial decisions such as those that created the situation whereby 'relatively fewer journalists are now required to write more stories to fill the ever-expansive pages of the national press', meaning that 'many of the elements of rigorous, independent journalism are inevitably depleted when reporters are obliged to produce more stories in less time' (Lewis et al., 2008b: 27–28, 42). Any equation of a free press with a free market is challenged by academic Colin Sparks, who argues that, because of the constraints imposed on journalists operating within mainstream media, a truly free press is 'an impossibility in a free market' (Sparks, 1999: 59).

For many scholars and observers influenced by Marxism, the media in general and journalists in particular tend to play an ideological role, irrespective of the intentions of the individuals involved. By ideology is meant 'some organised belief system or set of values that is disseminated or reinforced by communication' (McQuail, 2000: 497). A Marxist critique suggests that, in western, capitalist societies, the media in effect help to spread and reinforce a ruling class ideology; that is, a way of seeing the world that tends to accept some ideas as natural, 'common sense', and others as extreme, off-the-wall. There will be exceptions, and the system is not foolproof, but many Marxists argue that today's mainstream newspapers continue to display the tendencies identified by Karl Marx and Friedrich Engels more than 160 years ago:

> The ideas of the ruling class are in every epoch the ruling ideas: ie, the class which is the ruling material force of society, is at the same time its ruling intellectual force. The class which has the means of material production at its disposal, has control at the same time over the means of mental production, so that thereby, generally speaking, the ideas of those who lack the means of mental production are subject to it. The ruling ideas are nothing more than the ideal expression of the dominant material relationships, the dominant material relationships grasped as ideas; hence of the relationships which make the one class the ruling one, therefore, the ideas of its dominance. (Marx and Engels, [1846] 1965: 61)

Ideological power has been described as 'the power to signify events in a particular way', although ideology can also be 'a site of struggle' between competing definitions (Hall, 1982: 69–70). Viewed from this perspective, for all the apparent diversity of the media, and taking into account various exceptions, the routines and practices of journalists tend to privilege the explanations of the powerful and to foreclose discussion before it strays too far beyond the boundaries of the dominant ideology (Hall et al., 1978: 118). Yet such an emphasis on the ideological content of journalism is frequently challenged for downplaying the agency of journalists and/or for failing to take account of the complex ways in which audiences may actually 'read' media texts. Nick Stevenson sounds a cautionary note about the tendency of media theorists to 'overstate the incorporating power of ideology' (Stevenson, 2002: 46). Questioning the assumption that the social background of journalists leads automatically to a middle-class perspective in their output, for example, he argues not that class composition has no influence, but that there are also ideological divisions and conflicts *within* classes which limit the degree of 'ideological closure' achieved by the structural dominance of the media by white middle class graduates (Stevenson, 2002: 33). In other words, real life tends to be messier than is allowed for in many theoretical explanations.

In their 'propaganda model' of how mainstream media operate, Edward Herman and Noam Chomsky identify five filters that, they argue, combine to produce 'the news fit to print' (Herman and Chomsky, [1988] 1994: 2). The filters are:

- Wealth and the concentrated ownership of dominant media firms.
- Advertising.
- Reliance on information from the powerful.
- Punitive action ('flak') against transgressors.
- Anti-communism.

Since the collapse of the Soviet Union, the fall of the Berlin Wall, and the growth of Islamic fundamentalism, Muslims could be seen as replacing communists as the bogeymen in the above model (Temple, 2008: 117). For Herman and Chomsky, debate and dissent are permitted within media – but only up to a point. Their model has been dismissed by many critics as nothing more than an unsubtle 'conspiracy theory', but Herman (2000: 102–103) rejects this, arguing that the propaganda model describes 'a decentralised and non-conspiratorial market system of control' in which the five filters 'work mainly by independent action of many individuals and organisations'. The result, it is argued, is that a form of consensus is manufactured which is all the more powerful for appearing to be arrived at freely:

> The elite domination of the media and marginalisation of dissidents that results from the operation of these filters occurs so naturally that media news people, frequently operating with complete integrity and goodwill, are able to convince themselves that they choose and interpret the news 'objectively' and on the basis of professional news values. (Herman and Chomsky, [1988] 1994: 2)

This concept of news values is one that has often divided journalists and academics. Whereas the former tend to speak of possessing an instinctive, almost mystical, 'nose' for what makes a good news story, the latter attempt to understand the process by breaking down news stories into abstract categories and by viewing everyday journalistic practice through the prism of theory. News values, writes Jerry Palmer (2000: 45) for example, are to be understood as 'a system of criteria which are used to make decisions about the inclusion and exclusion of material' and about which aspects of selected stories to emphasise. Such values 'transcend individual judgements, although of course they are to be found embodied in every news judgement made by particular journalists' (Palmer, 2000: 45).

Johan Galtung and Mari Ruge were perhaps the first – and certainly the most influential – to provide a systematic list of news values, in a paper presented at the Nordic Conference on Peace Research in Oslo in 1963 and published in 1965. In an effort to answer the question 'How do events become news?', Galtung and Ruge (1965: 65–71) presented 12 factors they regarded as being important in the selection process: *Frequency* (an event that unfolds within a publication cycle of the news medium is more likely to be selected than a one that takes place over a long period of time); *Threshold* (events have to pass a threshold before being recorded at all, and the greater the impact the more likely it is to be selected); *Unambiguity* (a clearly understood event without multiple meanings); *Meaningfulness* (culturally familiar); *Consonance* (expectations about an event); *Unexpectedness* (unusual events); *Continuity* (something remains news once it has become news); *Composition* (an event that fits with the overall composition or balance of a newspaper or news broadcast); *Reference to elite nations* (seen as more consequential than the actions of other nations); *Reference to elite people* (some people are more equal than others); *Reference to persons* (individual human interest rather than abstractions); *Reference to something negative* (bad news is good news).

Informed by – but not uncritical of – the work of Galtung and Ruge, Harcup and O'Neill (2001) later carried out an empirical study of the UK press and proposed a more contemporary set of news values. They found that potential news stories must generally satisfy one or more of the following requirements to be selected:

- *The power elite*: stories concerning powerful individuals, organisations or institutions.
- *Celebrity*: stories concerning people who are already famous.
- *Entertainment*: stories concerning sex, showbusiness, human interest, animals, an unfolding drama, or offering opportunities for humorous treatment, entertaining photographs or witty headlines.
- *Surprise*: stories that have an element of surprise and/or contrast.
- *Bad news*: stories with particularly negative overtones, such as conflict or tragedy.
- *Good news*: stories with particularly positive overtones such as rescues and cures.
- *Magnitude*: stories that are perceived as sufficiently significant either in the numbers of people involved or in the potential impact.
- *Relevance*: stories about issues, groups and nations perceived to be relevant to the audience.
- *Follow-ups*: stories about subjects already in the news.
- *Media agenda*: stories that set or fit the news organisation's own agenda. (Harcup and O'Neill, 2001: 279; Harcup, 2004: 36)

In this way, then, academic research around news values, informed by theoretical perspectives, can help us to understand the ways in which some things become identified as 'events' and the ways that some of those 'events' are selected and then processed to become what is known as 'news'.

Another pioneering academic study of the selection of news was that carried out sixty years ago by David Manning White, which resulted in what became known as the 'gatekeeping' theory. White ([1950] 1999: 72) observed the ways in which a wire editor at a US morning newspaper selected stories for inclusion and found that the choices were 'highly subjective' and based on the editor's own 'experiences, attitudes and expectations'. In turn, White's gatekeeping model was later challenged for its assumption that there existed an unmediated reality that newsgatherers could choose either to admit or exclude (McQuail, 2000: 279). A study by Walter Gieber ([1964] 1999: 223) suggested instead that news had no independent existence but was 'a product of men [sic] who are members of a news-gathering (or a news-originating) bureaucracy'. For Gieber, 'extrapersonal' factors could constrain the choices of individual journalists and the personal attitudes of journalistic 'gatekeepers' were of less importance than the bureaucratic routines involved in producing, processing and editing copy. This is what Golding and Elliott were driving at when they observed: 'News changes very little when the individuals that produce it are changed' (quoted in Curran and Seaton, 1997: 277).

Different theoretical traditions

Theorising about journalism such as has been discussed in this chapter tends to come from one of three broad sociological traditions, argues Bob Franklin (1997: 35): namely, the organisational approach; the Marxist approach (aka political economy); and the culturalist approach.

According to the organisational approach, the output of journalists is shaped by a combination of the ways in which journalism tends to be organised as an activity – the importance of deadlines, restrictions on time and space, relations with sources, and so on – and of the practices valued by journalists themselves, such as an understanding of news values and a commitment to at least the impression of objectivity (Franklin, 1997: 35–37). For Franklin, such an approach offers an insufficient explanation of the journalistic process:

> These rather prosaic, if not commonsensical, organisational accounts of media content make the explanations offered by other sociologists seem unduly sophisticated. Shortages of time and space, the availability of information and the errors committed by journalists working to deadlines provide a sufficient account of the constraints on journalism. Organisational theorists are content to explain ideological skew or bias in media content by reference to 'cock up' rather than 'conspiracy'; in this sense they let journalism off the hook. (Franklin, 1997: 37)

In contrast, a Marxist approach emphasises the ways in which journalists are constrained by the political and economic structure of society in general and of the media in particular; hence its alternative label of political economy (Franklin, 1997: 37–44). According to this approach, journalists are rarely the fearless, crusading mavericks of legend. Most lack real autonomy and independence within media industries dominated either by rich individuals or powerful corporations and 'the structure of the market usually guarantees a congruence between proprietorial and journalistic perceptions' (Franklin, 1997: 38). This point appeared to be made flesh when, in the run up to the US–UK invasion of Iraq in 2003, the war was supported by every single one of Rupert Murdoch's 175 newspaper editors across three continents (Greenslade, 2003b). Not that structural control of the media has to be so total to be effective, as Marxist theoretician Ralph Miliband put it:

> Radio and television in all capitalist countries have been consistently and predominantly agencies of conservative indoctrination ... that have done what they could to inoculate their listeners and viewers against dissident thought. This does not require that *all* dissident thought should be prevented from getting an airing. It only requires the overwhelming bias of the media should be on the other side. And that requirement has been amply met. (Miliband [1970], quoted in Franklin, 1997: 42; our emphasis)

The third broad tradition of sociological theorising about journalism identified by Franklin is the culturalist approach, which emphasises the relative or 'licensed autonomy' of journalists within mainstream media (Franklin, 1997: 44–47). According to variants of such thinking, neither governments nor media employers need to tell journalists what 'line' to take on important issues of the day because, broadly speaking and with exceptions which merely go to prove the rule, journalists 'have internalised the dominant societal values' (Franklin, 1997: 46). Thus it is regarded merely as common sense that falling house prices should be a cause for gloomy rather than celebratory coverage, even though cheaper housing might in reality be good news for many people, not least the low-paid journalists in the provincial press. Low air fares, on the other hand, tend to be reported as good news for consumers rather than bad news for the environment. Many people take an opposite point of view to the prevailing 'common sense' on such issues, but not only do their concerns rarely get an airing in the mainstream media, for the most part our newspapers also appear to be ignorant that such contrary thinking even exists.

Sociology has been one of the key methods used to examine 'the people, practices and behaviour, structures, and institutions' of journalism, but it is far from the only academic discipline to explore the various ways in which journalism matters, argues Barbie Zelizer:

> *History* targeted how journalism used to matter ... *Language studies* concentrated on the verbal and visual tools by which journalism matters. In focusing on its languages, it offered formal and informal templates for considering how the messages of news were structured. *Political science* developed a focus on how journalism ought to matter ... And *cultural analysis* described how journalism matters differently, seeing it as relative to the givens of those engaged in its production, presentation, and reception while dissipating the consensus that grounded more traditional inquiry. (Zelizer, 2004: 206; our emphasis)

To these five areas of academic inquiry with an interest in journalism could be added anthropology, communication studies, economics, law and philosophy (Zelizer, 2004: 8).

No one area has a monopoly on insight, argues Zelizer (ibid.: 213), who calls for journalism to be examined through an 'interdisciplinary lens' because 'the boundaries of what is and is not journalism remain necessarily unclear'. As the authors of a study into such research in the UK conclude:

> British media and communication research is a multidisciplinary field drawing on a range of fields in the social sciences and humanities as well as in the visual arts and computer science. The academic community fosters the multidisciplinary roots of media and communication studies and sees their maintenance as an asset for research. Many of the scholars interviewed for this study thought that this was a good thing, since what happens in the media cannot be studied as separate from the rest of society. (Hujanen et al., 2008: 119)

If journalism's boundaries are necessarily unclear, and necessarily inseparable from wider society, then arguably this is truer than ever today, in the era of blogging, user-generated content and so-called 'citizen journalism'. This very slipperiness in defining journalism only reinforces the argument that, just as there are many different journalisms, there can be many different ways of understanding journalism. Journalists, even members of the ex-editors' club who now fill the media pages of the heavy papers, need to recognise that they are not the only ones with worthwhile or insightful things to say about journalism. Whereas commentators such as Andreas Whittam Smith may dismiss journalism studies for borrowing the clothes of more respectable academic disciplines, hackademics such as Barbie Zelizer see this interdisciplinary approach not as a weakness but as a strength. As Martin Loffelholz notes approvingly: 'The current theoretical discourse on journalism is heterogeneous, multidimensional, and full of competing ideas' (Loffelholz and Weaver, 2008: 15). But it could benefit from being even more so, according to Herman Wasserman, who argues: 'Change and evolution in newspaper journalism is a heterogeneous and contextually dependent process. A multi-linear, multi-perspectival view on journalism studies should be followed, with more perspectives from the global South entering the debate' (Wasserman, 2008: 793).

No single academic discipline is likely to hold all the answers and no single theory will be able to explain everything. Academic inquiry and theoretical concepts are simply tools that we can use to help us to explore the practices and meanings of journalism; torches to help light up a path through the undergrowth. However, theorising that takes little or no account of the conditions in which journalism is practised is unlikely to offer much illumination. As Sir William Hope put it in 1692: 'Theorie without Practice will serve but for little' (quoted in OED, 2007). He was writing about understanding the skills of sword-fighting but, it could be argued, the same goes for understanding the craft of journalism and the future of newspapers. What kind of future that might be will be addressed in the next chapter.

10

NEWSPAPERS AT THE CROSSROADS

It is too early, far too early, to be writing the obituary for newspapers in their traditional form. They have been around for more than two hundred years in a number of variations on their present form. Yet there is no doubt that the early years of the twenty-first century witnessed greater uncertainty than ever before, compounded in 2008–2009 by a serious economic recession. There was hysteria, fear, even panic. It was a good time for pundits because they were offering 'analysis' and 'predictions' to a world that did not fully understand what was happening or going to happen. It was a time to doubt the 'certainties' of those who could not be certain. It was a time of talking down the future of newspapers and talking up a new age. It was a time of myth and rumour, of grand schemes, of emperors' clothes, of trying things, taking a punt, because 'to do nothing is not an option', the favourite cliché of the time.

Franklin (2008c: 633) refers to the 'precocious pessimism and unwarranted hyperbole of those who wish to proclaim the imminent demise of the newspaper, [which] is clearly unsustainable'. Such pessimism is demonstrated by Greenslade (2009) who predicted that 'the combination of structural and cyclical decline at a time of recession, a continuing credit drought, rising newsprint prices and the flight to the internet is transforming an already grim situation into a perilous one'. Also among the pessimists, this time over the prospects for the regional press, was *Guardian* chief executive Carolyn McCall (2008). She said many well-known regional and local newspapers would go out of business. 'The changes are structural – they are permanent and result from fundamental changes in consumer behaviour, communications and technology. The situation is exacerbated by the current cyclical downturn, but neither the readers nor the revenues are ever coming back, at least not to anything like previous levels'. The executive editor of the *New York Times*, Bill Keller (2007), is part of a more optimistic faction. He is unconvinced that the increasing mastery of web journalism, shown by his own and other newspapers, means that it will replace the newspaper. 'There is something tremendously appealing about a portable, authoritative package of dispatches from all corners of the world, from all corners of the culture, selected and written for you by intelligent people. [It] offers a reader serendipitous encounters that are hard to replicate in the quicker, reader-driven format of a website'.

Inevitably bubbles would burst and money would be lost. Yet still, in the UK in 2008, about 11.7 million national newspapers a day were being purchased (and many more given away – including 1.4 million *Metros* in the big conurbations and 900,000 free London afternoon papers) and in the UK regions some 60 million copies a week (of dailies and weeklies) were being sold or distributed (Audit Bureau of Circulations figures). This was a long way from 'death'. But there was crisis in the air and on the balance sheets. The *Media Guardian*, the online industry news website, on a single day in early 2009 (14 January) provided an indicative snapshot of the climate. Its home page alone provided the following stories: 'Economist Group axes 13 staff'; 'Archant (regional newspaper publisher) to cut up to 20 jobs on Suffolk papers'; 'Archant cuts its London offices'; 'MEN (*Manchester Evening News*) Media disbands motoring sales (advertising) team'; 'Jobs go as Trinity Mirror (largest regional newspaper publisher) merges divisions'; '*Financial Times* signals 80 job losses'. And there was the announcement that the *Times* and *Guardian* were following the *Telegraph* in putting their cover prices up to 90p (the ailing *Independent* was already £1), the *Observer* following the *Sunday Times* to £2, the *Mirror* rising to 45p, the *Sunday Mirror* and *News of the World* to £1. All this at a time of falling retail prices in the high street, and inevitably bad for circulation. Just one day, but it was typical of every day as the continuing crisis in the newspaper industry met the gathering recession head on. Recessions end; but will the crisis in the newspaper industry?

The crisis for newspapers in the United States was much worse, with famous major titles like the *San Francisco Chronicle* and *New York Times* facing cash crises. Other major publishers, like the Tribune Company (*Chicago Tribune*, *Los Angeles Times* and *Baltimore Sun*) and Philadelphia Newspapers (*Inquirer* and *Daily News*) filed for bankruptcy (BBC News online, 2⁻ February 2009 – http://news.bbc.co.uk/1/hi/world/americas/7913400.stm).

Not that the talk of a crisis within newspapers was a simple product of the recession, of course. Many have predicted the end of print since the advent of the internet and long before too. New words entered the language during the first decade of the twenty-first century: pods and blogs and touchpoints and downloads, hubs and spokes, VJs and content – some, like the last, were old words, but were used as though they were new. In fact much that was going on was not new at all, but was a rebadging, rebranding, repackaging (also buzzwords of the early twenty-first century) of old concepts to take account of a changing media world. The pace of change was frenzied. Publishers were investing in a new world that many did not fully understand. At the same time operating costs were cut to try to maintain the profitability which had been such a feature of the recent years of a decline in newspaper circulations. There was a breathlessness to it all; everybody was in a hurry.

Why? It was as though the shapers of the newspaper industry suddenly became aware around 2005 and 2006 that they had been given a second chance, having in most cases turned their backs on the first. Until 2005 there had been a decade of tinkering, of talking in a desultory way about what was going on, but in many cases doing nothing about it. The mantra, repeated time and again by the hard-headed chief executives while all around them the possibilities were expanding and the early adopters were adopting, was: 'But how are you going to make money out of the internet?' It was a rhetorical question, given credibility by the bursting of the techno-bubble. So while the first guru of internet media, Nicholas Negroponte, was touring the world making a speech based on his massively influential book *Going Digital*, and the disciples were trying to convince anybody who would listen that we had gone digital, and anyone who hadn't was making a big mistake, the financiers in the publishers' boardrooms were looking at their newspaper revenues, profits and share prices and closing their eyes to the future. Circulations were falling, yes, but gently and from a high base, and the decline was satisfactorily profitable. If proof were needed then it was provided by the queue of potential buyers every time a group or title came up for sale. The *Telegraph*, *Express* and *Mirror* were all sold during this decade of indifference to the new digital world.

Seminal moments for the twenty-first century newspaper

Among key points along the digital way, three stand out for their impact. Chronologically, they were Murdoch, the *FT* news story and the *Economist* cover story. The first was a speech, the other two words on paper. The irony was noted. Rupert Murdoch, the richest, most powerful, admired and despised media magnate in the world, had not been known for his embracing of the internet. He said little about it, and such is his control of his empire that neither did his senior executives across the world. Murdoch was happy to continue building said empire, turning his satellite television channel, Sky, into a commercial success, and making a fortune from his newspapers – in Britain *The Times*, *Sunday Times*, *Sun* and *News of the World*.

Then, suddenly, on Thursday, 13 April 2005, he went digital. He was not the first; in fact he may have been one of the last. But it was not really until his digital conversion that the world of print went crazy. If Rupert had finally been won over, then there had to be something in it. Murdoch's major strategic decisions – in the UK buying *The Times*, Wapping and Sky – were calculated business decisions. Murdoch doesn't do other kinds of decisions. There was a *Times* website, but it concerned

Murdoch only in the slightest, and was little developed. He had not taken a major strategic decision about the internet.

In April 2005 he made a keynote speech to the American Society of Newspaper Editors in Washington, DC. His theme was 'The role of newspapers in the digital age'. It was the speech of a convert, tantamount to a confession of past sins on the way to finally seeing the light. 'As an industry, many of us have been remarkably, unaccountably complacent', he said. 'Certainly, I didn't do as much as I should after all the excitement of the late 1990s. I suspect many of you did the same, quietly hoping that this thing called the digital revolution would just limp along'. He continued:

> I come to this discussion not as an expert with all the answers, but as someone searching for answers to an emerging medium that is not my native language. I'm a digital immigrant. I wasn't weaned on the web, nor coddled on a computer. Instead I grew up in a highly centralised world where news and information were tightly controlled by a few editors, who deemed to tell us what we could and should know. My two young daughters, on the other hand, will be digital natives. They'll never know a world without ubiquitous broadband internet access. (Murdoch, 2005)

The challenge for digital immigrants, he said, was to apply a digital mindset to a set of challenges that they unfortunately had limited to no first-hand experience of dealing with. The next generation of people accessing news and information, whether from newspapers or any other source, had a different set of expectations about the kind of news they would get, including when and how they would get it, where they would get it from, and from whom. He quoted the Carnegie Corporation report by Merrill Brown saying that consumers (in the USA) between the ages of 18 to 34 were increasingly using the web as their medium of choice for news consumption:

> 44% of the study's respondents said they used an (internet) portal at least once a day for news, as compared to just 19% who use a printed newspaper on a daily basis. More ominously, looking out three years, the study found that 44% expected to use the internet more to learn about the news, versus only 25% who expected to use traditional newspapers more. What is happening is, in short, a revolution in the way young people are accessing news. … They want their news on demand, when it works for them. They want control over their media, instead of being controlled by it. … In the face of this revolution, however, we've been slow to react. We've sat by and watched while our newspapers have slowly lost circulation. We all know of great and expensive exceptions to this – but the technology is now moving much faster than in the past. (Murdoch, 2005)

Murdoch said the industry had to awaken to the changes in technology and reader habits or newspapers would be relegated to the status of also-rans. He was confident about the future of newspapers; he thought they were uniquely positioned to deliver news, as long as they took advantage of their 'great new partner – the internet'. This would require cultural changes, a complete transformation of the way we think about newspapers. Murdoch's wake-up call to himself and his empire was quickly taken up by his senior executives around the world. Others, like the *Guardian* editor, Alan Rusbridger, who had seen the light several years earlier and developed online journalism at his newspaper in ways Murdoch had suddenly recognised, allowed themselves a modest smile, but realised that the age of serious competition was about to begin.

Murdoch, whose Washington speech (above) had done so much to concentrate debate, quickly turned his 'conversion' into a strategy. He bought MySpace, the social-networking website, for £330m in 2005 and set in motion the development of the online operations of his newspapers. By 2008 the *Times* and *Sun* websites were the third and fifth respectively most visited UK newspaper-based websites (ABCe figures), and in an Australian radio lecture that year, echoing and developing his themes of three years earlier, he said:

> Unlike the doom and gloomers, I believe that newspapers will reach new heights. In the 21st century people are hungrier for information than ever before. If you discuss the future with newspapermen you will find that too many think our business is only physical newspapers. I like the look and feel of newsprint as much as anyone. But our real business isn't printing on dead trees. It's giving our readers great journalism and great judgement. It's true that in the coming decades the printed versions of some newspapers will lose circulation. But if papers provided readers with news they can trust, we'll see gains in circulation – on our web pages, through our RSS feeds, in emails delivering customised news and advertising, to mobile phones. In short we are moving from news papers to news brands. For all of my working life I have believed that there is a social and commercial value in delivering accurate news and information in a cheap and timely way. In this coming century, the form of delivery may change but the potential audience for our content will multiply many times over. (Murdoch, 2008)

The next seminal moment came with a half-page story in the *Financial Times* of 30 May 2006. Across the top of page three ran the characteristically restrained headline 'Net poised to overtake national press'. More significant was the single word in small type above it: 'Advertising'. Murdoch, in his speech, had referred to the prediction from Bill Gates, the owner of Microsoft, that the internet would attract $30 billion in advertising revenue within the next five years (from 2005). Now, just a year later, the *FT* was giving prominence to a report from GroupM, a WPP holding company, which drew on data from a number of its media buyers representing 30 per cent of global media advertising. It predicted that in the UK the internet would shortly be overtaking national newspapers to become the third biggest advertising medium by spend, after TV in first place and the regional press in second place. Like all such forecasts, it was challenged by others. Media consultant Jim Chisholm of iMedia, a British consultancy, predicted that a quarter of print classified advertising would be lost to digital media in the next ten years, with newspapers that were taking 36 per cent of global advertising in 1995 now taking 30 per cent, and the figure falling to 25 per cent by 2015 (*Economist*, 1 September 2006, p. 57).

The *FT* story recorded a turning of the tide. In the late 1990s, after the stumbling internet start by the *Daily Telegraph*, there had been widespread scepticism that online news would challenge traditional printed forms for the simple reason that it would not attract advertising. Competitors regularly noted that the two most rapidly developing and most respected news websites based in the UK were the BBC's and the *Guardian*'s. Why? Because one was state funded (through the licence fee) and the other was owned by a trust. Neither had shareholders to report to, a share price published. But by 2006 the prospects for advertising on the web were finally taken more seriously.

The third moment that concentrated minds and the debate, by now raging, was the publication by the *Economist* on 1 September 2006 of a cover story entitled 'Who Killed the Newspaper?' The international news and business magazine is an example of the fact that print is alive and very well; it sells 1.1 million copies a week worldwide, and has a much visited website. The 2006 issue of the *Economist* devoted four pages to the death of newspapers debate. It observed that newspaper sales had been falling continuously in America, Western Europe, Latin America, Australia and New Zealand (while conceding they had been rising everywhere else). 'In the rich world newspapers are now an endangered species. The business of selling words to readers and selling readers to advertisers, which has sustained their role in society, is falling apart'.

The *Economist* viewed the decline of newspapers not only as an internet issue, but also as one relating to content, price and spin-off businesses from the newspaper. However the emphasis was on the rise and rise of the newspaper derived website. More newspapers treated these as a priority these days, said the magazine, and website advertising revenues were increasing, some by as much as 30 per cent per year. It should be noted these are percentages of very small numbers. In the end it came down to maintaining revenues in the broad while declining circulations meant lower revenues from sales, lower advertising revenues resulting from reduced sales, as well as other factors. The most important of these was the migration of lucrative classified advertising from print to the web, and a developing interest by advertisers in using the web now that audiences were growing so rapidly and the sought-after younger audiences were increasingly using websites as their preferred source of news.

According to the *Economist*:

> Having ignored reality for years, newspapers are at last doing something. In order to
> cut costs they are already spending less on journalism. Many are also trying to attract

younger readers by shifting the mix of their stories towards entertainment, lifestyle and subjects that may seem more relevant to people's daily lives than international affairs and politics are. They are trying to create new businesses on and offline. And they are investing in free daily papers, which do not use up any of their meagre editorial resources on uncovering political corruption or corporate fraud. So far, this fit of activity looks unlikely to save many of them. Even if it does, it bodes ill for the public role of the Fourth Estate. (*Economist*, 2006)

Waking up to the need for change: a false dawn

The World Editors Forum held its second conference in May 1995, in Paris. The subject was digital technology and its impact on newspapers. It was not like the debates of the early twenty-first century, because then newspaper publishers were still confident and their products were still selling. But we had been through the first digital revolution. Reporters were transmitting their copy from portable computers; hot metal was dead and digital newsroom systems had been installed across the industry; pages were being made up on screen and sub-editors were formatting; there was still plenty of paste-up around; and few journalists had web access at their desks. The newspaper librarians were usually more familiar with the possibilities than the journalists, and tended to do the journalists' searching for them. At the same time the early adopters were vocal and there was a band of the newly digital who were apocalyptic, for their time, about the prospects for newspapers. Debate with them was difficult because so many, ignoring the evidence of their eyes, insisted that newspapers had already been replaced. Even to suggest, in 1995, that there was life in newspapers was to be called a Luddite, but if you have decided on a mission (often lucrative) of telling the old guard what they do not want to hear, but think they probably ought to if only to impress at the next board meeting, then you do not deal in shades of grey. Their presentations sparkled; the only question they ducked was where were the revenues coming from? At the time there weren't any. And they hadn't time to notice that their conference was being run by an organisation entirely focussed on newspapers.

But one speaker was noticeably more grounded than the others. Ben Rooney was the editor of the then recently launched *Electronic Telegraph*, the first online offshoot of a British national newspaper. He called his contribution 'The Story of *ET*'. He said the most important thing about him was that he was not a computer scientist, he was a journalist. And he gave a definition of his product that would not gain respect in the boardroom today: '*ET* is not an internet product that happens to be a newspaper; it is a newspaper that happens to be on the internet. That is important'.

The *Daily Telegraph* was then, as now, the largest-selling serious newspaper in the UK, selling more than it does today, with an ageing readership, as it has today. They sought out new readers among young professionals, and Rooney described them by using the same words we hear so often today, not least from the *Telegraph*'s latest editor, Will Lewis.

> They are busy. They lead full, busy lives, and they do not have the time to read a newspaper in the traditional way. They are selective. Typically they will have a portfolio of resources to get their news and entertainment – they might read one magazine for one feature, get their news summary from the television, but want to get sport news from a paper. They are computer literate. They have a computer screen at their desk; they are used to getting information from it. This was key. These are people who, if you looked in their briefcase under the mobile phone and beside the CD player you might find a copy of yesterday's newspaper still neatly folded, still unread.

ET took *Daily Telegraph* copy and, in the current vernacular, repurposed it for the web. They launched the service on 15 November 1994. They were ahead of the game but they did not follow through. They produced a ground-breaking, competent website, but did not develop it. So much so that the *Telegraph*'s 'digital revolution' of 2005, marketed as something so new and mould-breaking, could be seen as catching up on what might have come many years earlier. But the mood of the 1990s – and the technology then was much more crude – was a lack of conviction on the part of the publishers. Like Murdoch, they delayed their conversion on the basis that they couldn't see the revenues. Better to concentrate on wringing a profit from the medium they understood.

Alan Rusbridger became editor of the *Guardian* when *ET* was one year old. Of all the newspaper editors of that time he was the least in need of convincing where the future lay. *Guardian Unlimited* was launched that year. It was given money and staff to develop, and with no shareholders asking awkward questions about returns quickly became the dominant newspaper-based website in the UK. Rivals showed little concern, and often little awareness. *Guardian Unlimited* grew and grew, exploited subject areas such as media and education that the newspaper had developed as classified advertising goldmines under Rusbridger's predecessor, Peter Preston, and made the *Guardian* an international brand, particularly in the United States.

Newspaper journalists, including those on the *Guardian*, seldom engaged. Although their 'repurposed' copy might appear on the website, they did not 'write for the web', and indeed usually did not read their copy there. Rusbridger took a close and constant interest in the web. In this he was very different from his rival editors on other titles, and from most of his own journalistic staff, apart from those, usually young, usually unknown to the journalists on the paper, in the other building where they 'did the web'. All this would change, but not quickly.

Following Murdoch's Washington speech of 2005 the newspaper world woke up. In 2006 advertising revenues and circulations, in both the national and regional press, were falling. As we have seen in Chapter 5, various strategies were adopted to deal with these newspaper problems which were now feeding down to the bottom line. Formats were changed, with positive results. Some publishers started giving away their newspapers. Marketing and promotion through add-ons – CDs, DVDs, posters, books, wall-charts – were seen across all titles and were quickly regarded by managements as an essential part of the national newspaper package. But however significant or successful these strategies were, they had one thing in common: they represented fiddling with the traditional product, the newspaper.

But now was the time to get serious about the web. The impact of the *Telegraph* in this area was significant. That most traditional of newspapers, with its ageing readership, its preoccupations with field sports, military matters, royalty, private education, country houses, Agas, and what it saw as middle-class values increasingly represented an old order that was increasingly absent from life as the rest of us experienced it. The *Telegraph* was an unlikely place to find the new media order, but that was the way it turned out. The *Telegraph* had stood back from the compact revolution, probably rightly considering its readers would resist a smaller format. But its move from traditional family ownership to modern corporate newspapering had ended in disaster through the financial scandal that had engulfed the ownership of Conrad Black. The *Telegraph* had more to worry about than its format; it was seeking new owners. In came the Barclay brothers, the quiet, low-profile media moguls. In came a dose of *Daily Mail*-bred executives. In, most significantly, came William Lewis, the new editor. His background was in business journalism. He was less stuffy than most of his predecessors; blokeish and rugby loving, he talked more about the future of the group than its traditions. He presided over a shake-up as radical as any newspaper has witnessed, starting with the physical environment in which the *Telegraph*, both daily and Sunday, was produced. Before he became editor he was charged in 2006 with moving these papers from the 'new Fleet Street' of Canary Wharf in London's docklands to offices by Victoria station previously occupied by a finance house. Symbolically, the old trading floor became the new newsroom.

It was purpose built for the new media age. It started with the name on the door: the *Telegraph* was no longer a newspaper group but a media group. It continued with a massive and controversial shake-out of staff; there was no longer a place for the traditionalists or the sceptics. The layout of the newsroom with its central hub (where conferences take place in public, as opposed to executives filing into the editor's office) and spokes radiating from it, all dealing with different facets of multi-media publishing, was designed to integrate them. A huge 'media wall' dominates, displaying website pages, charts of the most 'visited' stories of the day, videos ... and the newspaper. The digital editor, Edward Roussel, was almost as important as the editor, and executive conversation was as much about eyeballs, brand

and hits as it was about readers and stories. The *Telegraph* hired broadcast journalists as well as those with a background in print. It formed a relationship with ITN to provide video content for its website. It launched online television, podcasts, blogs and totally revamped its website. And through all the change Lewis maintained that the newspapers remained central as the trusted brand on which all the new developments were based. And the printed product was still, of course, the source of most of the revenue.

For months the *Telegraph* was the most talked about newspaper and new media publisher, partly because the change was so rapid and so radical, partly because it was the *Telegraph*, of all papers, making these changes. It remained the case that the average age of the newspaper readership was 56 and of the web audience 41, and the crossover between the two platforms was 25 per cent (interview with Will Lewis by Cole, *Independent on Sunday*, 18 February 2007). The questions remain. Is the *Telegraph* seeking to develop two rather different audiences – old paper for old readers, new media for new young readers – or is the aim to progressively unite them? The future of the newspaper depends on the answer, and Lewis maintains – and it is demonstrated daily in the paper with its constant cross-referencing – that different platforms provide different services, that both are equally important, and that integration is for the benefit of both.

That sentiment would be echoed by his rivals. At the 2007 Society of Editors conference, in a discussion of 'The 2020 Vision', Lewis, Anne Spackman, editor of *Times Online*, Peter Wright, editor of the *Mail on Sunday*, and Mark Dodson, chief executive of GMG Regional Media, all maintained that newspapers would survive in a much changed multi-media environment. The *Times*, *Mail* and *Sun* websites underwent considerable development in 2006–7 and saw great growth in audience. Approaches vary, and tend to reflect the character of the newspaper, another indication that brand influences website use and brand is set by the newspaper.

Those newspapers that came late to taking their websites seriously were soon recording huge figures for usage, as shown in the table below. No longer was the *Guardian* alone and completely dominant. The *Telegraph*, *Times*, *Mail* and *Sun* were competing hard. The *Guardian* had steadily built up its audience over ten years or so, during which it had made a large impact in the United States. The *Mail*, particularly, came from a standing start, and also built up a considerable US audience. The UK sites all gain between 30 per cent and 40 per cent of their users from the UK, and it is this figure that is of most interest to advertisers who target their spend nationally. The *Guardian* remains the most popular newspaper-based website in the UK, followed by the *Telegraph*, *Times* and *Sun*. Globally the ranking is the same, apart from the *Mail*, which replaces the *Sun* in fourth place.

The websites listed in Table 10.1 all publish charts of the most read stories, demonstrating clear differences between the interests of each newspaper and

Table 10.1 *Audience for newspapers and their websites, November 2008 in (000s)*

Title	Newspaper average daily sale	Website global unique users in month	Global unique users a year ago	Website UK unique users in month 2008	Percentage of unique users who are in UK 2008
Guardian	358	26,044	17,500	9,548	37
Mail	2,194	20,870	14,416	6,442	31
Sun	3,046	16,428	11,609	6,936	42
Telegraph	835	22,959	12,801	7,395	32
Times	622	21,599	12,283	7,231	33
Independent	201	8,888	4,619	n/a	n/a

Individual figures for corresponding Sunday newspapers are excluded, as some websites are shared between daily and Sunday titles. Unique user figures are gathered and reported over monthly periods. Newspaper sales are reported as an average per publication day over the month, and in each case exclude the sale of a corresponding Sunday newspaper.

Sources: ABC and ABC Electronic

website audiences. On one day in January 2009, for example, the second most read story on the *Mail* website was 'Feeling blue? Today – January 19, 2009 – is the most depressing day in HISTORY, say experts'. True, the collapse in bank shares was the most popular, but this website regularly records most hits for showbiz/celebrity stories. The *Times*'s second most popular website story was 'Wealthy men give women more orgasms' following only the bank story, while the *Guardian*'s second most popular web story was 'Charlie Brooker on the absurdity of calorie counting'. Every indication there that the serious readers of serious newspapers change their reading preferences when they go online, or more likely that the websites attract a different kind of reader.

The question of web-advertising revenue remains paramount. Despite investment and a management and editorial emphasis on website development, more than 90 per cent of advertising revenues still come from the print product and publishers admit that online advertising rates tend to be about 20 per cent of those for advertisements on the printed page. While classified advertising for cars, jobs and property is migrating to websites which offer greater range and convenience, what newspapers call display advertising – consumer goods, financial, corporate – is still being developed for the internet. Picard (2008: 714) found that the relationship between GDP and newspaper advertising was weakening, particularly for classified advertising, and that the growth of newspaper advertising overall was not keeping pace with inflation. Display advertising remained relatively healthy while classified advertising trends were problematic.

Although the shifts in newspaper advertising are removing the unusually high profitability of the industry, they are not yet dooming it to demise or altering the basic structural element of newspaper markets in the United States. The changes, however, would seem to be moving the industry back to a period in which the newspaper industry was less financially interesting to investors who were primarily interested in profits and asset growth.

While website publishers argue about the relative importance of different forms of audience measurement – unique users or page impressions – the advertisers will decide. Their prime concern is that an advertisement is seen, and with the huge range of pages available on websites the fact that a site has been visited can be no guarantee that the page containing that advertisement is being seen by a particular visitor. Increasingly advertising is likely to be directed at particular interest groups and page impressions of particular web pages will be measured to establish what is charged for an advertisement.

The regional and local press faces its own distinct problems over the faith they can place in websites to compensate for the loss in sales and advertising revenues. With property and car classified advertising moving to websites run by the estate agents, car dealers and various aggregators – although some regional publishers are trying to compete with their own sites in these areas – website advertising revenues are hard to come by. And will the former or current readers of local news in local papers visit the local website? Great efforts are being made, with local papers seeking to offer the stories which once proved so popular with their newspaper readers, the very local, community news. One successful example here is Gazettelive.co.uk, the site run by the Middlesbrough *Gazette*. Visitors to this site can click on postcodes to find news from their own district. But the news still has to be gathered, and editorial staff reductions on local papers all over the country make this difficult, particularly when reporters have to be 'multi-skilled' in order to be able to provide audio and video content for the website as well as text.

The *Manchester Evening News*, which has also made staff cuts, seeks to integrate editorial on the *Telegraph/Guardian* model. A central desk allows decisions to be made about the content both for the paper and website – which stories go where, and when, and who covers them. There is also an associated TV channel – Channel M – represented at the same command desk.

All publishers of national newspaper websites are concerned about Google and the share of the advertising cake it takes. Google is a news aggregator, massively popular and scoring very highly on measurements of trust. For many, Google is the gateway to news, aggregating news stories from many sources and routing visitors to the source; increasingly journalists are required to write stories with key words included in headlines and intros, in what has quickly become known as 'search-engine optimisation'. The concern is that Google News plays no part in the expensive process of gathering news. It feeds off others' costs and yet gathers huge advertising revenues from its search engine. Google claims that it 'democratises news' by allowing 'multiple perspectives on the same topic' and sending visitors who might otherwise not go there to particular news websites. The publishers of those sites say they have invested in their sites and their reporting but Google is creaming off the advertising. This debate continues, and has been described by Anne Spackman of Times Online (Society of Editors conference 2007) as her 'main preoccupation'.

Who does the reporting?

This brings us back to the heart of the future of newspapers matter. Websites, like newspapers, television and radio, require content, news and other material. So do mobile phones and RSS feeds. Providing editorial matter, as we called it before 'content' became the word, has traditionally been the job of journalists. Most bloggers and so-called citizen journalists are not professional journalists, are not trained, and do not have the researching, reporting, interviewing, writing and editing skills of the professionals. Anybody can have an opinion and write it down – the blogger is sometimes no more than an old fashioned, opinionated letter writer with unlimited space, the citizen journalist a member of the public with a mobile phone. As Temple insists: 'There is no doubt that blogging and online journalism challenge established traditional perceptions of journalism, but the lazy assumption that just because someone has an opinion they are a journalist needs to be contested' (Temple, 2008: 212). New media provide access to more contributors, which can be welcomed, but most consumers of media will want to know something about provenance. Is the source of any consequence, or reliability? Authority, credibility and trust come from knowing where these have come from. Which brings us back to brand, and trust: loyalty to a particular news website will be developed by the perceived integrity of its reputation for accuracy, reliability and fairness, which in the case of newspaper-based websites, will come from the reputation of the newspaper that preceded it.

Broadcast journalist turned web evangelist Charlie Beckett (2008: viii) puts less emphasis on the professional provenance of news information, celebrating the fact that 'the tools journalists can use are constantly expanding. Links and search enable journalism to be found. Blogs allow anyone to publish and contribute. Mobile devices share what they see – even as it happens – in the form of text, photos, audio and video. Databases and wikis enable large groups to pool their knowledge'. Beckett (2008: 4) espouses what he calls 'networked journalism', a concept claimed by Jarvis (2007), meaning the 'public can get involved on a story before it is reported, contributing facts, questions and suggestions. The journalists can rely on the public to help report the story'. Beckett believes that 'by changing the way journalists work and the way journalists relate to society, we can sustain good journalism and in its turn journalism can be a force for good'. He sees networked journalism as 'a way of bridging the semantic divide between Old and New Media, reaffirming the value of the core functions of journalism. 'It means a kind of journalism where the rigid distinctions of the past, between professional and amateur, producer and product, audience and participation, are deliberately broken down'. Hall (2008: 218) describes this phenomenon as 'disintermediation, the removal of intermediaries in the journalistic supply chain: the realisation that journalism had lost exclusive access to its primary sources of news and that its own readers were frequently beating it to the important stories'. This disintermediation, argues Hall, coincided precisely with the fall in advertising revenues and circulation as newspapers ceased to be the true mass-media form in the twenty-first century. Search engines, portals and peer-to-peer media-sharing applications, auction sites, even, on occasions, blogs, seemed able to draw as much traffic as the newspapers' websites.

Although none of these writers is explicitly seeing these new forms of journalism as replacing newspapers there is a clear implication that they change journalism. Is that simply by expanding it, by broadening the range of people who contribute to it? Is it simply technology-driven change? For example the camera in the mobile phone broadens the likelihood of pictures, moving or still, of news events being available, be it an air crash or a celebrity misbehaving in a nightclub.

Journalism has always taken advantage of technological change, for the printing of newspapers, the transmission of words and pictures or the maintaining and accessing of archival material. But it has always exercised judgement – about which there is legitimate controversy, over what is published and who decides – and demanded expertise – that specialist reporters and commentators have a degree of knowledge of their subject. There is no parity between that and a citizen who simply decides to publish an opinion. The general public have access to much more information through the internet, and a greater ability to discuss it with as many people as choose to read it. But they do not necessarily have the journalist's direct access to the providers, or withholders, of such material, or the resources of those employed to interrogate the validity, intention or self-interest of those in power whose activities, decisions and policies are being reported. What is so often described as 'citizen journalism' certainly adds to the raw material available to journalists but it does not necessarily add the skills and techniques of inquiry to take it further. The role of the journalist to find out and expose is unlikely to be fulfilled by the self-motivated blogger sitting alone at the computer, any more than the assembling of other people's work by the news aggregator gathers stories. Somebody still has to go out there and find things out.

So while the advent of new media raises questions about the future of specific platforms – which is about how and where the information is published – it should not threaten the future of journalism, which is about what is published. In the present cacophony of debate about media futures this much more important fact tends to be ignored. Google produces nothing; it distributes the work of others. Mobile phones do not have teams of reporters behind them; the same is true of most websites. The *Guardian* and *Telegraph* may be obsessed with Facebook and Twitter – and perhaps this amounts to more than sending out signals that they are abreast of current fads – but these social networking accessories rarely unearth information, still less authenticate it. The strength of newspapers, whatever their individual weaknesses, is that they employ reporters, as do news agencies and broadcast news organisations. Without them there would be no content worthy of the name.

A continuing need for journalism

No new technology, no new medium, has ever replaced an old one. In 1475 we had the first book. Books are still with us, and selling in vast quantities. In 1663 we had the first magazine. We've never had more than we have today. In 1922 we had the first radio. In 1926 we had television, although in reality not until after the Second World War. In 1975 we had the first personal computer. All of these were expected to sound the death knell of existing media at the time. But all are still around. New media have added to, and changed, old media. More information is available, and being consumed, in more ways than ever. Our newspapers may be of a smaller format, they may be free, they may be referring us to other platforms run by the same publisher and using the same pool of content as is available to the newspaper, the range of content may have changed, not always for the better – but the newspaper still fulfils the definition we offered in the opening pages of this book. It remains an easily scanned portable reading medium with large doses of serendipity. And it still depends on journalism.

Journalism still produces content that matters. And the quality of journalism should remain our primary concern. New technologies, new platforms, have expanded and changed the ways we access information. Some of the new platforms have not always improved the quality of the information. And some publishers have given more thought, and investment, to *how* it is published rather than to *what* is published.

Temple (2008: 216) maintains that the future health of newspapers depends on one thing – content, content, content. Not a billion bloggers bleating in cyberspace, but distinctive comment and analysis that have faced the rigours of a well-honed editorial process. 'That has been the newspaper's unique selling point (USP) for centuries and it will continue to be its USP for the future, whether in print, online or in technologies yet to be invented'.

Good journalism has never been cheap. It takes time and tenacity and talent to explore and expose what others would prefer left buried. Good journalism holds those with power and influence to account. This is not easily done using the screen of a mobile telephone. Good newspapers have traditionally, if not always, done it well.

'Does news matter?', asks Peter Preston, rhetorically. He continues:

> Does it matter if you know what's going on in your world, your street, your town, your country? If it does, then you'll want someone to discover, collect, edit and distribute that news – and you'll want it done with some professionalism. Facts that bear some relation to the truth are better than facts confected or simply got wrong. There is a need for solid facts. Therefore there is a continuing need for organisations that can dig out those facts. Therefore there will – on screen or in print – be a continuing need for journalism and journalists. It doesn't matter much whether the facts that the news factory produces are put down on paper or transmitted on the net. Killing forests is only one ancient way of approaching a task that may be far better done digitally. Journalism itself – good, responsive journalism, meeting a need – is not threatened by the net. Indeed, its opportunities and possibilities are much enhanced. It won't die, though more trees may live. (Preston, 2008: 647)

Newspapers have many rivals for attention, and some will not survive the competition. Others may be killed by owners only interested in the bottom line. Still others will change or adapt to new conditions. There will be free newspapers, e-newspapers, newspapers on computer screens and mobile telephone screens and i-pod screens. At least there may be, because – despite the cries of confident predictors – nothing is very certain. Only those on top of the subject have the confidence to say they don't know what things will be like in ten or twenty years' time.

But what has changed as the late adopters have engaged with online news in their search for a new economic model for the publication of news, is that they have mostly stopped saying it is all over for the newspaper. Of course newspapers will still be around they say, as though they had never doubted it. Well they did, and some still do. But the big players, building their twenty-first century media businesses, have developed a sense of history that tells them you do not simply consign a traditional medium to the dustbin. You adapt it. Add to it. Apply new technologies to it. Recognise anew what it can do better than other forms of media. Hold on to its good name, its brand. Maintain trust in it. And keep turning the pages.

Philip Meyer, in his book *The Vanishing Newspaper* (2004:16), predicts that the last newspaper will be read in 2043. By that time he is likely not only to be dead, but also wrong.

11

READ ALL ABOUT IT: A CRITICAL
BIBLIOGRAPHY OF NEWSPAPER JOURNALISM

Just as reports of the death of newspapers have been greatly exaggerated, so there is no sign of any imminent demise of books about newspapers. Quite the reverse, in fact. There appears to exist a more extensive literature about journalism than ever before, although it is not all written in the same language. The transformation of UK journalism into an overwhelmingly graduate trade – not, it should be noted, a profession – and the emergence of journalism studies as a subject within higher education have prompted academic publishers to compete with each other to see which can produce the longest list of journalism titles. Also, a book occasionally emerge from outside the 'hackademy' to find a larger audience and touch a more public nerve about the perceived falling standards of our news media. Whatever the particular merits of such books, the very fact that they find a readership and prompt a debate that reaches far beyond journalists and journalism students is an indication of just what an important role journalists – including those clinging on to the inky world of newsprint – play within society.

Journalism under the microscope

Two such crossover books in recent years have been *Flat Earth News* by Nick Davies (2008) and *What the Media are Doing to Our Politics* by John Lloyd (2004a). Both are laments for what the authors see as a loss of journalistic integrity and both have been much discussed, yet they have each come up with two totally different views of what the problem is and where the blame lies. For Davies, most journalism no longer asks the hard questions because it has been fundamentally corrupted by a corporate takeover that results in too few journalists with too little time to check things thoroughly and too little incentive to do so. Much of the UK media's willingness to swallow the Blair government's misleading line that Iraq had weapons of mass destruction was just one example of how journalism has been compromised by an unhealthy emphasis on the bottom line, he argues. For Lloyd, in contrast, too many journalists ask the wrong questions, because they begin from the false assumption that politicians are likely to be attempting to conceal or distort the truth. Some of the UK media's willingness to challenge the Blair government's honest belief that Iraq had weapons of mass destruction was just one example of how journalism has been compromised by too many journalists assuming that politicians are liars, he argues. A critical reading of both books is recommended for anyone wishing to better understand arguments about the state of the newspaper industry in the early years of the twenty-first century. It is worth noting that, despite their different perspectives and conclusions, Davies and Lloyd share the view that good journalism takes time: Davies criticises the growth of 'churnalism' (first introduced by Waseem Zakir in Harcup, 2004: 3–4), in which too many journalists simply repackage PR and agency material, while Lloyd calls for 'slow journalism', similar to the 'slow food' movement, that puts quality before speed. A not dissimilar critique has emerged from within the academy, where Professor Bob Franklin (2005) uses the terms 'McJournalism' and 'McDonaldization' to signify the 'flavourless mush' produced by what he contends has become a predictable and standardised newspaper industry.

When journalists write about journalism they tend to do so without a bibliography or detailed references. This is the case with Nick Davies's book, but unusually he does draw on academic research: a specially commissioned study that attempts to quantify the reliance of major UK national newspapers – the *Times*, *Guardian*, *Independent*, *Daily Telegraph*, and the *Daily Mail* – on a combination of public-relations and news-agency material. The research itself, by Lewis et al. (2008a), can be read in the journal *Journalism Studies* with a companion study from the same stable in *Journalism Practice* (Lewis et al., 2008b). Such detailed empirical academic research about aspects of journalism is rarely read by journalists or welcomed by newspaper editors, but it is one of the strengths of peer-reviewed journals such as *Journalism Studies* (Taylor and Francis), *Journalism: theory, practice and criticism* (SAGE) and *Journalism Practice* (Taylor and Francis). These journals all publish research from scholars around the world and should be essential reading for serious students of journalism, not only for the original studies they contain but also for their book reviews. An especially valuable resource are the special issues of *Journalism Studies* (Vol. 9, No. 5) and *Journalism Practice* (Vol. 2, No. 3) published in October 2008, which are both packed with illuminating papers discussing the future of newspapers. Other journals that publish material relevant to newspaper journalism include *Ethical Space* (Institute of Communication Ethics), *European Journal of Communication*

(SAGE), *Journal of Media Practice* (Intellect), *Journalism and Mass Communication Quarterly* (Association for Education in Journalism and Mass Communications) and *Media, Culture and Society* (SAGE).

However, because there is often a significant time lag before research can be published in academic journals and books, students should also be aware of other locations for a discussion of the state of newspapers and other forms of journalism, including academic conferences and seminars, annual guest lectures, and conferences of organisations such as the Society of Editors, the Association for Journalism Education and the National Union of Journalists. Journalists can be observed discussing their craft in *British Journalism Review* (SAGE) and *Press Gazette* (Progressive Media), among other places, and also worth monitoring are the media pages of the *Guardian, Observer* and *Independent*, the *Media Talk* podcast available via the *Media Guardian* website, BBC Radio 4's *The Media Show*, and blogs such as those by Jon Slattery (http://jonslattery.blogspot.com), Roy Greenslade (www.guardian.co.uk/media/greenslade), Paul Bradshaw (http://onlinejournalismblog.com), Alan Geere (http://alangeere.blogspot.com), the anonymous Grey Cardigan (http://blogs.pressgazette.co.uk/greycardigan) and the self-styled Gentlemen Ranters, who are not all gentlemen and can be found in an online version of 'the last pub in Fleet Street' (www.gentlemenranters.com). Other useful websites include those of *Press Gazette* (www.pressgazette.co.uk), the media ethics charity Mediawise (www.mediawise.org.uk), the National Union of Journalists (www.nuj.org.uk), the Campaign for Press and Broadcasting Freedom (www.cpbf.org.uk), Hold the Front Page (www.holdthefrontpage.co.uk), Journalism (www.journalism.co.uk) and Fifth Estate (www.fifth-estate-online.co.uk). Keeping an eye on such outlets and their international equivalents can help students keep abreast of issues and debates as they emerge in real time, rather than waiting for the academic machine to creak into action.

Lessons from history

As debates rage around us in the blogosphere and elsewhere, it is worth remembering that what can be gained in terms of speed can sometimes be lost in terms of perspective. An understanding of the history of newspapers can help guard against being swept along with the latest fad that promises to change everything; reading history can also dispel the myth of a golden age when journalism was just perfect. Thankfully there are some excellent history books that can help do just that. What better place to start than with John Milton's *Areopagitica* (1644), a plea for press freedom that has recently been republished with an illuminating essay by Granville Williams (2005), which places Milton's work within the context of today's media? Michael

Bromley and Tom O'Malley's (1997) collection *A Journalism Reader* may not go back as far as Milton but it does bring together a fascinating range of historical accounts of journalism from 1800 to 2000, including John Stuart Mill, W.T. Stead, C.P. Scott, George Orwell, Francis Williams and Nicholas Tomalin.

Readable histories of newspaper journalism in the UK are included in Andrew Marr's thoughtful (2005) *My Trade*, Gopsill and Neale's lively (2007) account of the NUJ's first century, *Journalists*, Temple's refreshingly upbeat (2008) *The British Press*, and Kevin Williams' splendidly titled (1998) *Get Me a Murder a Day!* Engel (1996) tells an entertaining tale of the growth of newspapers as popular journalism, while Conboy (2002) covers similar ground from a more academic perspective. Conboy (2004) has also written an analytical history of journalism that would be a useful theoretical companion to the substantial press histories by Greenslade (2003a) and Griffiths (2006). Curran and Seaton (2003) discuss the history, economics and politics of the newspaper industry in the UK alongside the development of broadcast and online journalism and within the context of sociological and political economy explanations.

For a description of the UK press, and an understanding of why it is the way it is, Jeremy Tunstall's (1996) *Newspaper Power* remains a solid starting point despite its age. For a more up-to-date analysis of the press by a range of practitioners and scholars, see Bob Franklin's edited (2008a) collection *Pulling Newspapers Apart*. Another major academic contribution to an understanding of newspaper journalism, in addition to its broadcasting and online cousins, is *News Culture* by Stuart Allan (2004), which also includes useful chapters on 'race' and gender. Franklin (1997) offers an eloquent critique of the tabloidisation of the UK media, countered by McNair's (2000) case that coverage of politics in particular has *not* been dumbed down. Because the regional press tend to be little more than an afterthought in most of the books mentioned in this chapter, it is just as well that there is at least one substantial work out there that focuses specifically on the journalism of local and regional media, with an emphasis on newspapers: *Local Journalism and Local Media*, edited by Franklin (2006). *Understanding the Local Media* by Meryl Aldridge (2007) is a useful addition to this rather small field. For a more historical exploration, see the special issue of *Journalism Studies* (Vol. 7, No. 3, June 2006) that was guest edited by Andrew Walker, which includes eight contributions on the subject of the development of the provincial press in England between 1780 and 1914.

Media histories by Jane Chapman (2005) and Burke and Briggs (2005) extend their gaze beyond the UK to place the growth of newspapers within an international context, whilst William Huntzicker's (1999) *The Popular Press, 1833–65* is an appropriate starting point for a study of the historical development of journalism within the USA. Further exploration of comparative press history in different national contexts can be found in another special issue of *Journalism Studies* (Vol. 4, No. 4, November 2003), which traces the development of news-based journalism in Scandinavia, Germany, France and Spain, in addition to the USA and UK.

Journalists at work

There are a number of good books concerned with newspaper journalism written by current or former practitioners and aimed at journalism students. One of the best is *The Universal Journalist* by David Randall (2007), which is now in its third edition. Devoid of a bibliography and references it might be, but it is full of insight and good advice from a reflective practitioner who is currently assistant editor of the *Independent on Sunday*. As a companion volume, Randall's (2005) *The Great Reporters* is a highly readable romp through the lives of some reporters who left their individual marks on journalism in assorted ways. Compared to Randall, Richard Keeble's (2006) *The Newspapers Handbook*, now in its fourth edition, offers a much more academic take on the press, albeit one that is also rooted in an understanding of practice. For an optimistic – some might say hyperbolic – discussion of the ways in which new online technology and so-called citizen journalism can be utilised to 'save' newspaper and other traditional forms of journalism, see Charlie Beckett's (2008) *SuperMedia: saving journalism so it can save the world*.

Academic critiques of news values are explored in Jackie Harrison's (2006) book *News* as well as in a journal article by Harcup and O'Neill (2001), who present the results of a content analysis of news values at work in the UK national press. Further discussion of news values and news selection can be found in O'Neill and Harcup's more up-to-date contribution to Wahl-Jorgensen and Hanitzsch (2009). Challenging the news values of the mainstream press has been one of the drivers behind the production of what have been termed 'alternative media', and interesting work in this field includes Atton and Hamilton (2009), Atton (2002), Harcup (2005, 2006), Rodriguez (2001) and Whitaker (1981). Chapter 5 of Chambers et al. (2004) explores the extent to which the increase in the proportion of women journalists may have impacted upon news values and newsroom culture.

There is a growing literature concerned with the ethics of journalism, and a useful starting point is Harcup's (2007) *The Ethical Journalist*, which discusses ethical considerations as integral to all journalistic practices rather than as restricted to a discrete set of ethical issues. Frost (2007), Keeble (2009) and Sanders (2003) all provide suitable companion volumes, with Karen Sanders taking the most philosophical approach; she argues that most journalists work in a market in which they are faced with 'multivarious moral dilemmas' and in which a concern for a profitable bottom line means that most newsroom decisions are taken in 'a climate where reflection on the practices and principles of journalism is actively discouraged'. See Shannon (2001) for a rather uncritical semi-official history of the Press Complaints Commission, O'Malley and Soley (2000) for a more hostile account of press self-regulation, and Frost (2004) for an academic analysis of the first decade of PCC adjudications. For a specifically US perspective on journalistic ethics and responsibilities, see Bill Kovach and Tom Rosenstiel's (2003) *The Elements of Journalism* – worth reading despite its austere restatement of principles which led it to be described as the 'book of lists' (Weinhold, 2008: 478) – and *Ethics in Journalism* by Ron Smith (2008), now on its sixth edition. Also from the USA, to see quite how badly things can go wrong when a newspaper takes its eye off the ball, read the sorry tale of Jayson Blair's career at the *New York Times* in *Hard News* by Seth Mnookin (2005).

For a practical account of newspaper journalists at work on investigative reporting, there is still no better place to start than the classic *All the President's Men* by Carl Bernstein and Bob Woodward (1974), which details the painstaking work involved in the *Washington Post*'s Watergate exposés. The seedier end of UK tabloid investigative journalism is covered in *Exposed!* by former *News of the World* hack Gerry Brown (1995) and *Confessions of a Fake Sheikh* by Mazher Mahmood (2008). For more reflective discussion of the contested roles, contexts and meanings of investigative journalism, see Foot (1999), Pilger (2004), Spark (1999) and Chapter 11 of Keeble (2006); all of which are informative contributions despite making little attempt at engaging with any of the relevant academic literature that could add a different dimension to the discussion of investigative journalism. For a discussion of the practicalities of investigative journalism alongside more theoretical perspectives, try de Burgh (2008), Chapter 6 of Harcup (2009b) and Chapter 4 of Harcup (2007) and, from a more specifically US perspective, Ettema and Glasser's (1998) *Custodians of Conscience*; some more recent academic research on investigative journalism was collected in a special issue of the journal *Journalism: theory, practice and criticism* (Vol. 8, No. 5, October 2007), which draws on work from far beyond the UK and USA.

The language used within newspapers is another area that journalists and academics tend to write about as if in parallel universes – not only using a different vocabulary and grammar, but also frequently using them to discuss wholly different concepts. The classic practitioner text on newspaper style is *Essential English for Journalists, Editors and Writers* by Harold Evans (2000), mercifully renamed from its earlier incarnation as *Newsman's English*. Anna McKane's (2006) *News Writing* is more up to date, discursive and student-friendly, and *Good Writing for Journalists* by Angela Phillips (2007) reproduces and discusses examples of longer, more feature-based material from a range of publications. Keith Waterhouse's (1989) *Waterhouse on Newspaper Style* is essentially the old style guide of the *Daily Mirror* and, although the specifics change faster than the rise and fall of a Z-list celebrity, it remains a delightful introduction to the thinking behind the style of the redtop tabloid press – if you can find a copy of it anywhere. Tabloid language and ideology are subjected to more critical scrutiny in Conboy's (2006) *Tabloid Britain*. Further detailed analysis of the language of newspaper journalism can be found in Fowler (1991), Bell (1991), Cameron (1996), Conboy (2007) and Richardson (2006). A sample newspaper style guide is reproduced and discussed from both practitioner and academic perspectives in Chapter 12 of Harcup (2009b).

Journalists' memoirs tend to be characterised by 'omissions, self-justifications and fallabilities', argue Sally Bailey and Granville Williams in a rare and insightful academic analysis of the genre; however, they add that 'journalists' memoirs have been an underused source in helping us to understand some of the dilemmas, pressures and practices facing journalists in their work' (Bailey and Williams, 1997: 352, 375). Easily the best-selling is *The Insider* by Piers Morgan (2005), former editor of both the *News of the World* and the *Daily Mirror*, despite the fact that many of his 'diary' entries were reconstructed long after the events they describe. Another big-hitter in the self-justification business is Andrew Neil (1996), former editor of the *Sunday Times*, whose *Full Disclosure* has been described by John Pilger (1998: 456) as 'arguably one of the most sustained boasts in autobiographical history'. However, it is worth reading for an inside account of the 'calculated terror' of Rupert Murdoch's ownership and management style. Some rather more reflective memoirs include those by Knightley (1998), Marr (2005), Hastings (2002), Stott (2002) and, from an earlier era, James Cameron ([1968] 2006).

Theory and practice

Journalists, ex-journalists and academics all contribute chapters about various aspects of newspaper and magazine journalism in Richard Keeble's (2005) edited collection *Print Journalism: a critical introduction*. Another edited volume worth exploring is Stuart Allan's (2005) *Journalism: critical issues*. For a more sustained theoretical analysis of journalism, try Sheridan Burns (2002), Zelizer (2004), McQuail (2000) or Campbell (2004). Howard Tumber's (1999) *News: A Reader* includes extracts from many key studies, including Herman and Chomsky on their propaganda model, Golding and Murdock on the influence of economic power, Galtung and Ruge on news values, and Stuart Hall on news values as ideology. Manning (2001) reviews relevant research into, and explores theoretical frameworks that seek to explain, the relationship between journalists and sources.

Stevenson's (2002) exploration of Marxist explanations of the media, not just journalism, includes a discussion of objectivity, truth, hegemony and moral panic, whilst Critcher (2002) applies the concept of moral panic to the *News of the World*'s 'name and shame' campaign on paedophilia. Lynch and McGoldrick (2005) use the work of Derrida and other critical theorists to explore the ways in which journalism is biased in favour of event over process, effect over cause, and dominant discourse over critical reflection.

A comprehensive overview of different academic approaches and methods for researching journalism around the world is provided by Martin Loffelholz and David Weaver's (2008) edited collection *Global Journalism Research*, which includes contributions from active researchers in a range of different countries. As such, it provides a more international – and more up-to-date – treatment of many of the areas discussed in the useful if US-focused *Qualitative Research in Journalism*, edited by Sharon Iorio (2004). A further range of international perspectives on the press can be found in *The Function of Newspapers in Society*, edited by Shannon Martin and David Copeland (2003). Specially commissioned original contributions by an impressive cast list of international scholars have been brought together in the weighty *Handbook of Journalism Studies* edited by Wahl-Jorgensen and Hanitzsch (2009). However, despite the ever-expanding library of journalism studies, the extent of which this critical bibliography merely hints at, one of the few places in which practitioner and academic accounts of journalism can be found actually talking to each other – in dialogic fashion – remains *Journalism: Principles and Practice* (Harcup, 2004, 2009b). Finally, and arguably most important of all, students of journalism should read the newspapers – print and online editions; popular and heavyweight; local, regional, national and international – every day.

APPENDIX: PRESS COMPLAINTS COMMISSION CODE OF PRACTICE

The Press Complaints Commission is charged with enforcing the following Code of Practice which was framed by the newspaper and periodical industry. It was amended and ratified by the PCC most recently in 2009, with the current code taking effect on 19 October 2009.

The Code

All members of the press have a duty to maintain the highest professional standards. The Code, which includes this preamble and the public interest exceptions below, sets the benchmark for those ethical standards, protecting both the rights of the individual and the public's right to know. It is the cornerstone of the system of self-regulation to which the industry has made a binding commitment.

It is essential that an agreed code be honoured not only to the letter but in the full spirit. It should not be interpreted so narrowly as to compromise its commitment to respect the rights of the individual, nor so broadly that it constitutes an unnecessary interference with freedom of expression or prevents publication in the public interest.

It is the responsibility of editors and publishers to apply the Code to editorial material in both printed and online versions of publications. They should take care to ensure it is observed rigorously by all editorial staff and external contributors, including non-journalists, in printed and online versions of publications.

Editors should co-operate swiftly with the PCC in the resolution of complaints. Any publication judged to have breached the Code must print the adjudication in full and with due prominence, including headline reference to the PCC.

1) Accuracy

i)   The press must take care not to publish inaccurate, misleading or distorted information, including pictures.

ii) A significant inaccuracy, misleading statement or distortion once recognised must be corrected, promptly and with due prominence, and – where appropriate – an apology published.

iii) The Press, whilst free to be partisan, must distinguish clearly between comment, conjecture and fact.

iv) A publication must report fairly and accurately the outcome of an action for defamation to which it has been a party, unless an agreed settlement states otherwise, or an agreed statement is published.

2) Opportunity to reply

A fair opportunity for reply to inaccuracies must be given when reasonably called for.

3) *Privacy

i)   Everyone is entitled to respect for his or her private and family life, home, health and correspondence, including digital communications.

ii) Editors will be expected to justify intrusions into any individual's private life without consent. Account will be taken of the complainant's own public disclosures of information.

iii) It is unacceptable to photograph individuals in private places without their consent.

Note – Private places are public or private property where there is a reasonable expectation of privacy.

4) *Harassment

i)   Journalists must not engage in intimidation, harassment or persistent pursuit.

ii) They must not persist in questioning, telephoning, pursuing or photographing individuals once asked to desist; nor remain on their property when asked to leave and must not follow them. If requested, they must identify themselves and whom they represent.

iii) Editors must ensure these principles are observed by those working for them and take care not to use non-compliant material from other sources.

5) Intrusion into grief or shock

i)   In cases involving personal grief or shock, enquiries and approaches must be made with sympathy and discretion and publication handled sensitively. This should not restrict the right to report legal proceedings, such as inquests.

*ii) When reporting suicide, care should be taken to avoid excessive detail about the method used.

6) *Children

i) Young people should be free to complete their time at school without unnecessary intrusion.

ii) A child under 16 must not be interviewed or photographed on issues involving their own or another child's welfare unless a custodial parent or similarly responsible adult consents.

iii) Pupils must not be approached or photographed at school without the permission of the school authorities.

iv) Minors must not be paid for material involving children's welfare, nor parents or guardians for material about their children or wards, unless it is clearly in the child's interest.

v) Editors must not use the fame, notoriety or position of a parent or guardian as sole justification for publishing details of a child's private life.

7) *Children in sex cases

1. The press must not, even if legally free to do so, identify children under 16 who are victims or witnesses in cases involving sex offences.

2. In any press report of a case involving a sexual offence against a child –

i) The child must not be identified.

ii) The adult may be identified.

iii) The word 'incest' must not be used where a child victim might be identified.

iv) Care must be taken that nothing in the report implies the relationship between the accused and the child.

8) *Hospitals

i) Journalists must identify themselves and obtain permission from a responsible executive before entering non-public areas of hospitals or similar institutions to pursue enquiries.

ii) The restrictions on intruding into privacy are particularly relevant to enquiries about individuals in hospitals or similar institutions.

9) *Reporting of Crime

(i) Relatives or friends of persons convicted or accused of crime should not generally be identified without their consent, unless they are genuinely relevant to the story.

(ii) Particular regard should be paid to the potentially vulnerable position of children who witness, or are victims of, crime. This should not restrict the right to report legal proceedings.

10) *Clandestine devices and subterfuge

i) The press must not seek to obtain or publish material acquired by using hidden cameras or clandestine listening devices; or by intercepting private or mobile telephone calls, messages or emails; or by the unauthorised removal of documents or photographs; or by accessing digitally-held private information without consent.

ii)   Engaging in misrepresentation or subterfuge, including by agents or intermediaries, can generally be justified only in the public interest and then only when the material cannot be obtained by other means.

11) Victims of sexual assault

The press must not identify victims of sexual assault or publish material likely to contribute to such identification unless there is adequate justification and they are legally free to do so.

12) Discrimination

i)   The press must avoid prejudicial or pejorative reference to an individual's race, colour, religion, gender, sexual orientation or to any physical or mental illness or disability.

ii)   Details of an individual's race, colour, religion, sexual orientation, physical or mental illness or disability must be avoided unless genuinely relevant to the story.

13) Financial journalism

i)   Even where the law does not prohibit it, journalists must not use for their own profit financial information they receive in advance of its general publication, nor should they pass such information to others.

ii)   They must not write about shares or securities in whose performance they know that they or their close families have a significant financial interest without disclosing the interest to the editor or financial editor.

iii)   They must not buy or sell, either directly or through nominees or agents, shares or securities about which they have written recently or about which they intend to write in the near future.

14) Confidential sources

Journalists have a moral obligation to protect confidential sources of information.

15) Witness payments in criminal trials

i)   No payment or offer of payment to a witness – or any person who may reasonably be expected to be called as a witness – should be made in any case once proceedings are active as defined by the Contempt of Court Act 1981.

This prohibition lasts until the suspect has been freed unconditionally by police without charge or bail or the proceedings are otherwise discontinued; or has entered a guilty plea to the court; or, in the event of a not guilty plea, the court has announced its verdict.

*ii) Where proceedings are not yet active but are likely and foreseeable, editors must not make or offer payment to any person who may reasonably be expected to be called as a witness, unless the information concerned ought demonstrably to be published in the public interest and there is an over-riding need to make or promise payment for this to be done; and all reasonable steps have been taken to ensure no financial dealings influence the evidence those witnesses give. In no circumstances should such payment be conditional on the outcome of a trial.

*iii) Any payment or offer of payment made to a person later cited to give evidence in proceedings must be disclosed to the prosecution and defence. The witness must be advised of this requirement.

16) *Payment to criminals

i) Payment or offers of payment for stories, pictures or information, which seek to exploit a particular crime or to glorify or glamorise crime in general, must not be made directly or via agents to convicted or confessed criminals or to their associates – who may include family, friends and colleagues.

ii) Editors invoking the public interest to justify payment or offers would need to demonstrate that there was good reason to believe the public interest would be served. If, despite payment, no public interest emerged, then the material should not be published.

The public interest

There may be exceptions to the clauses marked * where they can be demonstrated to be in the public interest.

1. The public interest includes, but is not confined to:
    i) Detecting or exposing crime or serious impropriety.
    ii) Protecting public health and safety.
    iii) Preventing the public from being misled by an action or statement of an individual or organisation.

2. There is a public interest in freedom of expression itself.

3. Whenever the public interest is invoked, the PCC will require editors to demonstrate fully how the public interest was served that they reasonably believed that publication, or journalistic activity undertaken with a view to publication, would be in the public interest.

4. The PCC will consider the extent to which material is already in the public domain, or will become so.

5. In cases involving children under 16, editors must demonstrate an exceptional public interest to over-ride the normally paramount interest of the child.

(www.pcc.org.uk)

REFERENCES

Aldridge, Meryl (2007) *Understanding the Local Media*. Maidenhead: Open University Press.

Allan, Stuart (2004) *News Culture*. Maidenhead: Open University Press.

Allan, Stuart (ed.) (2005) *Journalism: critical issues*. Maidenhead: Open University Press.

Alton, Roger (2007) 'Alton backs "perceptive" Blair speech', http://www.guardian.co.uk/media/2007/jun/12/pressandpublishing.politics

Atton, Chris (2002) *Alternative Media*. London: SAGE.

Atton, Chris and James Hamilton (2009) *Alternative Journalism*. London: SAGE.

Bailey, Sally and Granville Williams (1997) 'Memoirs are made of this: journalists' memoirs in the United Kingdom, 1945–95', in Michael Bromley and Tom O'Malley (eds), *A Journalism Reader*. London: Routledge. pp. 351–377.

Barnett, Antony (2005) 'Guess who's coming to Chequers? Pop stars and tobacco bosses', *Observer*, 2 January, www.guardian.co.uk/politics/2005/jan/02/uk.freedomofinformation

Barnett, Steven (2006) 'Reasons to be cheerful', *British Journalism Review*, Vol. 17, No. 1, pp. 7–14.

Bayles, Ros and Hilary Macaskill (2004) *Journalism and Public Trust*. London: NUJ.

Beales, Ian (2005) *The Editors' Codebook*. London: Newspaper Publishers Association, Newspaper Society, Periodical Publishers Association, Scottish Daily Newspaper Society, and Scottish Newspaper Publishers Association.

Beckett, Charlie (2008) *SuperMedia: saving journalism so it can save the world*. Oxford: Blackwell.

Beckett, Francis (2006) 'Media studies? I'd prefer a law Degree ...', *Guardian*, 4 September.

Bell, Allan (1991) *The Language of News Media*. Oxford: Blackwell.

Bell, Emily (2007) 'Fix yourself first', *Guardian blog*, 12 June, http://www.guardian.co.uk/commentisfree/2007/jun/12/thecounterculturalviewof

Bernstein, Carl and Bob Woodward ([1974] 2005) *All the President's Men*. New York: Pocket.

Blair, Tony (2007) 'Our nation's future – public life', speech at Reuters, London, 12 June, http://www.pm.gov.uk/output/Page11923.asp

Bohman, James (2004) 'Expanding dialogue: the internet, the public sphere and the prospects for transnational democracy', in Nick Crossley and John Michael Roberts (eds), *After Habermas: new perspectives on the public sphere*. Oxford: Blackwell. pp. 131–155.

Boyce, George, James Curran and Pauline Wingate (1978) *Newspaper History: from the 17th century to the present day*. London: Constable.

British Social Attitudes Survey (2008) *24th British Social Attitudes Survey.* London: SAGE.

Bromley, Michael and Tom O'Malley (eds) (1997) *A Journalism Reader.* London: Routledge.

Brooke, Heather (2007) *Your Right to Know*, second edition. London: Pluto.

Brown, Gerry (1995) *Exposed!* London: Virgin.

Brown, Lucy (1985) *Victorian News and Newspapers.* Oxford: Clarendon.

Bundock, Clement J (1957) *The National Union of Journalists: a jubilee history.* Oxford: Oxford University Press for the NUJ.

Burke, Peter and Asa Briggs (2005) *A Social History of the Media: from Gutenberg to the internet.* London: Polity.

Burrell, Ian (2006) 'Newsroom revolt forces "Star" to drop its "Daily Fatwa" spoof', *Independent,* 19 October.

Cameron, Deborah (1996) 'Style policy and style politics: a neglected aspect of the language of the news', *Media, Culture & Society,* Vol. 18, pp. 315–333.

Cameron, James ([1968] 2006) *Point of Departure.* London: Granta.

Campbell, Duncan (2008) 'The judge Mr Justice Eady: private man who "dislikes bullies and hypocrites"', *Guardian,* 11 November.

Campbell, Vincent (2004) *Information Age Journalism: journalism in an international context.* London: Arnold.

Chambers, Deborah, Linda Steiner and Carole Fleming (2004) *Women and Journalism.* London: Routledge.

Chapman, Jane (2005) *Comparative Media History: an introduction – 1789 to the present.* London: Polity.

Chippindale, Peter and Chris Horrie (1992) *Stick It Up Your Punter! The rise and fall of the Sun.* London: Mandarin.

Chisholm, Jim (2006) in *Economist,* 1 September, p. 57.

Clarke, Bob (2004) *From Grub Street to Fleet Street: an illustrated history of English newspapers to 1889.* Aldershot: Ashgate.

Cole, Peter (1997) 'Quality Journalism: an oxymoron?', professorial lecture, University of Central Lancashire, 16 April.

Cole, Peter (2001) 'What chance serious debate in the modern media?', inaugural lecture, University of Sheffield, 7 February.

Cole, Peter (2005) 'The structure of the print industry', in Richard Keeble (ed.), *Print Journalism: a critical introduction.* London: Routledge. pp. 22–37.

Cole, Peter (2006) 'A sting too far? Is this the end for the fake sheikh?', *Independent on Sunday,* 30 July.

Cole, Peter (2007) 'Meet the "new" Telegraph: fluent in modern geek', *Independent on Sunday,* 18 February, p. 15.

Conboy, Martin (2002) *The Press and Popular Culture.* London: SAGE.

Conboy, Martin (2004) *Journalism: a critical history.* London: SAGE.

Conboy, Martin (2006) *Tabloid Britain: constructing a community through language.* London: Routledge.

Conboy, Martin (2007) *The Language of the News.* London: Routledge.

Conboy, Martin and John Steel (2008) 'The future of newspapers: historical perspectives', *Journalism Studies,* Vol. 9, No. 5, pp. 650–661.

Conlan, Tara (2006) 'MacKenzie "reignites Hillsborough row"', *MediaGuardian,* 1 December, http://media.guardian.co.uk/presspublishing/story/0,,1961877,00.html

Cozens, Claire (2004) 'Sun apologises for Hillsborough', *Guardian,* 7 July.

Critcher, Chas (2002) 'Media, government and moral panic: the politics of paedophilia in Britain 2000–1', *Journalism Studies,* Vol. 3 No. 4, pp. 521–535.

Curran, James and Jean Seaton (1997) *Power Without Responsibility*, fifth edition. London and New York: Routledge.

Curran, James and Jean Seaton (2003) *Power Without Responsibility: the press and broadcasting in Britain*, sixth edition. London: Routledge.

Curtice, John and Ann Mair (2008) 'Where have all the readers gone? Popular newspapers and Britain's political health', in British Social Attitudes: the 24th Report. London: SAGE.

Dacre, Paul (2007) 'Cudlipp lecture', London College of Communication, 22 January.

Dacre, Paul (2008) Speech to the Society of Editors conference, Bristol, 9 November, http://www.societyofeditors.co.uk/userfiles/file/PaulDacreSpeech91108.doc

Dash, Jack (1970) *Good Morning, Brothers!* London: Mayflower.

Davies, Nick (2008) *Flat Earth News*. London: Chatto and Windus.

de Burgh, Hugo (ed.) (2000) *Investigative Journalism: context and practice*. London: Routledge.

de Burgh, Hugo (ed.) (2008) *Investigative Journalism*, second edition. London: Routledge.

Dico, Jo Lo and Francis Elliott (2006) 'Journalists have no morality, PM's wife tells students', *Independent*, 26 November.

Dorril, Stephen (2000) 'What is investigative journalism?', *Free Press* No. 116, May/June.

Downing, John with Tamara Villarreal Ford, Geneve Gil and Laura Stein (2001) *Radical Media: rebellious communication and social movements*. London: SAGE.

Edelman, Maurice (1966) *The Mirror: a political history*. London: Hamish Hamilton.

Engel, Matthew (1996) *Tickle the Public: one hundred years of the popular press*. London: Gollancz.

Errigo, Jackie and Bob Franklin (2004) 'Surviving in the hackademy', *British Journalism Review,* Vol. 15, No. 2, pp. 43–48.

Ettema, James S. and Theodore L. Glasser (1998) *Custodians of Conscience: investigative journalism and public virtue*. New York: Columbia University Press.

Ettema, James S. and Theodore L. Glasser (2007) 'An international symposium on investigative journalism: introduction', *Journalism: theory, practice and criticism,* Vol. 8, No. 5, pp. 491–494.

Evans, Harold (2000) *Essential English for Journalists, Editors and Writers*. London: Pimlico.

Feldman, Sally (2008) 'Taking the Mickey out', *Times Higher Education*, 24 January.

Feldstein, Mark (2007) 'Dummies and ventriloquists: models of how sources set the investigative agenda', *Journalism: theory, practice and criticism,* Vol. 8, No. 5, pp. 499–509.

Finkelstein, David (2008) 'Investigative journalism: Elena Poniatowska (1932–) and Anna Politkovskaya (1958–2006)', *Journalism Practice,* Vol. 2, No. 1, pp. 130–134.

Foley, Michael (2007) 'Book review: *The Ethical Journalist*', *Irish Communications Review,* Vol. 10, pp. 67–68.

Foot, Paul (1999) 'The slow death of investigative journalism', in Stephen Glover (ed.), *The Penguin Book of Journalism*. London: Penguin. pp. 79–89.

Fowler, Roger (1991) *Language in the News: discourse and ideology in the press*. London: Routledge.

Franklin, Bob (1997) *Newszak and News Media*. London: Arnold.

Franklin, Bob (2004) *Packaging Politics: political communications in Britain's media democracy*. London: Arnold.

Franklin, Bob (2005) 'McJournalism: the local press and the McDonaldization thesis', in Stuart Allan (ed.), *Journalism: critical issues*. Maidenhead: Open University Press. pp. 137–150.

Franklin, Bob (ed.) (2006) *Local Journalism and Local Media*, second edition. London: Routledge.

Franklin, Bob (ed.) (2008a) *Pulling Newspapers Apart: analysing print journalism*. London: Routledge.

Franklin, Bob (2008b) 'The future of newspapers', *Journalism Practice,* Vol. 2, No. 3, pp. 306–317.

Franklin, Bob (2008c) 'The future of newspapers', *Journalism Studies*, Vol. 9, No. 5, pp. 630–641.

Franklin, Bob and David Murphy (1991) *What News? The market, politics and the local press*. London: Routledge.

Frost, Chris (2000) *Media Ethics and Self-Regulation*. Harlow: Longman.

Frost, Chris (2004) 'The Press Complaints Commission: a study of ten years of adjudications on press complaints', *Journalism Studies,* Vol. 5, No. 1, February pp. 101–114.

Frost, Chris (2007) *Journalism Ethics and Self-regulation*. Harlow: Pearson.

Galtung, Johan and Mari Ruge (1965) 'The structure of foreign news: the presentation of the Congo, Cuba and Cyprus crises in four Norwegian newspapers', *Journal of International Peace Research,* Vol. 1, pp. 64–91.

Gibson, Owen and Helen Carter (2009) 'The truth: 20 years after Hillsborough, Liverpool has still not forgiven the newspaper it calls "The Scum"', *Guardian*, 18 April.

Gieber, Walter (1964) 'News is what newspapermen make it', in Howard Tumber (ed.), *News: a reader*. Oxford: Oxford University Press. pp. 218–223.

Glover, Stephen (1994) *Paper Dreams*. London: Penguin.

Glover, Stephen (2006) 'What on earth was the *Daily Star* thinking of?', *Independent*, 23 October.

Gopsill, Tim and Greg Neale (2007) *Journalists: a hundred years of the National Union of Journalists*. London: Profile.

Gordon, David (2008) 'Role of FOI legislation in minister's downfall', *Belfast Telegraph*, 19 February, www.belfasttelegraph.co.uk/news/politics/article3445136.ece

Greenslade, Roy (1992) *Maxwell's Fall*. London: Simon & Schuster.

Greenslade, Roy (2003a) *Press Gang: how newspapers make profits from propaganda*. London: Macmillan. [Also 2004 revised paperback edition.]

Greenslade, Roy (2003b) 'Their master's voice', *Guardian*, 17 February.

Greenslade, Roy (2004) 'It's the most effective promotion in the history of newspapers', *Media Guardian*, 26 July.

Greenslade, Roy (2006) 'Why I am out to nail Mazher Mahmood', *Independent on Sunday*, 16 April.

Greenslade, Roy (2008a) 'Subterfuge, set-ups, stings and stunts', in Hugo de Burgh (ed.), *Investigative Journalism*, second edition. London: Routledge. pp. 319–339.

Greenslade, Roy (2008b) 'The digital challenge', *Guardian*, 7 January, http://www.guardian.co.uk/media/2008/jan/07/pressandpublishing.digitalmedia

Greenslade, Roy (2009a) 'Britain's Vanishing Newspapers', *Media Guardian blog*, 19 February http://www.guardian.co.uk/media/greenslade/2009/feb/19/local-newspapers-newspapers/print

Greenslade, Roy (2009b) 'Online is the future and the future is now', *Media Guardian*, 5 January, http://www.guardian.co.uk/media/2009/jan/05/recession-newspaper-industry-online-innovations

Grey Cardigan (2006) 'Dispatches from down table', *Press Gazette*, 27 October.

Griffiths, Dennis (2006) *Fleet Street: five hundred years of the press*. London: The British Library.

Grun, Jonathan (2008) 'Press Association hits back at Nick Davies' claims', *Press Gazette*, 26 February, http://www.pressgazette.co.uk/story.asp?sectioncode=6&storycode=40334

Guardian News and Media (2007) *Living Our Values: sustainability report*. London: Guardian.

Habermas, Jurgen (1974) *Theory and Practice*. London: Heinemann.

Habermas, Jurgen (1984) *The Theory of Communicative Action*. Cambridge: Polity Press.

Habermas, Jurgen (1989) *The Structural Transformation of the Public Sphere: an inquiry into a category of bourgeois society*. Cambridge: Polity.

Hackett, Robert A. (2005) 'Is there a democratic deficit in US and UK journalism?', in Stuart Allan (ed.), *Journalism: critical issues*. Maidenhead: Open University Press. pp. 85–97.

Hall, Jim (2008) 'Online editions: newspapers and the "new" news', in Bob Franklin (ed.) *Pulling Newspapers Apart*. London: Routledge, pp. 215–223.

Hall, Stuart (1982) 'The rediscovery of "ideology": return of the repressed in media studies', in Michael Gurevitch, Tony Bennett, James Curran and Janet Woollacott (eds), *Culture, Society and the Media*. London: Methuen. pp. 56–90.

Hall, Stuart, Critcher, Chas, Jefferson, Tony, Clarke, John and Roberts, Brian (1978) *Policing the Crisis*. London: Macmillan.

Hanna, Mark (2005) 'Investigative journalism', in Bob Franklin, Martin Hamer, Mark Hanna, Marie Kinsey and John Richardson (eds), *Key Concepts in Journalism Studies*. London: Sage. pp. 122–124.

Hanna, Mark (2008) 'Universities as evangelists of the watchdog role', in Hugo de Burgh (ed.), *Investigative Journalism*, second edition. London: Routledge. pp. 157–173.

Hanna, Mark and Karen Sanders (2007) 'Journalism education in Britain', *Journalism Practice*, Vol. 1, No. 3, pp. 404–420.

Harcup, Tony (2003) 'The unspoken – said: The journalism of alternative media', *Journalism: theory, practice and criticism,* Vol. 4, No. 3, pp. 356–376.

Harcup, Tony (2004) *Journalism: principles and practice*. London: SAGE.

Harcup, Tony (2005) '"I'm doing this to change the world": journalism in alternative and mainstream media', *Journalism Studies,* Vol. 6, No. 3, pp. 361–374.

Harcup, Tony (2006) 'The local alternative press', in Bob Franklin (ed.), *Local Journalism and Local Media: making the local news*. London: Routledge. pp. 129–139.

Harcup, Tony (2007) *The Ethical Journalist*. London: SAGE.

Harcup (2009a) 'Fair enough? Ethics and regulation in broadcast journalism', in Jane Chapman and Marie Kinsey (eds), *Broadcast Journalism: a critical introduction*. London: Routledge. pp. 247–256.

Harcup, Tony (2009b) *Journalism: principles and practice*, second edition. London: SAGE.

Harcup, Tony and Deirdre O'Neill (2001) 'What is news? Galtung and Ruge revisited', *Journalism Studies,* Vol. 2, No. 2, pp. 261–280.

Harrison, Jackie (2006) *News*. London: Routledge.

Hastings, Max (2002) *Editor*. London: Macmillan.

Hattenstone. Simon (2005) 'Looking for trouble', *Guardian Weekend magazine*, 5 March.

Herman, Edward (2000) 'The propaganda model: a retrospective', *Journalism Studies,* Vol 1, No. 1, pp. 101–112.

Herman, Edward and Noam Chomsky [1988] (1994) *Manufacturing Consent: the political economy of the mass media*. London: Vintage.

Higgins, Michael (2006) 'Substantiating a political public sphere in the Scottish press: a comparative analysis', *Journalism: theory, practice and criticism*, Vol. 7, No. 1, pp. 25–44.

Hildick, Edmund Wallace (1966) *A Close Look at Newspapers*. London: Faber & Faber.

Hipwell, James (2006) 'Prison diary: In this place you lose your name. I'm PA6164', *Guardian*, 27 February.

Hobsbawm, Julia and John Lloyd (2008) *The Power of the Commentariat*. London: Editorial Intelligence, in association with Reuters Institute for the Study of Journalism.

Hold the Front Page (2006) 'Media were told about less than one per cent of crime, Echo probe finds', 13 November, www.holdthefrontpage.co.uk/day/foi/061113lin.shtml

Hold the Front Page (2007) 'Regional writer shares Paul Foot Award', 16 October, http://www.holdthefrontpage.co.uk/AWARDS/071016foot.shtml

Hold the Front Page (2008) 'Regional press continues to push for information under FOI', 9 January, www.holdthefrontpage.co.uk/day/foi/080109roundup.shtml

Holland, Patricia (1998) 'The politics of the smile: soft news and the sexualisation of the popular press', in Cynthia Carter, Gill Branston and Stuart Allan (eds), *News, Gender and Power*. London: Routledge.

Howe, Melvyn (2006) 'Former Mirror journalist Hipwell jailed for share tipping conspiracy', *Press Gazette*, 10 February, http://www.pressgazette.co.uk/article/100206/mirror_journalist_hipwell_jailed

Hujanen, Jaana, Ninni Lehtniemi and Riiki Virranta (2008) *Mapping Communication and Media research in the UK*. Jyvaskyla: University of Jyvaskyla.

Humphrys, John (2006) 'The future of newspapers', *Independent*, 13 November, *Media Weekly*, p. 5.

Huntzicker, William (1999) *The Popular Press, 1833–65: history of American journalism*. Westport, CT: Greenwood.

Independent (1996) 'How not to be a journalist', *Independent*, 31 October.

Iorio, Sharon Hartin (ed.) (2004) *Qualitative Research in Journalism*. Mahwah, NJ: Lawrence Erlbaum.

Jarvis, Jeff (2007) 'For the record', 30 November, http://www.guardian.co.uk/commentisfree/ 2007/nov/30/fortherecord

Jempson, Mike (2007) 'The ethics business', *Journalist*, April: 22–23.

Jewkes, Yvonne (2004) *Media and Crime: A Critical Introduction*. London: SAGE.

Johansson, Sophia (2008) 'Gossip, sport and pretty girls', *Journalism Practice*, Vol. 2, No. 3, pp. 402–413.

Journalism Training Forum (2002) *Journalists at Work*, London: NTO/Skillset, http://www.skillset.org/uploads/pdf/asset_262.pdf?1

Journalist (2006) 'Star chapel stops gross Muslim slur', *Journalist*, November/December: 9.

Keeble, Richard (2001) *Ethics for Journalists*. London: Routledge.

Keeble, Richard (ed.) (2005) *Print Journalism: a critical introduction*. London: Routledge.

Keeble, Richard (2006) *The Newspapers Handbook*, fourth edition. London: Routledge.

Keeble, Richard (2009) *Ethics for Journalists*, second edition. London: Routledge.

Keller, Bill (2007) 'Not dead yet: the newspaper in the days of digital anarchy', Hugo Young lecture at Chatham House, London, http://www.guardian.co.uk/media/2007/nov/29/pressandpublishing.digitalmedia1

Knightley, Phillip (1998) *A Hack's Progress*. London: Vintage.

Kovach, Bill and Tom, Rosenstiel (2003) *The Elements of Journalism*. London, Atlantic.

Kunelius, Risto (2006) 'Good journalism: on the evaluation of some interested and experienced actors', *Journalism Studies,* Vol. 7, No. 5: 671–690.

Lewis, Justin, Andrew Williams and Bob Franklin (2008a) 'A compromised fourth estate?', *Journalism Studies*, Vol. 9, No. 1, pp. 1–20.

Lewis, Justin, Andrew Williams and Bob Franklin (2008b) 'Four rumours and an explanation: a political economic account of journalists' changing newsgathering and reporting practices', *Journalism Practice*, Vol. 2, No. 1, pp. 27–45.

Lewis, Justin, Andrew Williams, Bob Franklin, James Thomas and Nick Mosdell (2008) *The Quality and Independence of British Journalism*. Cardiff University School of Journalism, Media and Cultural Studies, http://www.cardiff.ac.uk/jomec/en/school/39/419.html

Lister, Sam (2006) 'MacKenzie: I'm not sorry about Hillsborough comments', *Liverpool Daily Post*, 1 December.

Lister, Sam (2007) 'Angry fans demand justice', *Liverpool Daily Post*, 8 January.

Lloyd, John (2004a) *What the Media are Doing to our Politics*. London: Constable.

Lloyd, John (2004b) Reuters Memorial Lecture, Oxford, 22 October, http://www.guardian.co.uk/media/2004/oct/22/broadcasting.pressandpublishing

Loffelholz, Martin and David Weaver (eds) (2008) *Global Journalism Research: theories, methods, findings, future*. Oxford: Blackwell.

Luckhurst, Tim (2008) 'Old school values for news', *Times Higher Education*, 7 February.

Lynch, Jake and Annabel McGoldrick (2005) *Peace Journalism*. Stroud: Hawthorn Press.

MacArthur, Brian (1988) *Eddy Shah Today and the Newspaper Revolution*. London: David and Charles.

MacDonald, Linda (2006) 'Mahmood set-ups: hits and misses', *Guardian*, 26 July.

Mahmood, Mazher (2008) *Confessions of a Fake Sheikh: the king of the sting reveals all*. London: HarperCollins.

Man, John (2003) *The Gutenberg Revolution*. London: Review.

Manning, Paul (2001) *News and News Sources: a critical introduction*. London: SAGE.

Manning, Paul (2008) 'The Press Association and news agency sources', in Bob Franklin (ed.), *Pulling Newspapers Apart*. London: Routledge.

Mansfield, Frederick (1936) *The Complete Journalist: a study of the principles and practice of newspaper-making*. London: Sir Isaac Pitman and Sons.

Marr, Andrew (2005) *My Trade: a short history of British journalism*. London: Pan.

Martin, Shannon and David Copeland (eds) (2003) *The Function of Newspapers in Society: a global perspective*. Westport, CT: Greenwood.

Marx, Karl and Friedrich Engels ([1846] 1965) *The German Ideology*. London: Lawrence and Wishart.

Mayes, Ian (2006) guest lecture at University of Sheffield, 28 November.

McCall, Carolyn (2008) 'Papers will go out of business warns GMG chief', www.holdthefrontpage.co.uk/news/081105mccall.shtml

McKane, Anna (2006) *News Writing*. London: SAGE.

McLaughlin, Greg (2006) 'Profits, politics and paramilitaries' in Bob Franklin (ed.), *Local Journalism and Local Media*. London: Routledge. pp. 60–69.

McNair, Brian (2000) *Journalism and Democracy: an evaluation of the political public sphere*. London: Routledge.

McNair, Brian (2003a) *An Introduction to Political Communication*. London: Routledge.

McNair, Brian (2003b) *News and Journalism in the UK*. London: Routledge

McNair, Brian (2008) 'I , Columnist', in Bob Franklin (ed.), *Pulling Newspapers Apart*. London: Routledge. pp. 112–120.

McQuail, Denis (1994) *Mass Communication Theory*. London: SAGE.

McQuail, Denis (2000) *McQuail's Mass Communication Theory*. London: SAGE.

Melvern, Linda (1986) *The End of the Street*. London: Methuen.

Meyer, Philip (2004) *The Vanishing Newspaper: Saving Journalism in the Information Age*. New York: University of Missouri Press.

Milton, John (1644) 'Areopagitica: a speech for the liberty of unlicensed printing', in Granville Williams (2005) *Milton and the Modern Media: a defence of a free press.* Accrington: B&D.

Mnookin, Seth (2005) *Hard News: twenty-one brutal months at the New York Times and how they changed the American media.* New York: Random House.

Morgan, Jean (2001) 'Hellier on sick leave as row over Desmond stance grows', *Press Gazette,* 14 September.

Morgan, Ken (2007) 'NUJ code of conduct leads world in exposing hypocrisy', NUJ 1907–2007 Celebration Supplement, *Journalist,* April, pp. 10–11.

Morgan, Piers (2005) *The Insider: the private diaries of a scandalous decade.* London: Ebury.

Morgan, Piers (2006) 'The Future of Newspapers', *Independent,* 13 November, *Media Weekly,* p. 6.

Morgan, Piers (2008) 'Adventures of the comeback kid', *British Journalism Review,* Vol. 19, No. 4, pp. 17–29.

Mudhai, Okoth Fred (2007) 'Light at the end of the tunnel? Pushing the boundaries in Africa', *Journalism: theory, practice and criticism,* Vol. 8, No. 5, pp. 536–544.

Murdoch, Rupert (2005) 'The role of newspapers in the digital age', speech to American Society of Newspaper Editors in Washington DC, http://media.guardian.co.uk/print/0,3858,5170708-105240,00.html

Murdoch, Rupert (2008) 'The future of newspapers: moving beyond dead trees', third Boyer lecture, ABC Radio, Australia, 16 November, www.abc.net.au/rn/boyerlectures/stories/2008/2397940.htm

National Readership Survey (2007) *Time Spent Reading* report, October.

Neil, Andrew (1996) *Full Disclosure.* London: Macmillan.

Niblock, Sarah (2007) 'From "knowing how" to "being able": negotiating the meanings of reflective practice and reflexive research in journalism studies', *Journalism Practice,* Vol. 1, No. 1, pp. 20–32.

Norton-Taylor, Richard (2008) 'How Labour used the law to keep criticism of Israel secret', *Guardian,* 21 February.

OED (2007) 'Theory', Oxford English Dictionary Online, http://dictionary.oed.com

Ofcom (2006) *Communications Market Report,* www.ofcom.org.uk/research

Ojo, Tokunbo (2007) 'The Nigerian media and the process of democratisation', *Journalism: theory, practice and criticism* Vol. 8, No. 5, pp. 545–550.

O'Malley, Tom and Clive Soley (2000) *Regulating the Press.* London: Pluto.

O'Neill, Deirdre and Catherine O'Connor (2008) 'The passive journalist: how sources dominate local news', *Journalism Practice,* Vol. 2, No. 3, pp. 487–500.

O'Reilly, Gavin (2007) Speech to Society of Editors, http://www.societyofeditors.co.uk/page-view.php?pagename=TheSOELecture

Osborn, Andrew (2007) 'These are the faces of the 20 journalists who have lost their lives in Putin's Russia', *Independent on Sunday,* 11 March.

Palmer, Jerry (2000) *Spinning Into Control: news values and source strategies.* London, New York: Leicester University Press.

PCC (2000) 'City Slickers ruling', Press Complaints Commission, Report 50, http://www.pcc.org.uk/news/index.html?article=MTc4NQ==□□

PCC (2006a) *Complaints Report No 73: April 2006 – September 2006.* London: Press Complaints Commission.

PCC (2006b) *Complaints Report No 74: October 2006 – April 2007.* London: Press Complaints Commission.

PCC (2007a) *2006 Annual Review.* London: Press Complaints Commission.

PCC (2007b) *Complaints Report No 75: April 2007 – September 2007.* London: Press Complaints Commission.

Phillips, Angela (2007) *Good Writing for Journalists.* London: Sage.

Picard, Robert (2008) 'Shifts in newspaper advertising expenditures and their implications for the future of newspapers', *Journalism Studies*, Vol. 9, No. 5, pp. 704–716.

Pilger, John (1998) *Hidden Agendas*. London: Vintage.

Pilger, John (ed.) (2004) *Tell Me No Lies: investigative journalism and its triumphs.* London: Jonathan Cape.

Ponsford, Dominic (2004) 'The Sun gives full apology to Merseyside', *Press Gazette*, 9 July.

Ponsford, Dominic (2006) 'Mirror staff angry at Slicker judge's slur', *Press Gazette*, 15 February, http://www.pressgazette.co.uk/article/150206/mirror_staff_angry_at_slicker_judges_slur

Ponsford, Dominic (2008) 'Sharing with Mail "will safeguard future of Independent"', *Press Gazette*, 28 November, http://www.pressgazette.co.uk/story.asp?sectioncode= □1&storycode=42559&c=1

Press Gazette (2007a) 'Blair slams media's "ferocious hostility"', *Press Gazette*, 13 June, http://www.pressgazette.co.uk/story.asp?sectioncode=1&storycode=37909

Press Gazette (2007b) 'We ignore this issue at our peril', *Press Gazette*, 9 November.

Press Gazette (2008) 'Express Newspapers pays McCanns damages', *Press Gazette*, 21 March.

Preston, Peter (2008) 'The curse of introversion', *Journalism Studies*, Vol. 9, No. 5, pp. 642–649.

Preston, Peter (2009) 'Regionals face far more than a local difficulty', *Observer*, 4 January, www.guardian.co.uk/media/2009/jan/04/regional-press/print

Randall, David (2005) *The Great Reporters*. London: Pluto.

Randall, David (2007) *The Universal Journalist*, third edition. London: Pluto.

Richardson, John E. (2006) *Analysing Newspapers: an approach from critical discourse analysis.* London: Palgrave Macmillan.

Roberts, Gene (ed.) (2001) *Leaving Readers Behind: the age of corporate newspapering.* Fayetteville: University of Arkansas Press.

Robertson, Geoffrey (2008) 'In defence of human rights', *Guardian*, 11 November.

Rodriguez, Clemencia (2001) *Fissures in the Mediascape: an international study of citizens' media*. Creskill, NY: Hampton.

Rooney, Dick (2000) 'Thirty years of competition in the British tabloid press: The *Mirror* and the *Sun*', in Colin Sparks and John Tulloch (eds), *Tabloid Tales*. Oxford: Rowman and Littlefield.

Rusbridger, Alan (1999a) 'Who can you trust?', Aslib Proceedings, Vol. 5, No. 2, pp. 37–45.

Rusbridger, Alan (1999b) 'Dumbing down', Cobden Lecture, Manchester Metropolitan University, 17 April.

Rusbridger, Alan (2002) speech at Society of Editors conference, York, 14 October.

Rusbridger, Alan (2005) 'What are newspapers for?', Hugo Young Lecture, University of Sheffield, 9 March, http://image.guardian.co.uk/sys-files/Guardian/documents/2005/03/15/lecturespeech.pdf

Sampson, Anthony (1996) 'The crisis at the heart of our media', *British Journalism Review*, Vol. 7, No. 3, pp. 42–51.

Sanders, Karen (2003) *Ethics & Journalism*. London: SAGE.

Schofield, Guy (1975) *The Men that Carry the News*. London: Cranford.

Scott Trust (2008) 'Scott Trust updates structure', press release, 8 October, http://www.gmgplc.co.uk/media/pressreleases/tabid/213/default.aspx?pressreleaseid=121&cid=viewdetails

Searle, Chris (1989) *Your Daily Dose: racism and the Sun*. London: Campaign for Press and Broadcasting Freedom.

Sedley, Stephen (2006) 'Towards a right to privacy', *London Review of Books*, 8 June, Vol. 28, No. 11, pp. 20–23.

Select Committee (2003), House of Commons Select Committee on Culture. Media and Sport. Minutes of Evidence 11 March 2003, at: http://www.publications. parliament. uk/pa/cm200203/cmselect/cmcumeds/458/3031112.htm

Seymour Ure, Colin (1991) *The British Press and Broadcasting since 1945*. Oxford: Basil Blackwell.

Shannon, Richard (2001) *A Press Free and Responsible: self-regulation and the Press Complaints Commission, 1991–2001*. London: John Murray.

Sheridan Burns, Lynette (2002) *Understanding Journalism*. London: SAGE.

Silver, James (2006) 'What the NoW didn't say in court', *Guardian*, 17 April.

Slattery, Jon (2006) 'Slickers had no guidance from bosses, says judge', *Press Gazette,* 26 January, http://www.pressgazette.co.uk/article/260106/slickers_had_no_guidance_from_ bosses_says_judge

Smith, Andreas Whittam (2008) 'Media studies is no preparation for journalism', *Independent*, 25 February.

Smith, Ron (2008) *Ethics in Journalism*. Oxford: Blackwell.

Snoddy, Raymond (1992) *The Good, the Bad and the Unacceptable: the hard news about the British press*. London: Faber and Faber.

Society of Editors (2004) *Diversity in the Newsroom*, London: Society of Editors http://www.societyofeditors.co.uk/userfiles/file/Diversity%20in%20the%20Newsro om%20Report%20PDF.pdf

Society of Editors (2007) A Matter of Trust conference, http://www. societyofeditors. co.uk/pageview.php?page_id=181&parent_page_id=381

Spark, David (1999) *Investigative Reporting: a study in technique*. Oxford: Focal.

Sparks, Colin (1999) 'The press', in Jane Stokes and Anna Reading (eds), *The Media in Britain: current debates and developments*. London: Macmillan. pp. 41–60.

Specter, Michael (2007) 'Who's killing Putin's enemies?', *Observer*, 25 February.

Steed, Henry Wickham (1938) *The Press*. Harmondsworth: Penguin.

Stevenson, Nick (2002) *Understanding Media Cultures*. London: SAGE.

Stott, Richard (2002) *Dogs and Lampposts*. London: Metro.

Stott, Richard (2007) 'Ethics whirl', *British Journalism Review,* Vol. 18, No. 1, pp. 78–79.

Straw, Jack (1993) 'Democracy on the spike', *British Journalism Review*, Vol. 4, No. 4: 45–48.

Stromback, Jesper (2005) 'In search of a standard: four models of democracy and their normative implications for journalism', *Journalism Studies,* Vol. 6, No. 3, pp. 331–345.

Sunday Times (2009) 'Tim Bowdler: paper tiger who had too much to eat', *Sunday Times*, 4 January, http://business.timesonline.co.uk/tol/business/industry_sectors/media/ article5438625.ece

Sutton Trust (2006) *'The educational backgrounds of leading journalists'*, http:// www.suttontrust.com/reports/Journalists-backgrounds-final-report.pdf

Temple, Mick (2008) *The British Press*. Maidenhead: Open University Press.

Tong, Jingrong (2007) 'Guerrilla tactics of investigative journalists in China', *Journalism: theory, practice and criticism,* Vol. 8, No. 5, pp. 530–535.

Toynbee, Polly (2008) 'Judge Dacre dispenses little justice from his bully pulpit', *Guardian*, 11 November.

Tumber, Howard (ed.) (1999) *News: a reader*. Oxford: Oxford University Press.

Tunstall, Jeremy (1996) *Newspaper Power: the new national press in Britain*. Oxford: Clarendon.

Ungoed-Thomas, Jon and Yuba Bessaoud (2007) 'The eco minister's 11,000-mile car claim', *Sunday Times*, 18 February, www.timesonline.co.uk/tol/news/uk/article 1400673.ece

Van Dijk, Teun A. (1991) *Racism and the Press*. London: Routledge.

Vasagar, Jeevan (2006) 'Fake sheikh accused after terror plot acquittals', *Guardian*, 26 July.

Wahl-Jorgensen, Karin and Thomas Hanitzsch (eds) (2009) *Handbook of Journalism Studies*. Mahwah, NJ: Lawrence Erlbaum Associates.

Wainwright, Martin (2008) 'It is a fight we must win', *Guardian*, 17 November, www. guardian. co.uk/media/2008/nov/17/ray-tindle-local-press-newspapers/print

Walker, David (2000) 'Newspaper power: a practitioner's account', in Howard Tumber (ed.), *Media Power, Professionals and Policies*. London: Routledge. pp. 236–246.

Wasserman, Herman (2008) 'Attack of the killer newspapers! The "tabloid revolution" in South Africa and the future of newspapers', *Journalism Studies,* Vol. 9, No. 5, pp. 786–797.

Waterhouse, Keith (1989) *Waterhouse on Newspaper Style*. London: Viking.

Weinhold, Wendy (2008) 'Newspaper negotiations: the crossroads of community newspaper journalists' values and labor', *Journalism Practice,* Vol. 2, No. 3, pp. 476–486.

Whitaker, Brian (1981) *News Ltd: why you can't read all about it*. London: Minority Press Group.

White, David Manning [1950] 'The gatekeeper: a case study in the selection of news', in Howard Tumber (ed.) (1999) *News: a reader*. Oxford: Oxford University Press. pp. 66–72.

White, Michael (2007) on Blair speech, *Guardian*, 12 June, http://media.guardian. co.uk/print/0,,330014022-105414,00.html

Who Killed the Newspaper? (2006), Economist, 1 September.

Wilby, Peter (2008a) 'This reckless reporting cannot continue', *Guardian*, 24 March.

Wilby, Peter (2008b) 'A job for the wealthy and connected', *Guardian*, 7 April.

Wilby, Peter (2008c) 'Overhyped health stories? They're all pants', *Guardian*, 2 June.

Williams, Francis (1958) *Dangerous Estate: the anatomy of newspapers*. London: Readers Union.

Williams, Granville (2005) *Milton and the Modern Media: a defence of a free press*. Accrington: B&D.

Williams, Kevin (1998) *Get Me a Murder a Day! A history of mass communication in Britain*. London: Arnold.

Williams, Kevin (2003) *Understanding Media Theory*. London: Arnold.

Williams, Raymond (1976) *Keywords*. London: Flamingo.

Wintour, Charles (1972) *Pressures on the Press*. London: Andre Deutsch

World Press Trends (2006) World Association of Newspapers: Paris www.wan-press. org/article4473.html

Young, Hugo (2004) *Supping with the Devils*. London: Atlantic Books.

Zelizer, Barbie (2004) *Taking Journalism Seriously: news and the academy*. London: SAGE.

INDEX

Supporting researchers for more than forty years

Research methods have always been at the core of SAGE's publishing. Sara Miller McCune founded SAGE in 1965 and soon after, she published SAGE's first methods book, *Public Policy Evaluation*. A few years later, she launched the Quantitative Applications in the Social Sciences series – affectionately known as the 'little green books'.

Always at the forefront of developing and supporting new approaches in methods, SAGE published early groundbreaking texts and journals in the fields of qualitative methods and evaluation.

Today, more than forty years and two million little green books later, SAGE continues to push the boundaries with a growing list of more than 1,200 research methods books, journals, and reference works across the social, behavioural, and health sciences.

From qualitative, quantitative and mixed methods to evaluation, SAGE is the essential resource for academics and practitioners looking for the latest in methods by leading scholars.

www.sagepublications.com